# Portrait of Haldane
at Work on Education

Also by Eric Ashby

*Challenge to Education*
*Scientist in Russia*
*Technology and the Academics*
*Community of Universities*
*African Universities and Western Tradition*
*Any Person, Any Study*


Also by Eric Ashby and Mary Anderson

*Universities: British, Indian, African*

*Adam Sedgwick's Discourse on the Studies of the University* (edited, with introductory essay)

*The Rise of the Student Estate*

LORD HALDANE OF CLOAN
1856–1928
Lord Chancellor, Secretary for War,
philosopher

*Drawing by Sir William Rothenstein,* 1916

# Portrait of Haldane
# at Work on Education

ERIC ASHBY AND MARY ANDERSON

ARCHON BOOKS
1974

**Library of Congress Cataloging in Publication Data**

Ashby, Sir Eric, 1904–
    Portrait of Haldane at work on education.

    Bibliography: p.
    1.  Haldane, Richard Burdon Haldane, 1st Viscount, 1856–1928.
2. Education–Philosophy. I. Anderson, Mary, historian, joint author.
II. Title.
LB775.H2827A84          370.1'092'4          74-6316
ISBN 0-208-01463-2

*First published 1974 by*
THE MACMILLAN PRESS
*London and Basingstoke*
*and in the United States of America*
*under the imprint Archon Books by*
THE SHOE STRING PRESS, INC.,
*Hamden, Connecticut 06514*

*Printed in Great Britain*

# Contents

# List of Illustrations

# Acknowledgements

For the material in this book it was necessary to draw upon collections of private papers. These are the Haldane papers (National Library of Scotland), the Asquith and Fisher papers (Bodleian Library), the Passfield papers (British Library of Political and Economic Science), the Lloyd George papers (Beaverbrook Library), the Gosse papers (Brotherton Library, University of Leeds), and the Balfour papers (British Museum). We are grateful for the help we have received from members of the staff of the libraries where they are housed, and also for permission, where it was needed, to quote from some of these papers.

Sir David Stephens, clerk of the parliaments, and Mr Maurice Bond, clerk of the records in the house of lords record office, kindly helped us to trace some records of parliamentary proceedings. Mr Keith Percy, of the University of Lancaster, who is working on the history of civic universities, generously gave us some transcripts of the Chamberlain papers at Birmingham University and extracts from an unpublished autobiography of M. W. Travers in the University Library at Bristol. Mr Norman Higham, librarian at Bristol University, gave us a copy of Haldane's address to the University College Colston Society in 1902.

We are indebted to the Scottish National Portrait Gallery for permission to reproduce the drawing of Haldane by Rothenstein, and to the National Portrait Gallery for permission to reproduce the cartoon by F. C. Gould.

The book has been greatly improved as a result of criticisms by Sir William Mansfield Cooper, who read the first draft, and we are very grateful to him for these criticisms. We have benefited also from conversations with other scholars, especially Professor Talmon of the Hebrew University of Jerusalem. Through the generosity of the Rockefeller Foundation, one of us (E. A.) was able to finish writing the book as a resident scholar under idyllic conditions at the Villa Serbelloni in Italy.

Finally we wish to record our thanks to Mrs Bridget Boehm who did much of the preliminary typing of the book, Mrs B. K. Knights, who typed the whole of the final draft, and to Mrs M. M. Anderson for reading the proofs and arresting many small errors.

E.A.

M.A.

In February 1974 one of us (E.A.) was privileged to give the Gregynog Lectures in University College, Aberystwyth, under the title *Haldane and the University of Wales*. The lecturer is asked to incorporate the content of the lectures in a book. Chapters 1, 6 and 8 contain the substance of the lectures.

The true analogy to the historian is the portrait painter. No two portraits are alike or have the same meaning. The individual in the picture cannot be exhausted. All the painter can do is to take certain features expressive of his meaning and put them on canvas. That is all the historian can do.

from a report in *The Times* of 15 December 1926, of the opening remarks by Lord Haldane when he presided at a lecture given by Professor C. W. Alvord, at Bedford College, London.

# Introduction

The inscription on Lord Haldane's tombstone in the burial ground at Gleneagles records that he was secretary of state for war and lord high chancellor, and the specific achievement of his career selected to be carved in stone is: 'Through his work in fashioning her army he rendered invaluable aid to his country in her time of direst need.' It is not likely that Haldane composed his own epitaph. Thomas Jefferson, who did, preferred to omit the fact that he had been president of the United States, and to have instead on his tombstone the words: 'Father of the University of Virginia'.

The theme of this book is that Haldane's deepest and most enduring commitment was to the improvement of education and that, like Jefferson, he hoped to be remembered for his services to the cause of universities. '... I have lived', he told a meeting of former students eight years before his death, 'in the cause of education perhaps more than in any other of the several causes I have been engaged in for many years. ...' And on another occasion, two weeks later: 'I have lived for universities. They have been to me more than anything else. ...'

Yet at his death in 1928 scant recognition was given to his concern for education. Four and a half columns of obituary in *The Times* contained only one brief paragraph about his educational interests, and the long leading article in the same issue only one sentence. In the months afterwards some of his admirers redressed the balance: Mansbridge in a letter to *The Times* and Heath in a collection of commemorative articles in *Public Administration*. And Morgan, a fellow Scot familiar with Haldane's work, wrote: 'Great as were his merits in other fields, it may be that when the final estimate of his life-work is made, the first place will be given to his ungrudging services on behalf of education of every grade.'

Let us make it clear at the outset that we are not presenting a final estimate of Haldane's lifework. That is why we call this book a portrait. It is a portrait of Haldane's work for education, done in the interstices of a full life as lawyer, cabinet minister, lord chancellor.

It is surprising, over forty years after his death, that the story of Haldane's preoccupations with education has not been told already; though it is not surprising that when he died, barely ten years after the armistice, he should stand in public esteem as the man who reformed the British army in time – just in time – to meet the holocaust of 1914. His sister, Elizabeth Haldane, chose a soldier to write his official biography; and although the biographer, Maurice, guided by Haldane's autobiography, gave due attention to Haldane's educational work, it was as chronicler rather than as critic. Neither Maurice, nor any others who have written about Haldane's career, have assessed and interpreted his contribution to the organisation of education in Britain. Even around 1956, at the centenary of Haldane's birth, comparatively little was published about his concern with the cause which he himself said he had 'lived for'. There was a good general survey by Lockwood in a second series of essays about him in *Public Administration*, and in 1960 a lecture by Logan on Haldane and the University of London; and that was about all. Even those professional historians who have strayed into the field of university history do Haldane much less than justice; they leave an impression that they have not examined important sources and they have not resolved glaring inconsistencies. Assessments of Haldane's contribution range from unstinted admiration to sceptical disapproval. 'There is', wrote Hetherington in 1932, 'no University in these islands which is not in Lord Haldane's debt', and Duff wrote in 1961: 'No man in British history has done so much for so many university institutions.' To counter this encomium there is the innuendo propagated by two distinguished academics in Lancashire, Hopkinson and Muir, that Haldane in his autobiography exaggerated the influence he had on the rise of the civic universities, especially on the creation of the University of Liverpool. There are criticisms, too, by Hearnshaw and by Logan, of Haldane's proposals (or, rather, those of the commission under his chairmanship) for the University of London. And there is, in Sadler's correspondence, a clear hint that Haldane's scheming on behalf of educational reform was heartily disliked in some quarters. Even testimony about Haldane's style of working on royal commissions is conflicting. Thus Bellot, writing of his handling of witnesses at hearings of the royal commission on the University of London, said that Haldane pressed 'his view pertinaciously upon the medical witnesses'. But Henry Jones, writing of Haldane's handling of witnesses at hearings of the royal commission on the University of Wales, said: 'His treatment of the witnesses was perfect, for his questions brought out their views, and he never attempted to make them say what he would most like to hear.'

So anyone who decides to portray Haldane at work on education has a clear job to do. There is no shortage of material for the job. Among the rich sources are the verbatim records of the two university royal commissions over which Haldane presided, a form of literature which is unfamiliar because it requires unusual stamina to digest it. There are unpublished and largely untapped departmental records from the treasury, the privy council, and the board of education; important because Haldane exerted a great deal of his influence silently, behind the scenes. There are revealing passages in the memoirs of Fitzroy, Fisher, and the indefatigable Beatrice Webb, and in the private papers of the period. There are the many addresses which Haldane gave as apostle and propagandist to win public support for his schemes, and the many speeches he made in debates on educational issues in parliament. And there are reports of committees which have remained unexamined owing to the chronic apathy about education at the time and the neglect of educational history since. A remarkable instance is the record of the privy council 'trial' of 1902 which was summoned to determine whether the Victoria University should be divided into separate autonomous universities in Lancashire and Yorkshire (described on p. 6.4f) and which decided a vital issue of educational policy for Britain. It received perfunctory notice in the contemporary press and is now almost wholly forgotten.

One of Haldane's favourite maxims was written by his hero, Goethe: 'He who would accomplish anything must limit himself.' Our portrait of Haldane tries to catch the light from only one facet of his life. His prime educational interest was in the promotion of universities. But he wanted universities to be an integral part of a coherent system of education such as is only now, in the 1970s, beginning to develop in Britain. His vision was of a national system of education with universities at the pinnacle, permeating (as he used to say) the whole of education beneath them and, through adult education, beyond them. Even those who may be familiar with Haldane's work on universities are not likely to know about the part he played in paving the way for the Education act carried by Fisher in 1918, or about his preoccupation with the creation of educational provinces in Britain, or continuation schools, or the promotion of adult education. What we have tried to do is to assess – in the pattern of a portrait-biography – Haldane's contribution to the British system of education, illuminated by new material

and matured by the passage of time. And we have tried to put on paper
an impression of how he appeared to those of his contemporaries
who talked with him about education.

# 1 Appointment with Mr Haldane

The visitor is ushered in. Haldane is standing to receive him; grave, friendly, almost deferential. He is heavily built, broad pale face, rotund body. (Violet Bonham Carter called him 'spheroid' and Beatrice Webb wrote that he was more like a French seventeenth-century abbé than an English politician.) He speaks gently, in a thin smooth voice, and puts the visitor at ease. With disarming geniality he creates an atmosphere in which any business can be settled amicably. He lights a cigar and listens to the visitor respectfully. When the time comes for him to talk he speaks without emphasis but with a quiet, confident logic and an apparently effortless mastery of facts which astonishes many who come to consult him; never arrogant, though at times ponderous, assembling more evidence than the argument needs; occasionally standing by the fire and reinforcing his point with what Austen Chamberlain (when Haldane spoke in parliament) called 'penguin-like gestures'.

The compelling impression Haldane created was one of reasonableness and, as one of his admirers put it: 'Thought itself made flesh'. His pride was to use his mind as an intellectual mill. The mill ground too fine for some listeners – 'no-one can invest a subject in a more lucid fog' – but for over a generation people sought his help or advice on legal topics, defence, political schemes and above all, on education. During Haldane's last illness at the end of his life, Beatrice Webb, often his severe critic, sought to cheer him by calling him the 'great consultant'. It was an apt compliment, for much of Haldane's achievement in public life, except as war minister and lord chancellor, was not due to the direct exercise of power on his part, but to the subtle way in which he could infect other people with his enthusiasm, persuade them to his views, equip them with his advice, and enlist their loyalty and affection. What were the qualities which gave him this high reputation?

First, an astonishing capacity for work. As a young lawyer and MP he could speak for a couple of hours in court; travel to Bradford and address 3000 people; return the same night, reading briefs in the train; arrive at his chambers at 3.30 a.m. to find another urgent brief to be read; get up at 7.30 a.m. to read it, and appear in court again to speak at 9.45 a.m. After which, as he wrote to his mother: 'Not a bit tired, only hustled a little.' A second quality was to tackle decision-making from principle, not expedience. As war minister, reorganising the army, he spent the parliamentary recess in 1908 'studying the characters of Generals, ancient and modern, with the end in view of learning to choose my own young ones aright.' Working from principle can lead to a sterile academicism; but Haldane, although he was steeped in nineteenth-century German philosophy, remained solidly pragmatic in politics. He had some utopian visions – one of them was an integrated and coherent educational system – but when he was engaged in practical politics and not oratory he approached utopia by plodding step by step on the ground, rarely by heroic global designs; each step prepared by painstaking consultation and consolidated by fact. A third quality which gave Haldane such influence over affairs was the way he would mobilise his whole daily life – domestic and public – to achieve his purpose. He would become infected with an idea, often an idea got from someone else; for he was not an imaginative innovator. He would decide that the idea ought to be turned into a decision. He would then design a strategy to achieve this end. If the strategy required public propaganda, he would address meeting after meeting on the topic. If it required political backing, he would coax the key politicians, one at a time, at dinner parties, in committees, at week-end house parties. Hospitality to his friends was one of his relaxations. He was said to have the best chef in town and the finest cellar in Scotland. But the dinner parties and the after-dinner talk over cigars were not mere relaxation; often they were deliberate moves toward the translation of ideas into reality. It was an essential element in Haldane's technique that he should deliberately create for himself a central place in the web of society; never – and this is what gave people such confidence in him – to further his own personal ends, always to further ends with which he, quite objectively, identified himself. He was 'Public-spirit personified'.

Of course this technique invites criticism. Haldane did deliberately orchestrate his friends and acquaintances, and to some of them this looked like opportunism. And his pertinacity, when he had made up his mind to identify himself with an issue, was inseparable from the complete confidence he had in the issue itself and, as he rose from success to success, in the impression he created that he (perhaps *only* he) could cause the issue to be resolved. There was a certain puzzling inconsistency between his modesty (it was only in his letters to his mother that he slipped, to please her, into pardonable exaggeration) and a faith in himself which A. G. Gardiner said 'amounts to inspiration.' To the fulfilment of his designs he brought patience, and imperturbability, a relentless tenacity, which wore down resistance. It would be gross misrepresentation to say that Haldane was prepared to concede on matters of principle in order to get results, but within the framework of his principles he was never obdurate; he was always ready to conciliate opposition by compromise; sometimes (as in the episode when he persuaded Irish MPs to co-operate over reform in the University of London, which we describe on p. 38f.) by doing an undisguised political deal with them. But his supreme weapon was the number and accuracy of his facts, his candour in deploying them, and an unquenchable optimism. '*Toujours bien, jamais mieux*' was the motto attached to him.* He never bullied his opponents nor humiliated them; indeed it was a criticism of his life as a politician that he set out to enlist the sympathy of both liberals and conservatives rather than play the party game.

Also among the qualities which supported his reputation was his generosity in entering into the interests of friends and strangers alike and the soundness of the disinterested advice which he gave them. In bitter adversity shortly after the outbreak of world war I, when he was in political exile, rejected by the people and hounded by the press, he was still willing to spend time and trouble on those who came to him for advice. Christopher Addison, who was then parliamentary secretary to the board of education, wrote: 'On many occasions ... I went to Haldane for criticism and advice. He was ever ready to help, for he is too great a man to sulk, and did not scorn to assist a minor Minister in relatively small affairs.' It was his misfortune, John Buchan said some years before, that all men spoke well of him; though this of course was never in fact the case. Beatrice Webb was censorious about his addiction to good living, though by her standards most of

---

* Sometimes this attitude gave people the impression that he was complacent. It is related that he was present at a reception for those high-powered evangelists, Moody and Sankey. The evangelists asked the guests in turn: 'Are you saved?'. But to Haldane, 'standing with his back to the fire, calmly surveying the scene, Moody could only say in veneration: "I can see it is all right with you, brother".'

her friends must have appeared self-indulgent (Tawney, not himself exactly a sybarite, described the Webb's hospitality as 'exercises in asceticism described by Mrs Webb as dinners'). H. G. Wells peppered him with an envious irony (his 'urbane voice that carried his words as it were on a salver, so that they seemed good even when they were not so'). Among his contemporaries in parliament Lloyd George did not disguise his dislike of Haldane's scheming – but then Lloyd George was a virtuoso in a similar technique. Also Haldane frequently, and conspicuously over the Education act of 1902, irritated his fellow Liberals because he would not toe the party line. Even men with similar aspirations for education in Britain, like Sadler, regarded him as an ominous influence.

But Haldane's massive learning and composure and obvious dedication to the public good prevailed against such criticism. Even when he was no longer a powerful political figure people continued to seek his support or to ask his advice because of the sheer weight of his wisdom. In August 1928, two weeks before he died, Beatrice Webb wrote to Haldane's sister: ' . . . we still hope, as time goes on, the complete restfulness of life will bring Lord Haldane back as a leading Consultant for all young movements and their representatives.'

Haldane never held a portfolio in education. Indeed, when he was offered one in the first Labour government he turned it down. Nor did he ever hold either of two other ministerial offices where influence can be brought to bear on universities: the treasury or the privy council. Yet his work for education was sustained for a longer stretch of his life than was his work for the army or for the law; and his influence on education was as enduring as it was on the war office or on the lord chancellorship. His own writing repeatedly makes it clear that (like Jefferson) he set more value upon his contribution to universities than upon the glittering political prizes that he won. 'My whole soul', he wrote of the time he first took ministerial office, 'had been for years in the effort to bring about reform in higher education and in other departments of administration.' To understand how this concern arose, it is necessary to look back at Haldane's youth and upbringing.

Richard Burdon Haldane was born in the comfortable environment of Charlotte Square, Edinburgh, in 1856. His father was a prosperous lawyer, a writer to the signet. His mother came of Northumbrian stock with impressive legal connections, including a lord chancellor (Lord Eldon) and a distinguished judge (Lord Stowell). It is not possible to separate out nature, nurture, and the elements of chance which together determine a man's personality and his achievements. But we can discern how the combination of these three factors influenced Haldane's education; and it was his education which kindled the lifelong interest which we portray in this book.

Strict calvinism was the spiritual environment of Haldane's home. At their small country estate, at Cloan in Perthshire, Haldane's father would hold Sunday evangelical meetings alternately in a loft on the estate and in neighbouring villages; and Haldane's mother came from a home where the head of the family had become a convert to the Plymouth Brethren. So it was natural that Haldane should describe himself long afterwards as a 'grave and pious' youth. Had he been sent, as many upper class Scottish boys were in those days, to school and university in England (his cousin went to Eton and Balliol) his piety would doubtless have been somewhat alleviated by anglicanism. But Haldane's father chose to keep his son in the more puritan atmosphere of Edinburgh: he sent him to the Edinburgh Academy (which Haldane recollected as 'never an interesting period to me') and to Edinburgh University.

It was in this environment that Haldane had to release himself from the spiritual constraints of his upbringing; a release made all the more difficult because Haldane was deeply attached to his parents and they were wise and patient in the way they brought him up. But even at school, he tells us, he had religious doubts, and at sixteen, when he enrolled as an undergraduate, he had already the maturity and the courage to confront the assumptions under which he had been reared. At the university his personality unfolded rapidly. His fellow students, young like himself, were mostly serious and hardworking. He found himself sitting side by side in the lecture rooms with the sons of farm labourers. This democratic tradition of Scottish universities, and their emphasis on philosophy and logic, drew from Haldane a response which lasted throughout his life. He tramped the hills with his fellow students in search of 'spiritual ground', as he put it, 'on which we could firmly plant our feet.' He went through what would now be called an identity crisis. Law was to be his profession but it had no remedy for his perplexity. Theology at Edinburgh offered him no comfort. Only in philosophy was he able to see strands of thought which might resolve his doubts.

At this point in his career, only two years on his way to a degree, Haldane reached a cross-road of choice which influenced the whole of his subsequent career. Like all such crucial decisions, the choice was determined by a blend of nurture, nature and chance. He had to reconcile his own thought and conduct with his home environment. He had the innate integrity and intelligence not to compromise over this reconciliation, nor to patch over the cracks in his belief. And by chance one of his professors, Blackie, knew how to advise Haldane what to do.

The choice was either to stay in Edinburgh, where he could get professional training but (he believed) no prescription for the art of living; or to go on, as his cousin had, to Oxford; or to do something else. Blackie had trained in Germany and he advised Haldane to put himself under the great metaphysician, R. H. Lotze, in Göttingen. Haldane's parents – and this is a testimony to their liberality – allowed their son, still only seventeen years old, to make his choice. He chose Göttingen, and in April 1874 he set sail for Hamburg.

Under the unwritten code of *Lernfreiheit* German students led a very different life from those in Britain. They were two or three years older when they came to the university. Their social origins were more like those of undergraduates in the 1870s at Oxford and Cambridge than like those of Scottish students, but they were without the collegiate supervision imposed upon Oxford and Cambridge undergraduates or the constraints of regular examinations imposed upon Scottish students. There were student societies (the *Verbindungen*) notorious for riotous behaviour, drinking, and duelling, but co-existing with this brutal side of student life there was devotion to serious scholarship at a level which (according to one of Haldane's letters to his parents) put to ridicule '4 out of 5 of the working students who come from Oxford or Cambridge.'

Into this sophisticated and adult society Haldane came as a perplexed, serious boy, eight years younger (he wrote) than the average among his fellow students. His home still powerfully influenced his life in Göttingen. He wrote to his parents: 'I feel the want of Sunday very much, for the day does not exist here. . . . I should like to be in the loft at the fortnightly meetings and was thinking that you would be preaching as we came to Goslar on Sunday. Are Moody and Sankey gone to London or back to America? If there is an account of their last visit to Edinburgh in any paper I should like to see it very much and also should like a report of the great cricket match. . . . I am reading through the Romans and through John's Epistles with Candlish's sermons. . . . Everything is green and beautiful but it is not home and I long for Cloanden.'

But despite bouts of homesickness Haldane revelled in the intellectual life.

Only about twenty students attend each lecture, the lecture rooms being indeed very small and numerous and the number of professors being in the ratio of one to every ten students. The professors for the most part look as if they had seen more books than soap and tailors' shops, for most of them are men of about 60, wearing coloured spectacles, broad Tyrolean hats, with dirty, badly shaven faces, and their clothes almost tumbling off. They sometimes lecture in Latin, sometimes in German, it being much the same to them & to the students. . . . There are no such things as examinations in the classes, much less anything so contemptible in the German eye as prizes – a great improvement on us and which I think accounts for the fact that the Germans are so much better informed, since they do not cram things as with us, but really learn them. . . . The lectures are admirable, very clear & intelligible though on subjects difficult to explain.

Reading philosophy and Goethe, talking with students – he was made member of a *Verbindung* – listening to professors, walking in the hills round the town, Haldane dispelled his depression and came to terms with his doubts. Two people in particular were responsible for this enlightenment: Professor Lotze, to whom Blackie had introduced him, and Fräulein Schlote, who gave him language lessons and introduced him to the study of Goethe, a study which took him back to Germany year after year for a generation.

I spent a very pleasant afternoon [he wrote to his parents] with Professor Lotze on Monday. I had a long conversation with him on the relation of Philosophy to religion, on materialism, the immortality of the soul, and so on. He said that a lifetime's reflection on these subjects (he is 65 and about my father's build, and like him very active) had convinced him that no ascertained truth in philosophy clashed with religion. . . . He did not believe that philosophy and Christianity had much in common – they were not necessary to each other's existence, but the reason of this was that their spheres were different.

And a few weeks later he wrote:

I have just returned from a visit to Lotze who invited me to come and sit for a while with him. I had an exceedingly pleasant time and a long talk in which he expounded the nature of faith and pointed out the relationship between it and positive knowledge, at the bottom of which it lies. . . . I proposed to him some difficulties that had come up in an analysis that I have been making lately of Causation in Willing, whereupon he got quite excited in pointing out how by faith philosophy raised itself above such difficulties in the freedom of the will and yet took the most scientific course. . . . I told him that philosophy was my *Herz-studium* but that I felt it to be very insufficient unless it culminated in faith.

These quiet conversations with Lotze set Haldane's intellectual and spiritual course for a lifetime. Thirty-six years later, in 1910, when he addressed students in Aberystwyth, he paid a moving tribute to this.

. . . I was bidden [he said] to choose for myself whether I would go to Oxford or to a German university, and I chose Göttingen because Lotze was there. I was only seventeen, little more than a boy. I remember vividly how spiritually as well as intellectually anchorless I felt in the early days of my residence in the old University town . . . the figure that stood out above all the others was that of my old master, Hermann Lotze. I had the privilege, boy as I was, of seeing him often in his study as well as of listening in his lecture-room, and to the end of my life I shall hold the deep impression he made on me – of a combination of intellectual power and the highest moral stature. It seems to me but yesterday that he used quietly to enter the lecture-room where we students sat expectant, and, taking his seat, fix his eyes on space as though he were looking into another world remote from this one. The face was worn with thought, and the slight and fragile figure with the great head looked as though the mind that tenanted it had been dedicated to thought and to nothing else. . . . Our feeling towards him as we sat and listened was one of reverence mingled with affection.

A man can be judged from those he adopts as his heroes. It is not difficult to see why Haldane in maturity had an affection for Germany and a dedication to the cause of universities. A German university had led him out of the perplexity of youth into the assurance of manhood. A German professor had demonstrated to him how to combine intellectual rigour with moral principle. German *Gelehrter* – Kant, Hegel, Schopenhauer and, above all, Goethe – shone a light ahead for his career.

Haldane spent only about four months in Göttingen. He came back to Edinburgh in time to re-enrol at the University for the new academic year. How much Germany had done for him is evident from the temporary surge of disappointment he had on returning home. 'Can you believe it?', he wrote to a fellow student in Germany (Hugo Conwentz) in October 1874, 'I actually dislike my own country now. The people seem to think of nothing but how to make money and never how to attain to a high culture.' But this impulse of disillusionment soon passed. Haldane threw himself with enthusiasm into the study of Hegel (one of the legends about him was that he would rise and light his own fire between five and six on dark winter mornings in order to read *Wissenschaft der Logik*). In 1876 he graduated with first class honours in philosophy and carried off a medal and two scholarships, one of which signified that he was the ablest student in philosophy of his year in the whole of Scotland.

The moment had come to embark on a career. Haldane, with this excellent academic record, could doubtless have pursued his *Herzstudium* as a profession. He used to quote, nostalgically, the lines from Lucretius:

But sweeter far to dwell remote, aloof
In some high mansion, built on Wisdom's hill:
Thence watch the errant crowd go to and fro,
Matching their wits, striving for precedence,
Toiling and moiling, hurrying night and day
To rise to fortune and possess the world.

Many successful men entertain a similar placid pipe-dream, but currents of ambition or social responsibility sweep it away. Despite his protestations in favour of the contemplative life, Haldane was in no doubt that his place was with the 'errant crowd'. He did not forsake his affection for philosophy, but these frequently quoted lines from Lucretius were never his guide. From the outset his mind was set on law and, through law, on politics. Even when still an undergraduate at Edinburgh he had begun to read concurrently for a law degree as an external student in the University of London; but he failed the first examination. From graduation he went straight to read law in the offices of two Edinburgh firms of writers to the signet, and, so that he might qualify himself to become a barrister, to eat dinners in Lincoln's Inn; for London, not Edinburgh, was to be his stage. He moved there in the latter part of 1877 and was called to the bar in 1879.

Haldane was not a man of means. His father had recently died, and he had to make his living as a barrister. From almost the start of his career in London, however, he began to involve himself in politics and in what was in those days the essential concomitant of politics: society. In 1880 – he was still only twenty-four – he was electioneering for the Liberals. He became a member of Brooks's Club. He laid foundations for his political friendships, spending long evenings with his contemporary, Asquith, 'concentrated on ideas', and, during walks they took together at Cloan, talking over 'what could be made of the future.' It was at this very embryonic stage of his political life that Haldane made his first venture into organisation on behalf of the party. Eager to preserve the association of young Liberals which had been formed by Albert Grey to fight the 1880 election, he trudged through deep snow early in 1881 to rally support for what became the famous 'Eighty' Club, so named after the great Liberal victory of that year, and destined to play an active part in promoting the Liberal cause for another generation.

Haldane's Liberalism was, for those days, radical. He, along with other young progressive Liberals of his generation, became concerned with the future of the working classes. For him this was no remote, theoretical concern, for some of them had been his classmates in Edinburgh; though the farm labourer's son enrolled in a Scottish university was a world away from the masses of the poor, underpaid and ill-housed, in London slums. It had been commonly assumed that the shocking gulf between comfort and poverty was immutable and that – to resurrect the cliché – a man was expected to accept the state of life to which God had called him. But, perhaps as a backlash to the grim implications of Darwinism for the condition of man, there was in the 1880s a stirring of conscience. An economic recession in the late 70s and early 80s stirred up radical thoughts; some people recognised what Galsworthy called the 'grin on the face of Fate'. Complacency among the well-to-do was challenged by an introspective social conscience among some of their sons and daughters. It took material form in the establishment of 'settlements' in the East End of London, some of them sponsored by public schools or Oxbridge colleges. It took ideological form in socialist and anarchist propaganda, in the suffragette movement, and in all sorts of radical-eccentric societies such as the National Anti-vaccination League, the National Anti-vivisection Society, the Society for Psychical Research, the Theosophical Society. All these had one thing in common: they opposed conventional Victorian ideals. Edward Carpenter (who describes this transition vividly in his autobiography) called it 'a large social and intellectual restlessness that in turn made members of established society nervous. . . .' But not all became nervous. Others – Haldane among them – saw opportunity, not apprehension, in this social ferment. In 1890, five years after he had entered parliament, he wrote to Mrs Humphrey Ward: 'The thought has come strongly upon me for the last six months that there is near at hand the greatest opportunity for trying to make our public position one of real and noble influence that ever has been. These great social questions which have exercised the minds of men for so long are at last before us practically or presently will be so.'

Here was a convergence of Haldane's philosophical idealism (stimulated at that time by the writings of T. H. Green) with his desire for action. It was natural that he should see education as the panacea for the solution of class differences. He became a member of the Council of the Workers' Education League and he gave a course of philosophy lectures at the Working Mens' College. He lectured also at the St James's and Soho Radical Club (the centre of the 'International' in London) on the socialist theories of Lassalle and Marx. He was hotly criticised afterwards for his views, so he may already have been declaring his faith that it was neither Capital nor Labour which created wealth, but Mind.

But all these were part time interests. Haldane's main energies had to go into his work at the bar. It is a testimony to his industry and capacity that by 1885, only five years after embarking on his profession and still under the age of thirty, he was firmly enough established to stand for parliament. In June 1885 Gladstone resigned and a short-lived Tory administration followed under Lord Salisbury. In the general election at the end of the year, Haldane was returned to parliament for East Lothian, a seat which he captured from the Tories and held for twenty-five years. It was the first election under the new franchise act which raised the United Kingdom electorate from about three millions to about five millions. Haldane tramped his constituency to enlist support from the newly enfranchised householders. His electioneering among them reinforced his faith in education. 'When I went into those spotless and speckless cottages', he wrote, long afterwards, 'there I saw books, and there was an atmosphere of education there, and I used to feel that these men were not what was ordinarily understood by labourers but were people with mind and knowledge just

like what was possessed by their most highly educated neighbours. . . .
I learned a great deal there and I learned this: that no political creed is
worth anything that does not embrace the spiritual side as well as the
material side.'

It was with these earnest and noble sentiments that Haldane went into
politics: to uplift, to reform, and above all, to educate. He was never,
by his own admission, a good 'party man'; he believed for instance,
that the business of the Opposition was not to oppose, but to criticise;
but he did believe in the party system and his aim was to endow Liberalism with ideals for the moral and intellectual development of the nation.
These political ideals and this faith in education and progress must of
course be judged in the context of the 1880s, not the 1970s, otherwise
they would be condemned outright as intolerably priggish. But even to
Haldane's contemporaries there was a certain inconsistency between
the idealism of his principles and the pragmatism of his practice. On the
public platform Haldane was the austere visionary, unhurried by
emotion, propagating high ideals; in the lobbies of the house of
commons and over the dinner table in his own home he was the subtle
schemer, scheming indeed in the highest public interest – never for
himself – but ready to compromise, to seize the right moment, to
conspire in ways which sometimes generated mistrust, even from such
an arch-conspirator as Beatrice Webb.

So, in portraying Haldane at work on education, one has to interpret
his speeches with discernment. It is the duty of a speaker to select
themes appropriate to his audience. It follows, therefore, that when
Haldane speaks to students, he emphasises the high responsibilities of
being a student, when he speaks to the Workers' Educational Association, he emphasises the need for adult education; and so on. That these
professions of faith were not always consistent does not surprise anyone
who has to make public speeches. This is not to say that Haldane was
disingenuous; even less that he was deceitful: just that, like anyone in
public life, he had to be many-sided in opinions as well as in activities,
shifting his priorities to suit his hearers. Bernard Shaw put the inconsistency beautifully in a salty letter to Haldane, written in 1907 after
Haldane had delivered an address steeped in Hegelian sentiments, as
lord rector of Edinburgh University:

I read your address to those unfortunate students very carefully;
and I must say that it is like your right honourable cheek to talk
to them like that. Why will people not tell the truth? Here are

you, the most conspicuous living example in the kingdom of the realisation of all these students' ambitions – a Scotch philosopher who has beaten all the practical men and statesmen at their own game. This you have achieved by doing exactly what you liked; smoking a good deal too many cigars; eating in a manner that shocks Mrs Sidney Webb; and generally making the greatest possible success of the world, the flesh and the devil. And yet you go down and tell those unhappy young people, in lofty and inspiring periods, that you did it all by a life of contemplation, aloof from the world at Weimar.

This is comedy, but it illustrates the difficulty of portraying a public man from his own testimony. How, to turn to a serious question, is one to decide what Haldane's views were about the function of MPs as representatives of their constituents in a democracy? That Haldane regarded his membership of parliament as a high duty there is no doubt. But was it a duty to lead, or to reflect, opinion among the people? Addressing a meeting at Cambridge in 1891, he said:

> ... it is no function [of MPs] to mould ideas; that is to be done outside, that is your work at the University; that is the work of the thinkers, of the teachers, of the preachers, of the evangelists of the gospel of progress in every part of the country.... We MPs are the sons of our nation and our age. Behind that age we cannot remain, neither can we advance before it. The work has to be done outside before the House of Commons can take it up.

But among his political colleagues Haldane advocated a different emphasis. Writing to Ronald Ferguson in 1889 he said:

> What we have to do at home is to try to gain the confidence of the electors and to mould their opinions. To my dying day, I think, I shall maintain the proposition ... that a democracy has not got, as is assumed in practice, a body of definite opinion, for the expression of which in Parliament it seeks delegates, but that it is an assembly of human beings earnestly seeking guidance from those of whose sympathies it is sure.

And, in his maturity, a generation later, speaking in the house of lords: 'I have all my life believed in putting before the democracy, and pressing upon it, new conceptions, and in no department has that been more strikingly necessary than in the case of education.' And if the democracy did not respond to the conceptions, Haldane was prepared to go further. The nation, he told the house of lords in 1916, 'has been very unhappy with regard to ideas about education. This is reflected in the Cabinet, in Parliament and in the country. Therefore the only way is for the leaders to take a definite decision without waiting for any particular mandate. . . .'

Haldane's work on education was a sustained reconciliation of these two conflicting ideas: on one hand, that in a democracy it is the people, not their leaders, who decide; on the other hand, that in a democracy the minority who are educated have a responsibility toward the majority who are not, and must decide on behalf of the majority. The utopian solution was education for all.

'Chance', wrote Poincaré, 'comes to the prepared mind.' But the opposite is also true: a man may be fortunate enough to come into a scene as though it were prepared for him. This was certainly the case for a politician with strong interests in education beginning a career in 1885. For over two decades there had been a growing dissatisfaction with the schools and colleges and universities of Britain. The dissatisfaction had been voiced by three very articulate critics whom the public could not ignore: Lyon Playfair, Matthew Arnold, T. H. Huxley. Lyon Playfair returned from the International Exhibition in Paris deeply depressed about the backwardness of technical education in Britain; he wrote in 1867: '. . . the one cause upon which there was most unanimity of conviction is that France, Prussia, Austria, Belgium, and Switzerland possess good systems of industrial education for the masters and managers of factories and workshops, and that England possesses none.' Matthew Arnold's criticism covered a much wider field. His famous comparative study of schools and universities on the continent, published in 1866 and several times reprinted, led him to the indictment that Oxford and Cambridge were not universities in the continental and traditional sense at all, because the superior faculties (law, medicine, even theology) had atrophied there, but were 'places where the youth of the upper class prolong to a very great age, and under some very admirable influences, their school education. . . .' T. H. Huxley, concerned chiefly with what he called the 'state of barbarous ignorance of even the rudiments of scientific culture', used his brilliant eloquence in a string of addresses to awaken the public to the need for reform in education. Nor was the agitation confined to academic evangelism. Successive governments had responded by setting up commissions and committees of enquiry:

the commissions on Oxford and Cambridge which reported in 1852; a select committee on scientific instruction in 1868; the Devonshire commission, which worked from 1871 to 1875; the Samuelson commission in 1884; and, for Scottish higher education, a commission appointed in 1876 which included both Playfair and Huxley. During Haldane's novitiate in parliament this era of awakening led to some useful reforms. There was a growing consensus about need, but a sharpening controversy about means. The deeply divisive question – which nowadays seems quite unreal – was whether education should be a responsibility of the state or should be left as far as possible to private agencies encouraged by the state. Gradually legislation crept in the direction of state support. The Technical Instruction Act of 1889 empowered local authorities to levy a penny rate for this purpose; and the Local Taxation (Excise and Customs) Act of 1890 authorised the application of the so-called 'whisky money' for the same purpose. In 1889 theWelsh Intermediate Education Act transferred to local authorities the control of secondary education previously vested in the Charity commission; and in 1891, twenty-one years after the introduction of universal elementary education, it was made free. The most important step toward state patronage of education was taken in 1899 when, following a royal commission under the chairmanship of Bryce (which included Sadler, who appears later in this story), the government set up a central education authority under a minister (there had not been one before), and it was called the board of education.

Haldane took no part in these developments. Some of them were the achievement of A. H. D. Acland, whom Haldane watched at this time, obviously with some envy, for he confessed privately in 1894: 'I would rather be like Arthur Acland, with all his fanaticisms, than anyone else I know just now....' It was another sign of his instinct, even in his early years in politics, to make education his platform.

But his first educational preoccupation was not with schools, but with universities. Here, too, there was a fresh breeze of reform, but it was very gentle and it did not disperse the infirmities about which men like Playfair and Huxley had been writing for years. Oxford and Cambridge had freed themselves from the constraint of religious tests and were rising toward the crest of a renaissance in teaching and research. The initiative, with periodic jolts from royal commissions, came from within. From Trinity College, Cambridge, Henry Sidgwick wrote that 'the long, long, canker of peace is over and done; the only thing soon will be to avoid radicalism.' It was he who opened the campaign – still not quite over – to admit women to Cambridge on equal terms with men. In Oxford, Jowett and others like him had created the image of the college as a nursery for leaders in politics and administration; and most of Haldane's close colleagues in the party were from Oxford. Oxford was not only a school for character-building; the ideas sown by Mark Pattison's famous tract, *Suggestions on academical organisation*, published in 1868, were already restoring the university as a great centre for scholarship. But this revival of intellectual energy at Oxford and Cambridge touched only a tiny fraction of the population in England, and even that fraction was not selected primarily on scholarly merit. In the late 1880s the combined student population in the two universities did not exceed 5000. Scotland offered its sons and daughters better opportunities: there were then some 6800 students in the four universities; but reforms in teaching and organisation at the Scottish universities were overdue. What was happening in Britain was a delayed response to the forebodings of men like Playfair: that Britain would fall behind the Continent if she did not recruit into industry, commerce and administration men with more than a secondary school education. The institutions which needed encouragement were those in the industrial cities (in 1885 even Owens College, Manchester, had only just over 400 students apart from those in the medical school). The blueprint which influenced Haldane most at this time was the one proposed by Arnold (Haldane, as a student, had met him in Edinburgh and remained his fervent disciple). Arnold envisaged a national system of state-aided education, integrated from school to university, under a minister of state assisted by an advisory council. He advocated a regional organisation for higher schools, under 'provisional boards', co-ordinated with the universities. He did not want a proliferation of degree-giving institutions in England, but rather some eight to ten centres monitored by examinations under the University of London.

Arnold died three years after Haldane entered parliament, but Haldane eagerly inherited Arnold's legacy of ideas, though he modified some of them in the light of his experience. The task ahead – and this is true of much of Haldane's work – was to transmute these ideas into the gritty details of legislation. This – it appears again and again in his portrait – was Haldane's contribution to education: to work on splendid aspirations until they could be fitted into a practical and acceptable administrative framework. Apart from certain lapses, due to over-optimism, which will appear in our portrait, he was a master craftsman in the art of the possible.

But in 1885, Haldane had to apply the art of the possible to his own career. In the Victorian age a man could not devote himself to politics unless he had some assured source of income. So Haldane's first objective was to establish himself at the bar. He had neither the temperament nor the sense of histrionics to excel at criminal law or before juries; he felt, besides, the want of the humanistic training of the older universities for this type of work. So he chose to specialise in the sort of civil cases where he could turn his Scottish philosophical training to account: cases of appeal before the house of lords and privy council which called for skill in applying the psychology of advocacy, and skill, above all, in establishing the first principles of law from a mass of intricate fact. He soon acquired prominence in this type of pleading, and a reputation for enjoying the sympathy of the supreme tribunals. In 1890, ten years after being called to the bar, he was appointed a queen's counsel at the early age of thirty-three. He worked immensely hard, and was more and more in demand in the courts. Briefs came pressing in on him from industrial magnates and colonial governments. His fees, already in the region of £2500 a year, mounted rapidly. A clear road lay ahead: the road to a distinguished and affluent practice as a barrister; beyond that a judgeship, leading perhaps, to appointment as one of the lords of appeal. But this was not the road Haldane chose. Writing in 1894, he said he had no intention of allowing his legal practice to 'swallow' him up. His goal was still political office 'not legal office, but one like the Local Government Board or the Scottish Office'.

The strategy needed for success in politics has to be every bit as arduous and deliberate as the strategy needed for success at the bar. But it is a very different kind. A politician has to be known, and what he stands for has to be known. Haldane set about deliberately to fulfil these two requirements. What he stood for needed no contriving; his background, his temperament, his intellectual interests, his sensitivity to the human condition: all these predisposed him to align himself with social reformers; not, of course, revolutionaries or extreme radicals – their programmes were utopian and impractical and therefore not politically viable – but with those reformers who believed in progress, gradualism, a steady evolutionary change from what is, to what is somewhat better. Several other young members of parliament had similar interests. They were led by Asquith, who with Haldane's help, had been returned for a constituency adjacent to his own in 1886. One of the group, somewhat older than the others, but newly elected like them, was Arthur Acland, who as we have just mentioned shared with Haldane a special interest in education and a faith in its efficacy in a democratic society.

There were plenty of issues which needed an injection of liberalism (both in its political and philosophical meanings) in the late 1880s. At home there were the problems focused by the slump and the widening of the electorate: questions of urban social welfare and labour relations, votes for women and the payment of members, local government reform, and above all – education. Abroad there was the perennial problem of Ireland, and beyond, the problem of devising a bond of empire that would withstand the divisive forces of developing nationalism. These overseas interests brought Asquith's group in touch with two of the more senior politicians, Rosebery and Morley – Rosebery, imaginative, personable, progressive, architect of the concept of liberal imperialism, at that time the 'glittering hope' of the Liberal party; Morley, deeply interesting to Haldane and his friends for his political association with Gladstone and the wide range of his literary interests. But over home affairs the radicalism of both men proved too tepid for the younger group, and in 'thinking and working out an effective programme' they soon felt obliged to become their own pacemakers. In the sharing out of this work, Haldane took as his special subjects: 'the extension of university education, women's suffrage, and housing'.

His colleagues now knew what he stood for. They knew, too, that he was no obedient and compliant backbencher, but a man of independent views, with a gift for propagating those views by what his admirers called persuasion and his adversaries called intrigue. It was perhaps as much due to this reputation for independence, as to Haldane's shortcomings as a public speaker, that alone of his close colleagues he was not given office when Gladstone formed his last administration in 1892, or, indeed, when Rosebery succeeded to the premiership in 1894. He is on record himself as saying that he did not want office so soon. Whether or not this was so, we doubt whether he would have refused a post if he had been offered one. But he still had to consolidate his position at the bar, and anyway he was beginning to experience what was to be the enduring satisfaction of his career: the satisfaction of influencing events by remote control, often anonymously, through informal conversations, talks at weekend house parties, acting as go-between to convey embryonic policies, modifying them all the time so that consensus could be reached, narrowing gaps between opposing views, proposing names for appointments; in short, Haldane had become the confidant of a wide variety of people. He had become (in the words of Beatrice Webb) 'an influential man'.

The second requirement was to be known to the right people; and there is no doubt that between 1890 and the turn of the century Haldane did deliberately become a 'society figure'. It may be too cynical to suggest that Haldane acquired friends in order to make use of them, but his excursions into some sections of society were certainly not in search of soul-mates. That he was attracted in the early 1890s by the dazzling, though sometimes precious sophistication of the 'Souls' is not surprising. The mingling of birth and intellect, the new ideas, the brilliant talk: all these were likely to draw him. There was the added appeal of elegant and witty women, for women figured as prominently as men in these gatherings, and for Haldane, as for Goethe, women were among the best instructors in the ways of the world. It was through Lady Horner of Mells – the wife of a close friend – that Haldane was first introduced into this fashionable society, and though never a 'paid up' member, came to be invited to their dinners and house parties. He became a frequent guest of the Tennants at Grosvenor Square; often a visitor at Panshanger, Taplow and Stanway. In this way he developed contacts with those of different political persuasions – with Alfred Lyttelton, for instance, George Wyndham, and above all Balfour – and, as at the bar, made friends who were later to help him with his educational projects. That he mixed at other house parties with the racing set is surprising; though as Lady Desborough recalled later, the social sets of that period were by no means exclusive, and there was a good deal of intermingling between them. Through relaxed weekends with these varied people, Haldane had, by 1900, extended his circle of acquaintances, assimilated the opinions and conceits of some of the sharpest minds in British society, and gained an insight into convictions and prejudices other than his own.

It was, of course, not enough to frequent these coteries of the establishment. Haldane had to make himself the centre of a coterie. As early as 1886, he and Asquith started an annual dinner at 'The Blue Posts', a public house in Cork Street. Eight guests were invited: four distinguished in letters and four – irrespective of party – in politics. Throughout his career Haldane used the dinner party, lubricated by superb cooking, choice wines, and much admired cigars, as an instrument for discussing, refining and influencing political policies. That

Haldane was conscious of his new social status as a queen's counsel is evident from a letter to his mother, early in 1890: '. . . it is quite curious to see what social importance even people like Lady Rosebery and the Spencers attach to it.'

During the latter years of his apprenticeship to politics, the house parties, the dining clubs and the salons provided a colourful backcloth to Haldane's serious work at the bar and in parliament. But he had also to become as much an expert in social reform as he was already becoming in constitutional law. For this he drew upon the ideas of another coterie, utterly unlike the 'Souls' or the race parties or the assemblies of radical liberals. He was admitted to the circle of the Webbs, to the earnest and censorious company of Fabian socialists. It was an experience as significant in its way as his sojourn in Göttingen.

We do not know exactly when Haldane met Sidney Webb. They were born within three years of each other (Webb in 1859). In 1885, at the time Haldane entered parliament, Webb was introduced by Bernard Shaw to the recently formed Fabian Society. Webb was at that time a civil servant, but his ambition was to write and work for socialism. The Fabian creed – the politics of attrition, through fact piled on fact – exactly matched his temperament. By 1887, Haldane and Webb were acquainted and a year later they were exchanging ideas at a meeting of the Fabian Society. The friendship between these two men was to become a most fruitful partnership in the cause of higher education. About the same time, Haldane was also meeting another earnest and much more intimidating socialist, Beatrice Potter. There is even a legend that on one occasion, towards the end of 1890, Haldane, after discussing with her the possibility of creating a radical socialist alliance, turned to more personal matters and proposed marriage. But this rests only on a passage in Beatrice's diary which is susceptible of other interpretations and is in any case inherently improbable; and when Beatrice became secretly engaged to Sidney Webb in July of the following year, Haldane was warm in his congratulations. To Beatrice he wrote that this was 'no ordinary marriage' but 'a big event' from which 'great things' would result; and years later, when acknowledging a copy of her joint work with Sidney on *Industrial democracy*, he hailed it as 'a tribute to the real meaning of the marriage of you two'. To enlist human relationships in the cause of politics was something which Haldane found intelligible and fine. Reviewing the events of 1891, Beatrice wrote in her diary of Haldane and other political associates 'appearing on the horizon – comrades which a word or an act might

transform into friends'. After her marriage in 1892, Haldane had a
third coterie where he became a familiar figure; the socialist salon
over which Beatrice Webb presided at her home in Grosvenor Road.

But we have to add one more line to our portrait of Haldane in
1890. We wrote above that it was 'inherently improbable' that Haldane
ever sought to marry Beatrice. The ground for this is that in the year
when this conversation is thought to have occurred Haldane had been
shattered by an event which left a permanent scar on his inner life.
He was engaged to be married and his fiancée (for reasons which are
still obscure) broke the engagement. Haldane took this blow with
Roman courage; but every now and again in his correspondence,
especially when he wrote to console others in misfortune, he wrote
words which showed that the wound had never quite healed. Soon
after the break, in the summer of 1890, he wrote to Mrs Humphrey
Ward: 'But when a soul has missed the goal towards which it was
striving, and is still staggering, it naturally, in recovering its balance,
seeks to restore the prop which it knows of old and has never found
to fail.' His response to the shock was to drive himself into public
work, activity, even into the social round; but certainly not to offer
himself, in the same year, to another woman. Beatrice's own diary
bears witness to the depth of his feeling. 'In spite of the successful
professional life,' she wrote about him seven years later, '. . . he is a
restless, lonely man – in his heart still worshipping the woman who
jilted him seven years ago.' And when similar calamities befell other
people, Haldane offered the remedy by which he had cured himself.
Listen to his message to the young John Simon, written after Simon had
lost his wife: 'There is only one solace for personal grief, and that is
work for the country. Briefs at the Bar will not provide it. You must
throw yourself into public service of some sort. Why not find a
constituency?'

# 2 Apprenticeship

Haldane's first appearance on the educational stage was a modest one. In 1888, as a graduate of the University of Edinburgh rather than as a member of parliament, he took part in a deputation from the general councils of the Universities of Edinburgh and Glasgow which waited on the secretary for Scotland (the marquis of Lothian) to criticise and if possible influence the latest of a series of bills – all of them abortive – brought before parliament to achieve some of the reforms proposed by a royal commission which had reported as long ago as 1878. The graduates from these two universities were concerned to increase their own representation on the university courts, which were the small and powerful executive governing bodies of Scottish universities; but they also expressed sympathy with student pretensions to representation on these bodies. They did not recommend any increase in the existing representation – students were already represented by the rector whom they elected, and an assessor whom he nominated – but they did give support to the claims of the recently formed Students' Representative Councils to be associated in this representation. Haldane was particularly emphatic about this, urging the admirable way in which the student councils were working, and strongly pressing that students should be given indirect representation through the new machinery they provided. For he had a deep conviction in favour of the enlistment of students in the affairs of universities. Anyone from an Oxford or Cambridge college could be forgiven for regarding such a conviction as misconceived (indeed, Haldane's cousin, Lord Camperdown, thought it would be 'improper' even to give statutory recognition to the new Students' Representative Councils). But to anyone educated in a Scottish university and familiar with the tradition of *Lernfreiheit* in Germany, it was a perfectly natural attitude. '. . . I consider', Haldane said, when debating the issue of statutory recognition a year later, 'that a University should be regarded as a kind of democracy where there is citizenship and where all internal affairs should be under the control of the various classes interested.' He was, as later pages of this portrait show, somewhat ambivalent about what he meant by 'a kind of democracy'; but the experience of his undergraduate days – the crofter's son beside him in the lecture room, the independent and relatively unsupervised style of life of Scottish and German students, the way they were treated, and responded, as adults – all this experience was distilled into his concept of the university as a community of senior and junior partners engaged in a common pursuit; an idealised concept, perhaps, but one which served him as a guide to practical policies.

In 1889, the last of the series of Universities (Scotland) bills – the bill that was ultimately to reach the statute book – came before the house of commons. On its second reading in June, Haldane made his debut as a speaker on higher education. The reform of Scottish universities was a topic of minor interest to English members and Haldane spoke to a very thin House. This, as he told the empty benches opposite him, was one of the peculiar difficulties of the subject! But this did not detract from the vigour of his performance; nor had it deterred him from coming with a well prepared brief. The standpoint he adopted – which he made plain from the outset – was highly characteristic. He found much to criticise in the bill, and reserved full liberty of action in committee; but since on balance he judged the advantages 'enormously' preponderated, he felt unable to put the 'slightest obstacle' in the way of the second reading. As a Scottish member, he could not incur the responsibility of holding up reform on which so much of Scottish opinion had been agreed for so long.

The reforms most urgently sought were amendments to the constitution of the universities, and an extension of their teaching power. Haldane championed the cause of both and used them as a yardstick for judging the merits of the bill. On the constitution, he was largely satisfied. Responsibility for business and finance was to be transferred from the professors of the senatus to the court, for 'men cannot be made both judges and advocates in their own case without prejudice to the interests of justice.' He extended a special welcome for the provision that the rector, in nominating his assessor, might take the opinion of the Students' Representative Council. But his major concern was to have the teaching improved, to secure for the students of Scotland the immensely more varied and effective education which he had experienced in Germany. This, he insisted, called for two practical reforms. One was to abandon the system whereby professors augmented their salaries, sometimes to the level of affluence, by collecting the fees of their students. Paid into a' common university chest, the fees could be used to support a far greater number of teachers, with the added advantage that professors would be rid of the temptation to enlarge the size of their classes. (In England, he pointed out, there were few professors who received more than £700–1100 p.a.; whereas in Edinburgh the professor of anatomy in 1886–7 received £2811, a sum which in Germany would maintain seven professors, and in Scotland ought to maintain three.) The other reform was to extend the system, already pursued in the medical faculty, whereby students were able to prepare for degree examinations by attending the courses of private teachers (similar to the coaches common in Oxford and Cambridge); men who were not on the staff of the university. The purpose was simply to enable the universities to increase their staff–student ratio without having to pay for it. This in turn called for a complete revision of the examination system. Under the existing system the private teacher was unable to compete with the university professor. The professor was assisted in degree examinations by an associate examiner, who in theory enjoyed equal responsibility with him; but since the associate was invariably a younger man, he was unable to assert his authority. The professorial monopoly in examinations had long been the object of controversy in the Scottish press, and was one of the scandals the new legislation would be expected to redress. On these issues Haldane was more anxious; for they were left for decision to the statutory commission that was to give effect to the bill. The failure of the bill to give guidance on such matters of principle was, indeed, one of his main criticisms, especially in view of reservations he had about the composition of the commission. But he put his mind at ease over this particular misgiving with a reflection which was significant in view of his later activities: 'Were it not that the Chairman [Lord Kinnear] is a judge of distinction and of most judicial mind who will approach the matter in a thoroughly fair spirit, I should despair of the Commission doing any good,' he declared; but 'as the Chairman is, after all, the most important person on the Commission,' he was ready to admit the character of the president 'got over' the disadvantage 'to some degree'.

What is also interesting to those watching him at work on higher education is what he omitted to say in this speech. The English civic university colleges had just received an unprecedented treasury grant which was to become an annual event, and was the forerunner of the massive subvention now administered to all universities by the University Grants Committee. But unlike other speakers, he did not call for an increase in the state aid proposed for the Scottish universities. An annual grant of £42,000 had been provided in the bill; and whilst he admitted he would have been glad of a further £10,000 from the government, it was in keeping with his realistic approach and liberal instincts that he preferred to rely on the redeployment of the considerable resources already at the disposal of the Scottish universities, rather than hold out for additional sums which he saw no likelihood of obtaining. Nor did he take the opportunity which this speech offered (since MPs then, as now, were not obliged to stick closely to the point) to put in some propaganda about the need to extend university education in England, though this was later to become one of his common themes. Playfair, in the same debate, did press, as he had been pressing ever since the 1860s, for more public support to 'make sufficient provision for higher teaching in all our great towns'. But Playfair was thirty-seven years his senior, and was moved (as Haldane was not, until later on) by the need to expand higher education in order to promote industry, not just to enrich culture. Haldane may well have been influenced by his instinct to confine himself to immediate and limited goals, and to matters he understood, for his acquaintance with universities was confined to his student experience and his membership of the Edinburgh general council. At first hand he knew little at that time about the machinery of government or the conduct of academic affairs.

This immaturity was evident in his attitude to the much debated issue of 'extra-mural'* teaching in Scotland. Despite the emphatic warning of the commissioners of 1876 about the danger that any extension of the system would present to the quality of the teaching in Scottish universities, Haldane was not deterred from ranging himself with the substantial body of opinion amongst Scottish graduates which pressed for it; what he failed to see was that this was a recipe for a university on the cheap. And three years later, when he took the initiative of raising a debate on the early draft ordinances of the commission, he still sponsored the general councils' view, dismissing the provision that had been made for assistants and lecturers who were to be on the university payroll as wholly inadequate for the extension

* This had in the context of Scottish universities an entirely different meaning from the one now attached to it in British universities. It denoted the private teacher, the coach, who taught for university examinations (particularly in medicine) but was not on the university staff.

of teaching power that was needed. On this later occasion, he was again outshone by more experienced educationalists. Professor Jebb, Conservative member for Cambridge University, and latterly a professor at Glasgow, contributed a persuasive defence of the commissioners' attempt to promote the expansion of Scottish universities from within, maintaining that 'those who knew the Scottish and English universities' would agree that it was of the greatest importance to the efficiency of a university that its teaching should not be cramped by habitual regard to the examinations. The extra-mural system 'would surround the universities with an indefinitely large fringe of teachers ... each following the impulse of individual enterprise, each selecting his subject at will, less with a view to the interest of the academic commonwealth than to the prospect of successful competition' – an assertion which Jebb might well have made about the university he represented in parliament. Sir Henry Roscoe, himself one of the statutory commissioners, and then at the height of his renown as pioneer of the civic university, dealt even more effectively with the attack Haldane had mounted, taking specific issue with him on the score of his analogy with conditions in Germany. 'The number of professors in German universities is, as my hon. Friend has stated, very large', he declared, but it was well known that the German universities were supported entirely by the state, and it was 'obvious that it was perfectly impossible for the Commission to attempt to apply the German system to Scotland.' Haldane's motion was decisively defeated; and on the specific issue of extra-mural teaching the statutory commission, reporting in 1900, unreservedly endorsed the earlier opinion of their predecessors. (To substitute 'a widely ramified system of preparation for examinations' for university education would be an infinitely greater evil than the mischief it was proposed to redress.) But it was a sign that Haldane was beginning to understand the subject that when in 1892, he had continued to press for a 'very large extension' of the teaching power of the Scottish universities (which, indeed, they needed) he had gone on to explain: 'It is not extra-mural teaching I am insisting upon, though that is a good thing. What is wanted is a reorganisation of professorships and the extension of lectureships on a substantial footing'; and that when he had reiterated the need for a reform in the examination system, he had acknowledged that 'teaching is a very important part of the question' and that what was wanted in Scotland was 'the addition of a stronger examining body not entirely independent, but standing in a sort of reciprocal connection.' Moreover, although the voting had gone against him, the careful statistical comparisons he provided between the teaching facilities in Scotland and Germany produced a disturbing picture which Roscoe's riposte could have done nothing to remove.

That Haldane, along with other members of parliament familiar with Scottish education, should have taken part in debates on the reform of Scottish universities was, of course, no evidence that he had a commitment to the cause of higher education. But there is evidence that such a commitment was germinating: as early as 1887, Haldane was getting himself involved in an issue which daunted all but enthusiasts in that cause, namely the organisation of the University of London. I have, he told his mother, 'been closeted for hours with Arthur Balfour' (a kindred spirit despite his very different educational background – Eton and Cambridge – and his conservative politics). They were conferring about the problems of the University of London, which 'are giving me a great deal of trouble at this moment but the trouble is well worth taking.' Just what sort of trouble Haldane was taking is not clear, though the problems were clear enough. London, the heart of an empire, had no proper university. There were colleges of higher education, already with distinguished men on the staff: at University College, Ramsay, Lankester, Karl Pearson, Croom Robertson, and (until 1882) Haldane's own uncle, Burdon Sanderson; at King's, Lister, Millar Thomson, Hopkinson and S. R. Gardiner; at South Kensington, Huxley, Armstrong and Ayrton. But the University itself was an examination machine.* The value of such a machine at that time was immense, for admission to examinations for the external degree was open to all comers, and by guarding jealously its standards, the University was able to establish a high standard for the currency of its degree, and so to put on the gold standard of learning the awards not only of the London colleges, but of those civic university colleges which were established in half a dozen English cities at that time, and even some colleges overseas. But to segregate the responsibilities for teaching and examining was to run into a serious danger: that examinations would become the master and not the servant of higher education; and this is what happened.

* Cf. Professor Hales in a letter to *The Times*: '. . . Now the London University imparts no learning; it teaches nothing; it gives neither lessons nor lectures; it provides no information; it only asks questions. It is a rigorous and many voiced catechist.' Quoted by the principal of King's, in evidence to the Selborne Commission, June 1888.

*Lehrfreiheit* was shackled by the syllabus. So, on grounds of prestige for the Empire's capital, on grounds of educational philosophy, and in response to a rising dissatisfaction among many graduates of the University of London themselves, there was a need to form the London colleges into a teaching university. But there were disputes and difficulties in the way. All sorts of propaganda for reform were being circulated. On one hand the dilatory response of the university senate prompted the formation of an *Association for Promoting a Teaching University for London* in 1884 (backed by names as formidable as Bryce, Huxley, Lister, Playfair, Kelvin and Tyndall), which from an early stage began to favour the establishment of a second university; on the other hand the body of graduates (convocation) – or at any rate some of them – wanted to convert the existing institutions into a kind of federal university. By 1887, there were four separate schemes under discussion, and the confusion was such that it could only be resolved from outside. The trigger for a parliamentary enquiry was a petition from the two illustrious colleges, University and King's, to be called Albert University. Nothing short of a royal commission could handle this situation, and one was set up in 1888, under Lord Selborne, to consider the proposal. The commission rejected it; but no agreement could be reached on its own recommendations, and four years later a further royal commission (the Gresham commission), this time under Lord Cowper, was appointed to make another attack on the problem.

Haldane took no part – no visible part, at any rate – in these discussions; and he had not yet perfected his technique of manipulating educational policies invisibly from the wings of the political stage. There were proceedings in parliament in connection with the renewed proposals for a separate teaching university in 1891 and 1892; but Haldane neither initiated them, nor contributed to them. He was, however, consolidating his understanding of educational problems. His signature appeared – along with many others including Bryce and Edward Grey – below a public protest, printed in the *Nineteenth Century* in 1888, against the stranglehold of examinations over education. This was nothing new. Although examinations for the civil service, introduced in 1870, had rid Whitehall of nepotism, and (through the payment-by-results system) had lifted the standards of teaching in schools, they had for many years been under attack. A more significant incident occurred in 1890, when Haldane was invited to serve on the council of University College, London. Here was definite evidence of his growing commitment to the cause of universities. We do not know how he came to be invited; it may have been a suggestion from his uncle, Burdon Sanderson (now in the Waynefleet chair of physiology at Oxford), or it may simply have been that he was a young member of parliament who obviously had a distinguished career ahead of him and who was known to his fellow MPs to be keen and very well informed on university affairs. At any rate the significant fact is that Haldane, a very busy barrister and a man still establishing himself in English society, regarded this invitation as one to accept. He served for eight years, until 1899, but made no forceful impact on the college. It was still, for him, a phase of incubation for his educational ideas.

After ten years in parliament, Haldane was known, and what he stood for was known. In February 1896 he figured in 'Spy's' series of famous lawyers, contributed to *Vanity Fair*, under a title which must have pleased him: 'A Hegelian politician'; for it was as a politician-philosopher that he wanted to be known. Despite his busy life at the bar and in parliament and his week-ends in society, he found time to publish a translation of Schopenhauer, a biography of Adam Smith, and numerous articles in the reviews on themes of politics and philosophy. In the house of commons he identified himself with liberal principles whether or not they were wholly acceptable to his senior colleagues in the Liberal party. One colleague described him as a man 'who is not prevented by the ties of Party from taking that independent view of questions which his own research and his own judgement enable and call upon him to take.' He was spoken of as 'one of the ablest exponents of what has been called the New Liberalism.'

On what evidence did Haldane acquire this reputation? In the house of commons he espoused measures of reform that marked him out as radical and progressive: leasehold enfranchisement (where he helped to bring in a bill to empower urban authorities to make compulsory purchases of land, and to exclude any element of 'unearned increment'); women's suffrage (where he himself introduced a bill for the removal of women's disabilities in 1892); and death duties (where he chaired the committee which worked out the details of the measure that formed the central feature of Harcourt's budget in 1894, assisted in its drafting, and played an important part in seeing it through its various stages in the House). But perhaps the clearest indication of his commitment to the New Liberalism was provided

by the public addresses he gave outside the House: for it was here
that he expounded the philosophy behind his action in the legislature.
His utterances on these occasions added up to a testament of patrician
socialism, innocent of any revolutionary fervour, an affair of the mind
rather than of the heart, pursuing the principles of liberalism to their
logical conclusion – which was a lot further than some liberals were
prepared to go. Listen to him addressing Cambridge dons and undergraduates at a meeting of the 'Eighty' Club in the Lion Hotel on
30 May 1891. First, a hand held out to socialism:

> I hope to see the Liberal party throw far more energy into its
> sympathies with the labour movement than it has done in the
> past. . . . We need for our development as a Party not only universal
> franchise, the franchise which shall enable the labourers, be they
> male or female [at this point his audience cheered] to make their
> voices heard in the councils of the nation, but also a measure which
> shall enable them to send, through the medium of payment of
> representatives out of public funds, those people to do their business
> in Parliament who are best fitted to do so. . . .

Then a little sally of flattery to his audience: the Liberal party ought
to go more rapidly on social questions, but it was fettered by its
mandate and could not go ahead of its constituents. The business of
the house of commons was 'not to elaborate new ideas and put them
before the country and press for their acceptance. The business of
the house of commons is to give a practical shape and legislative
form to ideas which are sent to it from outside. . . .' Then came
Haldane's commitment to collectivism to which he had been converted
in what Beatrice Webb called 'a sort of vague metaphysical way':
'we no longer concern ourselves with individuals, however numerous
or important, but we devote our attention much more to the community as distinguished from the individuals who make it up. There is a
sense of the corporate life of the nation, and of the claim which that
corporate life has upon us, which it seems to me was almost
unknown. . . .' And he went on to talk about the virtues of the
'collectivist idea': the desire to vindicate the claims of labour to a
larger share in the produce of industry, as against capital. It was a
speech which drew characteristic comment from Sidney Webb,
who lost no opportunity to encourage and prompt. Over Haldane's
efforts on the land question, he had written:

Last night was a great success for you – will you pardon my saying
that you are unduly diffident about your own capabilities in the
House? . . . I am . . . very thankful that I have always believed in
you. If I were a woman it would seem natural that I should say
something pretty & encouraging. I cannot do that: but this I know –
the [? that] life brings with it its own encouragement. And I
*know* which side is right.

Now, less lyrically, but more purposefully, he wrote: 'I read your
Cambridge speech & liked much of it. May I commend to your
holiday reading an article by me in the July number of the *Economic
Journal* on "The Difficulties of Individualism"?'

Haldane was only thirty-four when he gave this address to the
'Eighty' Club at Cambridge. He had been called upon to deputise for
a more senior member of his party, Robert Reid, whose claims to
the woolsack were to thwart Haldane's plans in 1905. But it was
a rising reputation as much as his foundation membership of the
Club which earned him the invitation; and the custom of printing
the speeches given on these occasions enabled him to set his ideas
before a wider audience.

So at forty, Haldane was already a distinguished lawyer, an intellectual radical in politics, devoted to gradualism, but a gradualism
constantly kept on the move; a man who was out to democratise
society, smoothly and (so far as possible) imperceptibly, through
legislation and education. His political philosophy had its roots in
Edinburgh and Göttingen: the community of Scottish students where
distinction depended on intellect, not birth; the strenuous pursuit
of truth in discussions with Lotze; the light shed by Goethe on the
whole art of living. 'A man of advanced ideas . . . an exceedingly
profound thinker': this was *Vanity Fair's* verdict on him in his fortieth
year.

It was, all the same, a surprising honour to be invited by the students
of Edinburgh in 1896 to stand as a Liberal candidate for the coveted
office of lord rector of the University; lord rectors were usually
much higher up the ladder of fame. Its significance for our portrait
of Haldane is that this invitation came from students; it was a vote
of confidence from youth. Haldane's student sponsors set out his
virtues and qualifications in the *Student* magazine for 5 November
1896. It is a generous testimonial, though slightly apologetic because
the sponsors were themselves embarrassed about Haldane's youth:

the ablest student of philosophy in his year in the whole of Scotland . . .
the youngest Queen's Counsel in the last fifty years . . . conspicuous
as a political thinker . . . a man who regards politics 'not as a sphere
for the exercise of Machiavellian astuteness, but as a subject of high
seriousness' . . . 'the most distinguished ornament' of the school of
thought which had introduced Hegel to England. So (ends the testimonial) 'we do not enunciate any controversial proposition when we
say that Mr Haldane if elected to the Lord Rectorship would honour-
ably fill the high traditions of that office. He is still a young man, but
he has clearly shown himself possessed of abilities which argue well
for his future career . . . .'

Haldane was not elected, but this was, in part at any rate, a reflection
of the political scene. He was defeated by Lord Balfour of Burleigh,
seven years his senior, who was secretary for Scotland in the new
Conservative government which had driven out the Liberals in
1895. Haldane kept his seat in parliament, with an increased majority
in his constituency, but political office was now out of reach until
the Liberal party got back into power, and it was to be ten years
before that happened. But this was Haldane's opportunity to concentrate his interest in higher education. He seized the opportunity.
To be in opposition and not even to hold a shadow portfolio of education were not disqualifications: they were positive benefits for his techniques of persuasion. He was ready now to embark on the first major
educational campaign of his career. He entered upon it in close partnership (or, as some of his contemporaries would have put it, close
conspiracy) with Sidney Webb. Their objective was to make the University of London an institution worthy of the Empire's metropolis.

We have already (p. 27f.) introduced the reader to some of the
intricacies of the University of London. They form no part of a
portrait of Haldane, but the portrait must be given a background.
In 1894, when the Gresham commission reported on the University,
it was an institution without students or teachers: it comprised only
candidates and examiners. Graduates had a place on the governing
body, but not teachers from the institutions which prepared students
for London degrees. So those who taught had no control over syllabus
or examination.

The recommendations of the Gresham commission would have
gone some way toward remedying these grave defects if they had
been adopted. Three abortive attempts were made to give legislative

effect to them: one in 1895, which collapsed because Rosebery's Liberal government was defeated; another in 1896 and a third in 1897, when both bills were withdrawn owing to the opposition they generated largely from a militant section of the University's own graduates. 'The whole affair', T. H. Huxley had written about it, 'is a perfect muddle of competing crude projects and vested interests . . . anything but a patch-up is, I believe, outside practical politics at present.' It was in 1896 that Haldane began to exercise his growing skill in consensus politics on this thorny problem. He had no official standing over the issue. He worked backstage. Plans were hatched over austere dinners in the Webbs' house, in co-conspiracy with the indefatigable Sidney.

Sidney Webb had already become involved in higher education in the metropolis. He was chairman of the technical education board of the London County Council, and it fell to him to decide how to use the valuable endowment Hutchinson had given for socialist education. It was following Haldane's legal advice (and probably much more than legal advice) that it was used to found (or, as one observer put it, 'to conceive in sin') the London School of Economics.

Over the University of London, the political problem was to narrow the gap between the supporters and the opponents of the Gresham report until a bridge could be thrown across the gap. The supporters wanted to create a university empowered to teach as well as to examine, with its governing bodies (senate and academic council) controlled by teachers in the London colleges, and to relegate the direction of external examinations to an advisory committee of the senate. The opponents saw this as an eclipse of the University as an imperial examinations board with worldwide influence and its replacement by a predominantly local institution. 'All day long', wrote Haldane to his mother in the summer of 1896, 'I have been working at the London University Bill trying to get cantankerous people to agree. I think we are now in sight of a settlement but it has been a tough job.' And three days later: 'Alas the University Bill is dead. The Bishops have killed it.' But the bishops reckoned without the pertinacity of the reformers. In the following January Professor Ramsay (professor of chemistry at University College and shortly afterwards to be awarded a Nobel prize) had some good news for the advocates of a teaching university. This passage from a letter he wrote to William Allchin (another supporter of the Gresham report) testifies to Haldane's reputation: 'Things are taking a new devt wh it is impt – most impt – you should know of. Mr. Haldane is negotiating & I should be glad if you cd meet him if poss. & talk over the matter.'

The outcome of the negotiations was the University of London Commission bill of 1897. It would have been impolitic to reject the framework of the Gresham commission; so the negotiators' task was to find a formula of reconciliation within this framework. By July 1897 a formula had been found which was commended to convocation (i.e. the graduates) by their chairman and supported by various dignitaries including the University's member of parliament, Sir John Lubbock. In essence the formula gave equal status to both proposed roles of the University, but put each role under a separate governing body: a council for external students to preside over its function as imperial examiner and an academic council to preside over its function as a teaching university, both under the sovereignty of a senate on which representatives of both these interests sat.

Educationally, this constitutional compromise was the least interesting feature of the bill; the novel idea was to create a category of 'recognised teachers', a status which the university could confer on teachers of suitable distinction and seniority in any institution within a thirty mile radius. Since these institutions included polytechnics, teacher-training colleges, and the like, this was a device to incorporate into one system the best of all tertiary education in the metropolis, to create a new pattern of university which would cater for the traditional and the new studies, for external, evening, part-time and full-time students; in a word, to put all higher education in London under one immense umbrella.

It was Sidney Webb's novel idea, it seems, not Haldane's. The story is told that Haldane asked Webb: 'What is your idea of a University?' Webb smiled, 'I haven't any idea of a University. Let's sit down and see what we can make of it . . .': the deductive method over again! But what Haldane wanted was simple and clear; it was to provide in London that personal encounter between master and disciple which Lotze had given Haldane in Göttingen. Beatrice Webb, with her terrible candour, makes this clear. 'Haldane', she wrote in *Our partnership*, 'to gain his higher aim, would willingly have scrapped the system of external examinations by which alone London University awarded its coveted degrees.' (This was true, but ironical, considering that Haldane himself was once a candidate for one of these examinations!) 'But', she went on, 'he realised, under Sidney's influence, if not the undesirability, at any rate the political impracticability, of overthrowing what had already taken deep roots.' However, though Beatrice Webb might write thus condescendingly about Haldane's ideas, she had no hesitation in acknowledging his capacity to steer ideas through parliament. 'If [the bill] goes through', she acknowledged in her diary for 26 July 1897, 'it will be due to Haldane's insistence and his friendship with Balfour – but the form of the Bill – the alterations grafted on the Cowper Commission Report are largely Sidney's. . . .' We have a vivid insight into Haldane's strategy on this occasion for he wrote in detail about it to Fitzroy at the privy council:

> I still have hopes of the negotiations [he reported at the beginning of July]. A month ago I got the Convocation party to agree to accept the Bill if the enclosed amendments were inserted. I took them at once to Lord Herschell [chancellor of the University]★. He was favourably disposed towards them. The delay has been with the Senate party, but I understand that Ld Herschell has convened a meeting of their representatives for Monday. If they will agree to the substance of the amendments & the Lord President is disposed to adopt them in the H. of Lords, I think I can get the Bill accepted in the Commons with very little discussion. Mr Balfour tells me he can find time on this hypothesis. . . . The important thing is to proceed without delay. . . . Meanwhile I enclose – as a private document from myself – the amendments which embody what has been accepted by the Convocation opposition. . . .

> I ought to add that the composition of the Commission will be a very delicate point. Before the Ld President decides on this, I should like to come to talk with you. Ld Davey would be acceptable as Chairman, but if Ld Lister goes on I am inclined to believe that the best way of allaying the suspicions of the Convocation party is that – should the Duke approve – I should go myself. I have – I think – the confidence of the opposition party, & I am Vice President of University College. I need not say that I have no ambition to serve, but I have the feeling that it may avert difficulty.

The bill was due to be introduced into the house of lords on 20 July 1897. Up to the last moment Haldane and Sidney Webb were 'rushing about London trying to get all parties to agree', in a veritable offensive of conciliation. Herschell's consent had to be confirmed; Lubbock's vote had to be secured. But to no avail. The bill passed all

---

★ And a brother-in-law of Haldane's uncle, Professor Burdon Sanderson!

stages in the house of lords, but the session was already too far advanced for any protracted debate in the house of commons: on 2 August it was withdrawn without a second reading.

The next incident in the story throws into relief Haldane's obsession with the issues of higher education. Three times, proposals to reform the University of London on the lines of the Gresham report had failed. A busy and successful lawyer, a politician whose career could well lead to the high office of lord chancellor, a reasonably affluent bachelor, welcome at the salons and house parties of Victorian society – Haldane might well, after the failure in August 1897, have dropped his interest in universities for the time being. But on 16 October he wrote privately to Balfour, seeking a fresh place for the bill in the government's legislative programme. This time, Haldane wrote, not much opposition was to be expected.

> From letters I have seen I gather that the Senate stands in its approval of the Bill as arranged, and that the majority of Convocation take the same view. . . . The real opposition comes from Dr Collins and Fletcher Moulton. I do not think they can get any substantial support in the House, for the Bill is strongly supported by Herschell, Bryce, Acland, Stuart, Cozens-Hardy, and all are leading people. . . . Lubbock is of course in two minds, and he will have to make some show of opposition but I believe he would be heartily glad to have the matter disposed of. . . . Dillon says his Irish will not oppose and I think I can do something with Healy – whom I saw before the House rose.

Balfour was responsive. 'I should very much like to get this London University question out of the way, and on the whole what you say seems satisfactory and reassuring. As soon as I get to London in November I will have a talk to Devonshire upon the subject.' Having cleared the way with Balfour, Haldane lost no time over the preparation of a fourth version of the bill. The interested parties were called to a conference in the senate room on 14 December 1897. A re-draft of the bill – almost identical with the 1897 version – was agreed upon. Early in 1898 it had an easy passage through the house of lords; and in June it came up for the critical debate at a second reading in the house of commons.

Haldane was no orator. His piping voice, his 'penguin-like' gestures, his sometimes tortuous and over-subtle logic, put him at a disadvantage where opposition had to be silenced by eloquence. But this was an occasion – one of the rare occasions of drama in his political career – when his deep commitment to a cause lifted him above these disqualifications.

It was not quite as dramatic as Haldane (and some of his biographers, who followed Haldane's own version of it) made out. Haldane wrote in his autobiography that after a succession of speeches fiercely attacking the bill he sprang to his feet 'for once like one inspired' and turned the tide of opinion. In fact he had not waited for a hostile tide to establish itself. After only two members had spoken in opposition, he immediately weighed in with a powerful defence. The context of his speech was predictable. It was a careful and reasoned argument for a teaching university in London: to bring distinguished professors into the metropolis; to extend to the 'working classes' opportunities for higher education already enjoyed by their European cousins; to improve technical education so that Britain could stand up better against foreign competition in trade; a bill essential for 'catching up' (as he put it) with other capital cities.

> These are the reasons upon which those of us who are interested in the Bill appeal to the House to pass it. We feel that it is a Bill which is required, and which is absolutely necessary, and a Bill without which university education in London can make no progress. . . . We feel that we have got here a measure which in itself embodies the best tradition of the past and which completes the work of Bentham and Austin, of Mill and Grote, of the men who were the pioneers of university education in London; and that it is a measure which, if it is allowed to bear fruition, will place us in a position at least as good as that of any metropolis in the world.

Lubbock then spoke in opposition as Haldane had foreseen (his attack thus coming after Haldane's defence – not before as Haldane recalled in his autobiography); and with only two of the remaining speakers venturing to challenge the bill, it received its second reading without a division. Haldane certainly exaggerated the drama of the occasion, but he did not exaggerate the effect of his intervention. Asquith, in a graceful note of congratulations, wrote of never before having known a case in which 'a single speech converted hostile and impressed indifferent opinion in the House'; and Chamberlain, from the other side of the House, generously offered similar compliments. Although built on inaccurate detail, Haldane's claim to have tipped the balance was well enough founded. And what is significant for a portrait of

Haldane is the importance he himself attached to the occasion, when, years later, he wrote his reminiscence of it. He *wanted* to be regarded by posterity as the man who secured reform in the University of London. His own emphasis showed where his heart lay.

The unopposed passage of the bill at its second reading was not, of course, the end of the affair. There was detailed criticism right up to the last, in which Haldane himself was not spared. ('He has got Scotch universities on the brain,' taunted an old opponent, 'and he does not understand at all what we want in London.') But it was in committee that the bill ran into real danger. Haldane had agreed to take charge of it at this stage, and at first all went well. Quite suddenly a threat developed from a quarter which Haldane had thought covered. Tim Healy appeared at the head of the Irish members of the committee, and in private parley with Haldane made it clear that the vital Irish vote would be withheld unless something was done to improve higher education in Ireland, Haldane, with evident relish, describes the sequel in his autobiography. Very well; if this was to be the price of the Irish vote, he would pay the price. He would himself go to Ireland privately and of course unofficially, to discuss and work out reforms in the Irish Universities acts, and he would steer them through parliament. The story of his visit as he himself remembered it is worth re-telling, for it shows what lengths he would go to in pursuit of his enthusiasm for higher education. He approached Balfour and secured his authority to try his hand at direct negotiations with the Irish. During the summer of 1898 he made himself familiar – as familiar as anyone can become without having lived in Ireland – with the problem; and early in October he slipped away to Dublin with a plan (described on p. 59f.) in his pocket. There followed a series of meetings which were bizarre even for Ireland. First, the provost of Trinity College had to be assured that an Irish Universities bill would not interfere with that proud and venerable institution. Then the archbishop and the Dublin hierarchy had to be persuaded that the plan would in fact create a *de facto*, if not *de jure*, Catholic university. In both these missions Haldane was successful. Then he went on to Belfast for similar consultations. Here, moves to provide higher education for catholics would not be likely to generate enthusiasm. So (he wrote) 'I talked . . . only as an inquirer but guided the conversation on to the main points of the scheme.' Again, Haldane's scheme won general consent. So far so good. But there was still the cardinal at Armagh to be reckoned with, and Haldane was advised to approach him as inconspicuously as possible. He took this advice so literally that when he reached Armagh by rail, he went on foot from the station to the cardinal's residence, in the dark! And how he cleared this last hurdle – 'with toes in the air' – he reported triumphantly to his mother, as he waited for the Dublin mail to take him back to England:

I left Dublin with the warning of the Archbishop that I should probably fail with Cardinal Logue the Primate. I descended on him at Armagh, & lo – in half an hour we had settled everything in accordance with my scheme, & were settling down – he in his red hat & I – over two dozen oysters (it is Friday) & a bottle of Champagne. . . . Healy & Dillon are much moved over my mission, & I think I have a chance of a statue in the Phoenix Park.

This astonishing escapade propitiated the Irish members, and in fact it did much more: it laid the foundation for a reform of Irish higher education which was enacted ten years later. This was not the only occasion on which Haldane engaged in political trading. Over the previous bill he wrote to Wace, the principal of King's College, on 26 July 1897: 'I undertake, if you leave the Bill as it stands, to support a recommendation to the Commission . . . . I will use such influence as I have. . . .' The act to set up a statutory commission for the University of London received the royal assent on 12 August 1898. Immediately Haldane got down to the next task, which was to influence the work of the commission. His proposals for its membership had already borne fruit. Lord Davey, for whom Haldane had devilled as a junior, was chosen as chairman; and among the members were two of Haldane's other suggestions: Creighton, already associated with Haldane and Webb over the London School of Economics, and Busk, the chairman of convocation. Haldane's offer to serve on the commission himself was not taken up, possibly out of regard for his professed reluctance; but in any case he could exercise his influence just as effectively without being a member. Hewins (the first director of the London School of Economics and closely involved with the Webbs and the University) testified to Haldane's mole-like persistence: Haldane (he wrote) is 'very much behind the scenes' and exercising 'great influence' on the reconstruction of the University.

Haldane had accepted the compromise, that implanting a teaching function into the University should not be allowed to weaken its examining function; and the Gresham concept – that the senate should have authority to approve 'schools' of the University where its teaching could go on – was of course consistent with his policy to enlarge opportunities for higher education. But he evidently had misgivings about a proliferation of recognised schools, for in the following year (1899) he was advising the clerk to the privy council (Fitzroy, through whom Haldane exerted a strong vicarious influence on the council's educational decisions) to resist the application from Royal Holloway College to be recognised as a school, because it was away in Surrey, twenty miles out of London. But Holloway's importunity prevailed, and in the end Haldane advised Fitzroy on the amending legislation which was necessary.

At the turn of the century Haldane was still absorbed in the part he was playing in remodelling the University of London. No detail was too trivial, no effort too tiresome, no setback too dispiriting. With a sort of persevering buoyancy he carried the negotiations forward and sustained the morale of those who had to take responsibility. A word in the right quarter at Westminster, a dinner party to reconcile views, a letter to Fitzroy at the privy council: day by day progress was made. (Had he not reminded Sidney Webb a few years before how difficult it was to 'drive rapidly without the co-operation of the great personalities'?) So at each step, it was Haldane who secured co-operation.

In retrospect Haldane was less than satisfied with the compromise act. It was, he wrote in his autobiography, far from ideal. He told the house of lords, when the University's affairs were again before parliament a generation later, that the bill of 1898 was 'thoroughly second rate'; and on another occasion explained that it was 'the utmost we were then able to do for getting the teaching side brought within the University'. But at the time he was enthusiastic; indeed when he turned his energies to higher education in the north of England four years later he commended the new type of federal university as a model for Liverpool, Manchester and Leeds.

Four years of negotiation over the Gresham report, drafting, seeking to compromise between conflicting views, and occasional log-rolling, had deepened Haldane's understanding of academic affairs; it had also whetted his appetite for more. He had demonstrated to himself and to his colleagues his flair for the strategy and tactics of policy-making, his rare ability to turn those earnest discussions in Beatrice Webb's drawing room and the talk among carefully chosen companions round his own dinner table into practical political decisions. His apprenticeship was now completed.

# 3 Co-conspirators

At the turn of this century some social reforms were so obviously necessary – in the eyes of the 'New Liberals' at any rate – that the only problem was how to achieve the reforms. With education it was otherwise. That every citizen should be able to read and write and do simple arithmetic was a necessity. That some citizens (but how many?) should have schooling up to the age of eighteen, to become proficient in literary studies and mathematics: this, too, was a necessity. That local authorities should make provision for technical and commercial education in night schools, or part time; this, too, was acknowledged and its goal was clear: it was to train technicians. But over university education there was a need to re-define goals. Their traditional functions remained as important as heretofore: to cherish learning, to educate recruits for certain professions, to ensure (in the words of the bidding prayer at Cambridge) 'that there may never be wanting a supply of persons duly qualified to serve God both in Church and State.' But for a generation before 1900 there had been warnings (we mention them on p. 14) that to be qualified to serve the state required training in new professions, especially the professions of science and technology applied to industry. Since the 1860s there were signs that Britain was losing her competitive advantage over foreign countries in trade because the British were not applying science to manufacture and because their facilities for higher education in technology were inferior to those in Europe and America. Even in pure scholarship – as Haldane himself had discovered – the universities of Germany had an attraction which even Oxford and Cambridge could not rival. To spend a year in Giessen or Göttingen, Berlin or Heidelberg, was the aspiration of scores of young American and British academics.

The warnings had not gone unheeded. The virtual monopoly of Oxford and Cambridge for English higher education was already over. Stimulated by developments in London and Manchester these ancient universities were themselves responding to the mood of the time, and were including technologists among their graduates. The royal commission on technical instruction published in 1884 encouraging evidence of the response of the new universities and colleges to the needs of industry: applied chemistry under Roscoe in Manchester, in no way inferior to that in the Zurich Polytechnic; courses on laundry chemistry under Jackson at King's College, London; courses on brewing, bread-making, glass and pottery under Graham at University College (who had also 'a large consulting practice for brewers'); metallurgy in Sheffield; textile technology in Leeds, shipping in Liverpool: all colleges supported by local industrialists who contributed funds and encouraged – indeed expected – curricula and research to be relevant to local interests. So there certainly was some progress toward the adaptation of higher education to national needs; but it was fragmentary, empirical, often fortuitous. There was no national plan, and no sign of an articulated purpose between schools and universities, universities and employers, employers and government. Much remained to be done in England and Wales; and the Scottish universities, once models for the rest of the kingdom, had responded even less to the times. There was a simple reason for this. To have modelled themselves on the newer style of curricula would have weakened their treasured tradition of broad general education, and put in its place the specialisation in science and mathematics essential for professionals. But the price of holding on to the Scottish tradition was high: Scottish graduates were having to come south after graduation in order to qualify themselves for posts requiring specialist training. So the Scottish universities, by the end of the nineteenth century, were under fire even from their most loyal friends. '. . . the four Scottish universities [said Haldane in 1901] . . . in the main owing to their sluggishness and want of ideas of their governors [are] of little use from the point of view of the application of science to industry. . . .'

This was the climate of opinion which convinced Haldane that he had to think not only about means, but about ends in higher education if he was to influence government policy. Like many others before him he turned first to Germany. It was shortly before the close of the century that he began a series of annual visits to Weimar and later to Ilmenau, to help his friend Hume Brown, who cherished the ambitious project of revealing the greatness of Goethe to the English speaking world. Their joint enterprise was to collect material for a full scale biography. One of the remarkable features of British academic life in the nineteenth century – indeed until world war I cast its shadow over Europe – was our sustained enthusiasm for importing German culture.* As long ago as 1844, over fifty years before Hume Brown's Goethe pilgrimages, Jowett returned from a visit to Germany determined to bring the light of Hegel into Oxford. In Jowett's college, Balliol, the use of German became 'almost a Balliol affectation'. In 1868 some of the reforms which Mark Pattison urged upon Oxford in his *Suggestions on academical organisation* were inspired by Germany. And in the same year Matthew Arnold published his report to the Schools Enquiry commissioners, which included his impressions of the universities of Prussia and his terse conclusion: 'our university system is a routine, indeed, but it is our want of science, not our want of liberty, which makes it a routine. It is in science that we have most need to borrow from the German universities. The French university has no liberty, and the English universities have no science; the German universities have both.' In 1897, nearly thirty years after Arnold's report, came the reports from the special inquiries branch of the board of education under one of Haldane's near-contemporaries, Michael Sadler. These, too, found in German education patterns for Britain to copy. So there was nothing original about Haldane's tactic to call the German university as witness in the indictment of British universities; though he had the capacity, which Jowett and Pattison and even Arnold and Sadler did not have, to carry his case beyond advocacy into political action. He prepared his case as carefully as he prepared cases at the bar; first mastering the historical background as far back as Wilhelm von Humboldt; then extracting the basic features of German universities which (in his view) gave them their superiority; and then – the practical politician taking over – he worked the themes which came out of these studies into speeches and addresses and articles, to inoculate as it were, public opinion.

Haldane supplemented his first-hand experience of German higher education with reading about higher education in France and the United States. In France universities had barely recovered from their Procrustean centralisation imposed in 1808 by Napoleon, administered (as Playfair wrote) 'with the power of a military despot and with the

* Bryce, in an introduction to a book by J. Conrad (*The German universities for the last fifty years*) translated in 1885, remarks how, in the 1840s, German universities were regarded as parents of revolution; but that by the 1880s the danger was that England would be too keen to imitate them, forgetting the dissimilarity of conditions between the two countries, 'and ignoring in particular the great difference caused by their dependence on the State.'

professional instincts of a drill sergeant' and not withdrawn until the partial decentralisation introduced in 1896–8. Haldane found them, as Arnold had found them, paralysed under excessive state control. In America, however, a genuine viable mutation of higher education was taking place. The Morrill Act in 1863 created conditions for founding the land grant universities. They were a response to the new society of the American frontier, with a twofold aim: to teach 'useful arts' like agriculture and engineering and to transmit a literary and humanistic culture less precious than that in the Eastern colleges. By the turn of the century they had established themselves and were challenging the supremacy of older elitist institutions, just as institutions in London and Manchester were challenging Oxford and Cambridge. Haldane's interest was captivated by the concept of the land grant university and he had evidently met people familiar with the University of Wisconsin (one of the more successful ventures) for in an address to Scottish teachers he singled it out as a place which cherished pure culture and the applications of science to industry and which carried its educational mission beyond the campus to anyone willing to listen, by summer schools, extension lectures, and the like. Here was a paradigm for Haldane's thinking: the democratic tradition of the Scottish university, with a curriculum more relevant than the Scottish curriculum, and a concept of extension work quite unknown in Scotland. It is not surprising that Haldane wrote to James Thursfield in 1902: 'from the United States we have at least as much to learn as from Germany.' Later he had reservations about the relevance of the Wisconsin pattern for Britain, on the ground that it was one which distracted the university from its prime function. When representatives of the Workers' Educational Association held it up as a model in their evidence before the royal commission on the University of Wales, Haldane cautioned them, and added that Wisconsin 'is not really one of the first American universities' (see p. 164).

And so, in these years around the turn of the century, Haldane was engaged in an exercise which would now be labelled 'comparative education', as a deliberate preparation for a political campaign to improve the British universities. The experience which, as it were, completed his brief, was a visit in April 1901 (during his annual Goethe-pilgrimage) to the *Technische Hochschule* at Charlottenburg. It was one of nine polytechnics in Germany (the others were at Hanover, Aachen, Brunswick, Dresden, Darmstadt, Karlsruhe, Stuttgart, and Munich) set up for higher education in technology. He was lyrical in his admiration: 'by far the most perfect University I have ever seen', he said in evidence to the privy council; manned by a great staff, crammed with students and apparatus, and making a close study of every new invention. It was a surprising and somewhat uncritical enthusiasm for a man so dedicated also to philosophy and Goethe. At the time – although he changed his mind later on – Haldane was not even disturbed by the way the Germans had excluded technology from their universities and forced it to become segregated in polytechnics. This was an unexpected lapse in his judgement, for in fact the British universities, which brought students of technology and of the humanities together in the same institution, had chosen a pattern better than the German pattern. But Haldane's imagination was caught by the *relevance* of the Charlottenburg education and – compared with institutions trying to do similar work in Britain – with the lavish way the state had financed it. So the drawbacks of segregation were dwarfed by the exciting prospect (which we depict in the next chapter) of creating a 'London Charlottenburg'.*

After the impact of Charlottenburg in 1901 Haldane was ready to take his ideas to the public. He told teachers at Dumfries that education seemed to him 'the most important, without exception, of the great social reforms which await treatment at the beginning of the twentieth century', and proceeded to develop a blueprint for educational policy which he had first sketched a few months before to businessmen at Liverpool. It was inspired by his experience in Germany, but Haldane was always very careful to warn his hearers against mere imitations of foreign models. Any lesson learnt from a foreign country must – he always stressed – be adapted to the style and genius of the British people. The outline of the blueprint was as follows: First, Britain should have a genuine educational *system*, not the haphazard assemblage of schools, universities, and colleges which were so many unwoven threads of education, not a woven fabric. Second, it should be organised in regions, each with a university as 'the brain and the intelligence' of the whole, and

---

* It is interesting that Friedrich Paulsen, the great authority on German universities, took a different view. In his famous essay (translated in 1906, but Haldane is known to have been familiar with his writings before then) he says: 'It is to be regretted that the new professions requiring higher training were not articulated with the old "faculties" ... It was due to the ascendancy of philological-historical culture and the aversion of the new humanism to everything "realistic" and "utilitarian".'

with teacher-training as an important part of each university's function. Third, control of the organisation should be decentralised, under 'local administration and control, fostered and assisted by the State'. Fourth, the pattern of curricula should have the 'double aim' of pure culture on one hand and application of scientific and other knowledge to practical life on the other.

There was nothing dramatic about this; not even original, for it contained little more than a development of ideas worked out by Matthew Arnold thirty years before. Bryce, Morant, and Webb had called for expansion of higher education. Playfair, Huxley, and Roscoe had preached, with more eloquence than Haldane, the cause of science in the service of industry. But the very fact that Haldane's blueprint was undramatic is evidence of his political skill. Utopian schemes end up in the waste paper basket, not as acts of parliament. This scheme was, in the long view, politically practicable at every point and (equally essential) it would not need to be carried out all at once. It is likely, too, that Haldane deliberately fudged the issue of how education in higher technology was to be organised: whether in universities (most of which at that time were too poor to support it on the scale of Charlottenburg), or in newly created polytechnics on the German model. To have been doctrinaire about this would have been to limit the options for action.

The value of Haldane's blueprint, then, was not in its originality, but in its feasibility. This was his unique contribution to the reform of education in Britain, that nearly all the schemes he submitted had the credibility of an architect's design which is accompanied by a quantity surveyor's estimate. Hence the response of his friends when a little book containing his educational addresses was published in 1902. 'I am exceedingly glad', wrote Morant,

> to read your bold stirring of the dry bones – may it indeed make many of them live. You have said what needs saying over & over again, & you have said it pointedly and with illustrations which ought to make the Englishman listen if anything will. I cannot say how deeply I sympathise with your impatience at the smallness of vision which seems always to limit our education rulers and education speeches.

Two other letters from friends illustrate the emphasis in Haldane's message which appealed to enlightened academics. Pringle Pattison (a lifelong friend and then professor of philosophy in Edinburgh) wrote: 'I always read about Education with a sinking heart .... But your appeal is largely conceived & strikingly put. ... I think your insistence on what one might call the double-celled ideal of the University – the University of free culture and the technical high school – is full of guidance.' And – significant in view of Haldane's subsequent association with the problems of the University of London – Lord Davey, who had been chairman of the commission to make statutes for that university in 1898, wrote:

The conception of the double aspect or objective of the higher education is most important. Whether the two objects – culture and professional training – can be carried on concurrently in one University I have some doubt. In the London University we are in a perpetual conflict between the two conceptions of the work of the University and seem at present in danger of falling between the two stools and doing neither efficiently ....

During the ten years of eclipse of the Liberal party, which did not end until 1905, Haldane rose to a position of influence and importance. He was, technically, simple a member of the Opposition; one who had never held office, in a party bitterly divided over home rule and the Boer war, and weakened by a vacillating leadership. But in 1902 (he was still only forty-six years old) he was made a privy councillor. He was described in a letter written by his contemporary Asquith (whose political career was already more successful than Haldane's) as the man who 'does all the brain-work of the Liberal Party, and, though never in the Cabinet, thinks for those who are.' He did not achieve this standing by ingratiating himself with the rank and file of the party; just the opposite: Haldane had made himself unpopular by carrying his educational mission across party lines and openly fraternising with Conservatives; even with Balfour, with whom he shared so many interests. He was 'the intermittent astral control of the Unionist Cabinet.' His blueprint for a national system of education was an offer to either party. As he told the guests at one after-dinner speech: 'I do not care what Government is in – (laughter) – if it will only take up science.'

Even to chronicle his activities over these years gives some impression of the endless machinating intelligence: combining with Asquith and Grey to restore the Liberal party, scheming with the Webbs to promote a new movement for national efficiency – whether within the Liberal party, or in a new political grouping; figuring in the membership of bipartisan clubs as different as the 'Co-efficients' (dedicated to the Webb's campaign for efficiency in politics) and 'that curiously English coterie of men of all parties and callings recognised as distinguished in public life' called, simply, the Club. His growing relish for the ideas of the Webbs is evident from his eager response to Sidney's famous article in the *Nineteenth Century* of September 1901, with its challenge to the progressive Liberals to work out a programme of national efficiency, not least in the sphere of education, where he had called for a systematic scheme from infant school to university. 'We are delighted with the "Escape from Houndsditch"', Haldane wrote to Sidney on 5 September, after dining with Asquith and one or two other colleagues. 'That is *your* speech for the new movement & it is a very important one. . . . Well, no one can say that your line is stale or that it is not suggestive. The difficulty will be to live up to it. We begin our Campaign in the end of this month . . . I – in my humble rôle – go to Glasgow, Dundee & Liverpool (where I have to address them on Education) besides a go off in my own constituency.' '[I]f success does come', he added in a note to Beatrice shortly afterwards, '. . . SW should at once come into the House & take a leading part in directing his own part of the programme of Efficiency. It is your word – a large part of the items are yours – you have worked it out.' It was, indeed, as 'a link in our chain proposals', and an 'item of "Efficiency in Tertiary Education"', that Haldane viewed his speech to the industrialists at Liverpool: his first major pronouncement on educational objectives. All the time, too, he was catching in the net of his acquaintanceship people whose position or experience would promote his – Haldane's – labours in the national interest: civil servants like Fitzroy at the privy council and Morant at the board of education; philosophers through the Synthetic Society (another dining club); members of the Fabian circle through the salon now presided over by Beatrice Webb; and – at the other end of the social spectrum – the prince of Wales, who had first expressed a wish to meet him in 1894 as a potential lord chancellor of his reign, and who in 1898 invoked his help in overcoming the financial difficulties of the Imperial Institute by getting the University of London to establish its headquarters there. Haldane's social charm must have been formidable, for after the prince's accession Haldane was frequently amongst the guests invited to meet him at his special request.

Fortified by allies as diverse as the British throne and the Fabians,

Haldane was now ready for his next sally into the educational system. The initiative on this occasion came from Sidney Webb. In 1900 Webb became a senator of the University of London and he remained chairman of the London County Council's technical education board; so he was able to take an integrated view of London's educational needs. The new senate was engaged in remodelling the University on the lines laid down by the commissioners appointed by the 1898 act. It was Webb's aspiration to make the remodelled University a great centre for applied science. His first step – typical of him – was to draw up a memorandum; Beatrice records that he was doing this in March 1901. The next step was to test the temperature of public opinion. In June articles on the need to train scientists and engineers appeared from his pen, anonymously, in *The Times*. In September there followed the essay in the *Nineteenth Century*, signed this time, urging progressive Liberals to put their weight behind a comprehensive policy on education and particularly 'a large policy of Government aid to the highest technical colleges and the universities. The statesman who first summons up courage enough to cut himself loose from official pedantries on this point and demands a grant of half a million a year with which to establish in the United Kingdom a dozen perfectly equipped faculties of science, engineering, economics and modern languages would score a permanent success.'

Meanwhile, in the spring of 1901 Haldane made his seminal visit to the *Technische Hochschule* at Charlottenburg (p. 44), and in the following September he, too, was writing an article, to be given also as a lecture, on similar lines, inspired by Charlottenburg. The institution was only twenty-one years old. It had been created from the amalgamation of two technical institutes and lavishly financed by the Prussian government. By 1901 it was already famous throughout Europe. Again and again Haldane eulogised Charlottenburg in parliament, in addresses, and in reports and commissions. Here was an essential educational weapon to combat the growing international threat to Britain's industries. From different directions Haldane and Webb converged on the need to create a similar institution in London. Webb's next burst of propaganda is recorded in Beatrice Webb's diary; towards the end of April 1902, she wrote, Sidney was preparing an article on the University of London for the June issue of the *Nineteenth Century* 'in the hope of catching a millionaire', and here, in developing the theme of his *Times* articles, he made a specific plea for a 'British Charlottenburg'.

The stimulus to improve higher technological education in London came from Sidney Webb, and he continued to work with Haldane until the project was successfully launched. But from 1902 it was Haldane who took command. On 9 May he wrote to Webb (the letter is quoted in part below) about the opening moves to launch 'our big scheme'. Already it was 'our' scheme; before long it became 'my scheme': 'I have a big business on hand just now', Haldane wrote three months later to Pringle Pattison, 'which needs all the strength one has – the creation of a school for the Empire for the application of Science to Industry – which is to have its seat in the Metropolis.'

There was already a considerable development of applied science in London at University College and King's College (p. 42) but nothing on the scale of the German polytechnics. In South Kensington there were two institutions: the Royal College of Science, including the School of Mines (they were technically two divisions of one institution), both under the board of education, and the Central Technical College of the City and Guilds Institute of London (re-named in 1907 the City and Guilds College), managed by a board drawn from the city companies. Neither University College nor King's could be transformed into a Charlottenburg. But – and this was the leap of imagination which made the prospect exciting – there was a possibility that a great centre for science and technology might be created at South Kensington, if the institutions already there could be incorporated and if some of the land, which belonged to the 1851 Exhibition commissioners, could be made available for more buildings. This was the idea which germinated slowly in the minds of Haldane and Webb. To turn the idea into reality required money, government consent to surrender its colleges in South Kensington, co-operation from the City and Guilds, agreement on the part of the 1851 Exhibition commissioners to release land, and negotiations with the University of London so that any London Charlottenburg would not be separate from the University, as the German polytechnics were, but associated with the University, to comprise a focus for science and scholarship in the Empire's capital. A formidable set of obstacles; and the sort of challenge which Haldane welcomed. He designed his strategy and went into action.

First, finance. Rumours were going about that the firm of Wernher and Beit was contemplating making a gift to University College, London, to encourage applied science. On 9 May Haldane called on the London partners. The outcome of his call – and his remorseless persistence in pursuing a scheme once he had espoused it – is evident from the letter which he wrote to Sidney Webb the same day, the one about 'our' scheme:

> I saw the four London partners of W. B. & Co this afternoon & had an hour with them. It was just in time. There had been no talk of a million – but they were pondering giving £100,000 to U. Coll. This I have *stopped*. They will give the £10,000 only. But I have undertaken to prepare a scheme for a Committee or body of Trustees to *begin* our big scheme. They will give us £100,000 to start it, & help us to get more. The partners are keen to do something. Could you come at 5.30 on Monday to the H of C – & you & I will talk over the scheme of such a Committee, to be independent of, but to work along with the University Authorities. If I can get Rosebery and Arthur Balfour to serve on it I think we may get a million. I believe W. B. & Co. will give much more than £100,000 really. Will you think out the outline of such a scheme.

Haldane was in his element. By the end of the month he had secured support from Rosebery, Balfour, and the duke of Devonshire, who was lord president of the council; and at some stage in the summer he had received gracious permission to be able to write: 'The King himself is keen. . . .'

Haldane knew better than most men that the scheme would fail unless there were, behind these august dignitaries, support troops comprising the men who really draft the decisions to be made. One of these he had already enlisted: Fitzroy, clerk to the privy council. 'It is a great scheme', Fitzroy wrote, 'and worthy of the fertile and daring brain of its organiser.' In June there was a conference under the *aegis*, now, of Rosebery. Haldane, Webb, and Messrs Wernher and Beit were there; and new recruits to the venture: Rucker, on behalf of the University of London, and the permanent head of the treasury, Mowatt, in his capacity as a member of the 1851 commissioners, trustees of the coveted site in South Kensington. At this meeting Haldane 'explained succinctly the scheme so far as it could be outlined, under the peculiar conditions of its inception. . . .' Some progress was made: there was optimism as to the site, from the 1851 commissioners, and there was the prospect of a maintenance grant from the LCC and further aid from the Rhodes Trustees, for Cecil Rhodes and Alfred Beit had been associates.

In the Christmas recess of 1902 Haldane resumed his campaign.
The Webbs had now become his staff officers. He wrote from Cloan
on 3 January to Beatrice, asking that Sidney (who, it has to be
remembered, was a member of the LCC) should prepare a draft
letter for Rosebery to send to the LCC, to secure a promise of a
maintenance grant for the new institution. The letter, vetted by
Haldane, must have had a familiar ring to Webb's colleagues on the
LCC! After writing about the way the British had lagged behind
other countries in provision for advanced instruction in scientific
technology and facilities for research Rosebery's letter went on:
'Perhaps the most perfect instance of such provision is the great
College of Applied Science at Charlottenburg, alongside of the
University of Berlin, erected at an outlay exceeding £500,000 and
costing £55,000 a year. From its portals there issue every year some
1200 young men of 22 or 23 years of age, equipped with the most
perfect training that science can give. . . .'

The letter elicited an appropriate response: in July 1903 the LCC
promised a maintenance grant of £20,000 a year. Of course it was
not just the letter which persuaded the Council. The very choice of
Rosebery as sponsor silenced some critics. And then Haldane never
entrusted delicate negotiations solely to the written word; he appeared
himself before the LCC's subcommittee to explain the scheme. The
decisive factor was probably Sidney Webb's skilful presentation of
the case to his colleagues. Ramsay MacDonald, also a member of the
LCC, is reported to have said: 'Mr Haldane and Mr Sidney Webb had
presented a pistol at the head of the Council.'

By July 1903 the first objective was secured: the promise of enough
capital and recurrent funds to launch 'our big scheme'. But the scheme
itself was still no more than a sketch-plan. It was part of Haldane's
technique to begin with modest objectives, until enough people
were committed, and then to enlarge the objectives as opportunity
arose. That is what happened this time. If the specification for a 'London
Charlottenburg' had been too precise, the blueprint too detailed,
there would have been less room to compromise, less freedom for
adaptation. Haldane was a man who hung on to his options as long
as possible. 'Our big scheme' began simply as a new college in South
Kensington in addition to those already there. But by the summer of
1903 another powerful mind – Morant's of the board of education
– had got to work on the scheme with the question: Why not contemplate a massive consortium or merger or partnership (deliberately

left undefined) between all the institutions of science and technology at South Kensington? The board of education *might* be persuaded to hand over the Royal College of Science and the School of Mines, to become part of the London Charlottenburg; and the City and Guilds *might* be persuaded to do the same with their institution. The whole complex (still growing in the imagination of its founders) *might* (in ways still undefined) be brought under the jurisdiction of the University of London, for the administrative headquarters of the University had recently been moved to South Kensington and the Royal College of Science and the City and Guilds College were already schools of the University. There were other prospects for change on the site, too, for the School of Mines had found itself unable to cope with the demand for experts for the gold mines in South Africa, and the Institute of Mining and Metallurgy had appointed a committee to enquire into the education of mining engineers.

Haldane's technique was to leave options open, but not beyond the point when it was clear that a choice among options would be politically feasible; then he was quick to force the pace. Some time between July and October 1903 he produced a document marked 'private', undated and unsigned, which lifted 'our big scheme' to a higher level.* His aim, clarified in this document, was to co-ordinate and extend existing institutions in South Kensington to provide a system of instruction in technology worthy of the metropolis. He envisaged a central institution (or a group of institutions; that option was still kept open) which would be closely related to, and largely controlled by, the University of London. But one step at a time: for the present, all that was needed was sufficient money to set the scheme in motion, sufficient co-operation between the institutions to assure their common interest, and a sufficiently close co-operation with the University of London to make it an effective partner. This objective could be achieved by bringing all the interested parties round the same committee table to discuss the terms of a partnership: the government, the University, the LCC, the City and Guilds, the trustees, and representatives of the technological institutions who would be the 'customers' for the products of these colleges. It was only a first step; but Haldane could not resist giving a glimpse of the distant horizon: a mobilisation, ultimately, of all the educational resources in South

---

* The private and unsigned memorandum was a device he used again, in 1916, when he wanted to involve himself in planning post-war educational reforms (p. 136).

Kensington into one great college; to be an integral part of the University; extending its influence beyond London and the provinces, even to centres of industry in the colonies.

Having drawn up this anonymous document, Haldane was able to entrust its administrative follow-up to the ruthless energy of Morant in the board of education. Morant persuaded the president to widen the terms of reference of the proposed committee to review the School of Mines; its remit should now be to consider the future of the whole complex of colleges in South Kensington. In November 1903 Mowatt (who had just retired from the treasury) was secured as chairman, and in April 1904 a strong committee was appointed. It did not include Haldane himself, but his eyes and ears (and voice) were present, for Sidney Webb was there as the LCC representative and Mowatt was a member of the University Colleges grants committee whose chairman was now Haldane.

In the following December the committee ran into trouble: Mowatt, its chairman, fell ill and on 29 December had to resign. This was a misfortune which could not be allowed to hold matters up. Haldane was at Cloan for the recess. On the last day of the year he wrote to Morant:

> The situation is serious as regards S. Kensington, & an effort must be made .... My own burden, as you know, is not a particularly light one, but I gathered that you would possibly suggest my name if I could do the work. Well – I was to some extent responsible at the beginning of this business, & I have kept myself informed of what was going on. I am willing to try my hand if you wish it. ... I will *make* the time if it seems good to you.

Haldane's offer was eagerly accepted. The president of the board of education (Lord Londonderry) speaking of it afterwards, said: '... I was at my wits end to find a substitute. But my mind turned, and so did the minds of those associated with me, to one individual, and our only doubt was as to whether the gentleman in question could find leisure to devote his great mind and great ability to the discharge of the duties given up by Sir Francis Mowatt. ... '

In January 1905 Haldane took control of the committee. On 20 February a preliminary report was agreed and signed. The final report came a year later. The first report was designed to probe resistances and to measure their strength; the second report was designed to overcome or to circumvent them. There were three difficulties to be overcome. One was to persuade the board of education to part with two 'imperial assets', namely the Royal College of Science and its associated School of Mines. Not only would this be tantamount to giving taxpayers' money to the consortium and ultimately to the University; it might also arouse jealousy among provincial universities. Another difficulty was to reach some concordat about the government of the cluster of colleges; Haldane suggested no more, at first, than a composite council in which each co-operating institution had an 'adequate share in the general control'. The third difficulty was to design a link with the University of London which would on the one hand avoid the German pattern: the separation of higher technology from the university (Sidney Webb felt strongly about this; he discussed it when he gave evidence to the royal commission on university education in Ireland, in 1901), and on the other hand would leave the maximum initiative to the new institution, an issue on which other people felt equally strongly. Thus when T. H. Huxley was at the Royal College of Science he fought hard to keep the college 'clear of any connection with a University of any kind'; and when he thought the Gresham commission might recommend a take-over of the College, he wrote 'I am ready to oppose any such project tooth and nail. I have not been striving these thirty years to get Science clear of their school-mastering sham-literary peddling to give up the game without a fight.'

Huxley was gone, but there were others still at South Kensington who shared his views; so Haldane had to proceed warily. He said as much to the somewhat over-eager representatives of the University when they pressed at a conference with the committee for the immediate incorporation of the new institution. The difficulty of the turnover at once, he told them, was 'a difficulty which I do not think anybody can appreciate who has not got the miserable misfortune to be an MP negotiating with the Government and a lot of other bodies', a difficulty which necessitated 'proceeding diplomatically step by step'. And, as an illustration of what he meant by 'diplomatically', what could be clearer than Haldane's rebuke to one professor at the meeting. In order to bring the proposed college within the purview of government grants for research, it was necessary to stress that its purpose would be to teach *advanced* science and technology. Professor Pearson strongly objected – and more than hinted that this proposal came from someone who knew nothing about teaching students! We can see Haldane's disarming smile and hear his gentle voice as he replied:

'It is quite true as Professor Pearson says that the amateur has been at work in this report but he must remember that we are a special kind of professor called into existence for the higher education of the Treasury and therefore we have our own methods and language.'

By 31 March 1905, only one month after the preliminary report was issued, Morant was able to tell Haldane privately that the government had agreed to hand over the Royal College of Science and the associated Royal School of Mines. Official confirmation followed on 3 April and in June the treasury agreed to give an annual grant of £17,000 (raised in November to £20,000) to the new institution.

Haldane, having first attained all the objectives in the first report of his committee, released the report to the press in June, after taking a lot of trouble to ensure that it would have a good reception. Thus it was arranged that one member of the committee, Sir W. White, should 'see *The Times*' beforehand. The press coverage was enthusiastic, not only about the scheme but about Haldane, who was now identified as its originator (Sidney Webb having faded, as usual, into the background). Haldane is, wrote the *Morning Post*, 'perhaps of all public men the most single minded in his appreciation of the nation's educational needs'. And *The Times* drew attention to Haldane's apostolic writings in *Education and empire*, published three years earlier, and the prospect of their realisation in an Imperial Charlottenburg in South Kensington. It was a personal triumph, though in fact the credit deserved to be more widely distributed: to Morant, whose energy drove the scheme forward from within the board of education, to Mowatt, whose goodwill helped to ensure treasury support, and to Webb, whose influence on the LCC and the senate was critically important.

Not that 'our great scheme' was accomplished yet; but Haldane had secured government approval for it. He now undertook personally to negotiate with the many bodies whose interests had to be satisfied. On 7 July 1905 his committee met representatives of the University of London. His gambit was:

Well, now, that brings me to what we are here today to do. Some of you, I have no doubt, have wondered until now that we did not take evidence in a formal fashion. I have had a great deal of experience of these Committees, and I always find that the formal taking of evidence after a certain point is much the least profitable way of doing things, and therefore it occurred to us that . . . what would be most useful would be that we should meet today and have a friendly talk about the whole matter. . . . We are very ready to learn here, but I am in hopes that it may turn out that our purpose is your purpose.

*Toujours bien, jamais mieux!* Haldane got an unequivocal promise of support from the University, though they still pressed for immediate incorporation of the London Charlottenburg into the University, and on this Haldane had to drag his committee's feet, for the City and Guilds were not inclined to perform *hara kiri*, and it would have been imprudent to hand over the other two colleges, which were regarded as 'imperial assets', without at least some minuet of disengagement. The next objective was concurrence from the City and Guilds. Again, Haldane's gift of cultivating friends came in handy; for the chairman of the City and Guilds Council was Haldane's old colleague at the bar, Lord Halsbury. A compact was reached: the City and Guilds College could become part of the scheme, provided it did not lose its identity.

The government were won over; the City and Guilds were amenable; the LCC had blessed (and promised to finance) the scheme. The committee were unanimous that as an interim arrangement there should be a governing body representing all the co-operating interests and that the whole complex of colleges should be recognised as a school of the University of London. But some members of the·committee wanted to go farther and faster than this and to pledge that the new institution would become fully incorporated into the University. To go as far as that would inevitably diminish the independence of the institution and might well arouse hostility from the parties whose co-operation was essential. An irreconcilable split developed in the committee itself. With a less experienced chairman than Haldane this might have been serious. But Haldane knew what to do; he persuaded the committee to sign a unanimous report with an open acknowledgement of their disagreement! And to quell any apprehension that this disagreement might hold things up, the committee suggested that the question of full incorporation into the University might be considered later, together with changes which might become necessary in the constitution of the University itself, by that ultimate placebo for constitutional ailments: a royal commission.

Haldane was by training and predilection a philosopher. He would employ expediency or accept compromise in order to get a decision, but his mind returned to principles, and it is possible to discern principles – though somewhat eroded by political realism – in much of his writing on education. An early draft of the final report of this committee (abandoned probably on Morant's advice because it was regarded as doctrinaire) is unmistakably in Haldane's devious and ponderous style:

> We are well aware that a love of logical organisation is not specially characteristic of the people of this country, and we naturally have no desire to make recommendations which the existence of deep-seated national characteristics is likely to render ineffective. The recent Education Act, however, and still more the manner in which the Act is being administered over considerable parts of the country by the most enlightened local authorities are compelling, to an extent previously unknown, the recognition of the fact that education must be regarded as an organic whole and that its development is successful in proportion as it is guided by a policy which regards it in all its bearings and aims at settled objects. It appears, therefore, well worth considering whether, before this country largely extends her provision for this type of education, as she will have to do, and no doubt will do, in the immediate future, an attempt ought not to be made to get at some general recognition of the principles which should, theoretically at least, underlie any such extension.

The final report of Haldane's committee on the future of the South Kensington college was launched with as much care for press publicity as was the first report. Though signed on 8 January 1906, it was not issued until 5 February, for fear (according to a note in Haldane's handwriting) it should 'fall flat' in the excitement of the January general election.

It was an election which returned the Liberal party to power and brought Haldane into the office for which he is remembered in history: as minister not for education but for war.

# 4 Above the Snow-line

For any man of normal physique, a career which comprised practice at the bar, a leading role in opposition politics, the re-organisation of the University of London and the creation of a London Charlottenburg would suffice. But during these ten years when the Liberal party was out of office Haldane's campaign for higher education spread far outside London to issues in Ireland (as we have already noted on p. 38) and in the north of England. Our portrait of Haldane must now take account of these activities.

Haldane's interest in Irish universities was partly a bargain to secure the support of Irish MPs for the University of London bill in 1898. But it would be unfair to suggest that he had no higher motive than this. Six months before the passage of the bill he had spoken eloquently in parliament in favour of easier access to higher education for Irishmen. In the debate on the address, in February 1898, he boldly supported Dillon's plea for denominational university education for Irish Roman Catholics, pledging himself to support any steps the Conservatives might take 'free from Party bias' to solve the problems of Ireland. 'The question before the House', he said:

is, substantially, whether the Catholics of Ireland, four-fifths of the population of the island, are to go without University education. . . . It is no use saying they can go to the Universities, for experience has proved that they won't go . . . . When I think of the difference between my own country of Scotland and the condition of things that exist in Ireland in this matter I am ashamed. Honourable Members sometimes speak – I don't think that they really speak deliberately after having considered it – but they speak lightly of a University education as if it was a sort of luxury. Well, I can only say, speaking from my own knowledge, that it represents the life and backbone of the people of Scotland . . . .

The plan which he took on his cloak-and-dagger visit to Ireland was a replica of the London model. The Royal University of Ireland was an examining body; teaching was done in the Queen's colleges in Belfast, Cork and Galway. Haldane's proposal was to create two teaching universities, one in Belfast and one in Dublin; to give each of them an internal and an external (i.e. examining) function; to give each university *de jure* a non-sectarian constitution but to make sure that *de facto* the university in Dublin was governed by catholics and the university in Belfast by protestants.

Haldane returned from Ireland with sufficient backing for his plan to encourage the government to act. By the end of October – within two or three weeks of his visit to the cardinal at Armagh, Haldane had sent Balfour a confidential note of proposals for the cabinet, and before the end of December a draft of an Irish Universities bill was ready. But on Kings Cross station, where Balfour and Haldane met to travel together to Hatfield, Balfour had to confess that he could not get the support of his colleagues, and the proposals were dropped. Haldane's efforts were not in vain, for ten years later the proposals were exhumed (at Haldane's suggestion) by the Liberal government and they became the basis of the successful legislation in 1908 which established the Queen's University of Belfast and the National University of Ireland, with University College, Dublin, as a successor to Newman's Catholic University.

Our portrait now depicts an episode which – if Haldane had done nothing else for British universities – would have secured him a distinguished place in the history of higher education. A generation afterwards, in recollection of this episode, he wrote: 'My relations with Balfour [over the university question] had become rather close ever since the London and Irish problems had engaged our efforts. But with these results I could not rest, and I went to him again about what was new.'

'What was new' was nothing less than the whole pattern for university education in England and Wales. When the new century dawned in 1900 there were five universities in England (Oxford, Cambridge, London, Durham, and the Victoria University) and one in Wales. All, in a sense, were federations of colleges. Up to the middle of the nineteenth century even the universities of Oxford and Cambridge were primarily examining bodies for teaching done in the colleges, although by 1900 this was no longer true: university teaching had become important, especially in science. Durham's constituent colleges never had the independence of Oxford colleges, but there was a framework of federation, and Armstrong College in Newcastle taught for

Durham degrees. The universities of London, Wales and the Victoria University were all co-ordinating bodies, prescribing the curriculum but (except in London since 1898) not teaching it. Teaching for Victoria University degrees was done under the control of three constituent colleges: Owens College in Manchester, University College in Liverpool, and the Yorkshire College in Leeds. And teaching for degrees in the University of Wales was done in separate colleges in Aberystwyth, Bangor, and Cardiff.

In March 1900 a charter was granted for a new university, in Birmingham, to serve 'the Midland Districts of England'. Its champion was the MP for West Birmingham, Joseph Chamberlain. It was a symbol of civic pride and it stirred the imagination of civic leaders in other cities to contemplate having fully fledged universities in their own cities. In the autumn of 1901 the MP for one of the divisions of Liverpool, A. F. Warr, invited Haldane to address a group of business men in that city to support a movement to detach the University College from the Victoria University and to set it up as an independent University of Liverpool.

To create a new university to serve the Midlands was one thing; to start splitting up the Victoria University into separate independent universities was quite another. It raised a fundamental problem. Parliament was well disposed toward the creation of more centres of higher education; the bill for the University of Birmingham was passed without much opposition. But did this have to mean a proliferation of degree-giving bodies? Or could it be achieved by bringing all new colleges of higher education in England under the academic control of London, or of the Victoria University, or of Birmingham? In other words, should the English higher education system expand by maintaining only three massive universities, with many affiliated colleges teaching for one or other of their degrees? Or should the larger cities have their own autonomous civic universities?

Many eminent men ventilated their fears about an unrestrained multiplication of universities in England. Matthew Arnold wanted Oxford, Cambridge, and London to be the only bodies with authority to award degrees. The commissioners appointed by the treasury to inspect university colleges in 1896 (Warren of Oxford and Liveing of Cambridge) urged that universities should not 'needlessly' be multiplied; London colleges should all be brought under the University of London, and colleges elsewhere should be grouped, as the northern ones were under the Victoria University. In the debate on the University of London bill of 1898, Lubbock pointed out that if (as was proposed) colleges wanting to be affiliated with London had to lie within a thirty mile radius, then it would be almost impossible to resist demands for universities elsewhere, 'and whatever difference of opinion there might be in the House, all interested in the higher education of the country would agree that any considerable multiplication of universities would be very undesirable.' Mowatt, at the treasury, held similar views: any plea for a new university 'should be very closely scrutinized because the multiplication of degree-giving bodies in a State is the certain forerunner of a depreciation in the value of a degree.' These fears were crystallised into one epithet, attributed by Haldane to Bryce: the pejorative label of 'Lilliputian Universities'.

So Liverpool's campaign to hive off from the Victoria University, to have a university of its own, would obviously be strongly opposed. It raised an issue of great importance. The future of English universities would depend on how the issue was resolved. Haldane realised this and eagerly came to the support of Liverpool.

University College, Liverpool, had allies in its aspiration. Huxley had strongly supported the idea that a university 'should exist in every great centre of population' (his argument was quoted in the petition from Birmingham in 1899). Creighton, in one of the last utterances before his death in January 1901, and quoted in the Liverpool case for a university, wrote: 'There is an absolute need that the number of universities should be increased; that each locality that is of importance should have its own university adapted in many ways to suit local needs.'

Haldane defined his own attitude to the controversy when he addressed the Liverpool businessmen on 22 October 1901. We are proud, he said, of Oxford and Cambridge. We do not seek to disturb their splendid traditions.

> But that does not make the educational reformer desire the less to see the expansion of another kind of teaching which they are not adapted to give. . . . The Victoria University and the University of Wales have taken the way we want. Let us assist still further the magnificent private efforts which made them what they are today. Why should not Liverpool and Manchester . . . possess, as in Germany they certainly would, their own Universities? How ridiculous it is to dread that such Universities would prove Lilliputians! Why should Leeds not be the headquarters of a Yorkshire

University? Why should not Birmingham, where the energy and influence of Mr Chamberlain have brought about a remarkable fresh development, be the centre for the Midlands; and why should not Bristol, where the soil so far has proved somewhat less fertile, be made by State cultivation the centre for the South-West of England?

It was beginning to be clear, now, what was emerging in Haldane's mind. It was a grand scenario of regionalism, with universities benignly presiding over the educational systems in each region, reminiscent, perhaps, of the way each German state had its presiding university, but, unlike German universities, a scheme to be financed by local civic spirit supplemented by aid from parliament. At a dinner in his honour after his Liverpool speech he went so far as to say that the days of federated universities were 'over'.* It was not to be so simple as that. In an episode of seminal importance, the claim of University College, Liverpool, to break away from the federal Victoria University and to award its own degrees was put on trial by the privy council.

Haldane's main objective was to multiply centres for higher education. Blocking the path to this objective was the unresolved controversy between the expansionists, who wanted each of these centres to be able to award its own degrees, and the restrictionists, who wanted the centres to be affiliated to one or other of the existing universities, and to confine degree-granting power to these existing universities. The restrictionists rested their case on the belief that a proliferation of degrees would debase the currency. The expansionists rested their case

* Haldane's frequent allusions to federalism in universities support the charge that 'no-one can invest a subject in a more lucid fog'. On occasion he commended the pattern of the University of London, which was at that time undoubtedly federal in structure. In his evidence to the privy council committee over Liverpool (p. 65ff.) he affirmed '. . . that the particular form of federal constitution which Victoria University has is cramping and restricting the development of the constituent Colleges, and ought to be abandoned.' It was not until he was concerned with the University of Wales that he distinguished clearly between federation and devolution in a collegiate university. By that time he had come to regard federation as a pattern in which the university neither finances the colleges nor has a hand in appointing their teachers, but which may exert a stranglehold on their teaching by controlling the curricula and the examinations. By contrast, devolution in a collegiate university was a pattern in which the university had overall control of the finances of the colleges and influence over the appointment of their senior academic staff, but which entrusted to the colleges a much greater degree of autonomy over curricula and examinations.

on the belief that each city would support (and finance) a university granting its own degrees with more enthusiasm that it would support a college affiliated to a university in some other city.

Haldane's next task, therefore, was to remove this obstacle in his path. The petition from Liverpool, submitted on 23 April 1902, was an opportunity to force a decision. But Haldane was laying his plans before then. Fitzroy, at the privy council, records (on 28 February 1902) that he had 'another talk with Haldane on the Northern University question. He is very keen for a hearing before the Privy Council and will take his coat off for the occasion, notwithstanding the amount of work with which he is occupied in other directions . . . .' Meanwhile Haldane had put the same idea into Balfour's ear. He advised Balfour to take advantage of the situation at Liverpool to appoint a 'very strong Committee of the Privy Council' to report on the issue.

The alternative was to have a royal commission. Haldane, backed by Fitzroy, opposed this; their objections emerge clearly from the wording of the confidential memorandum which the lord president put to the cabinet:

> It would, I think, be possible to appoint a fairly impartial Committee of the Council who would not have any strong preconceived opinions on the question, whereas if the Royal Commission were appointed in the ordinary way, it would probably be necessary to place upon it men with strong opinions one way or the other with the result of an inconclusive Report or of separate Reports.

The cabinet came down in favour of a privy council hearing, and by November the members of the committee had been chosen. It was composed of privy councillors who might have seemed to be innocent of preconceived opinions: the earl of Rosebery, Lord James of Hereford, Lord Balfour of Burleigh (secretary for Scotland), Sir Edward Fry (an ex-lord justice of appeal), with the lord president himself, the duke of Devonshire, in the chair. But was it entirely coincidence that two of the members (Balfour and Rosebery) were familiar with the non-federal pattern of the Scottish universities, another (Fry) had supported the recent reconstruction of the University of London, and none were publicly identified with what Haldane, in writing to Chamberlain at this time, referred to as 'Oxford notions of what a University ought to be'? And was it entirely coincidence that Rosebery, as Haldane recalled later, was 'not unnaturally much interested on my account', or that Fry, as a result of a long association with Haldane at the bar, was on terms of close friendship with him?

Haldane offered to lead the case on behalf of Liverpool himself, without a fee; but before the case came on he was made a privy councillor, which disqualified him from doing so. Instead, therefore, he appeared as leading witness and he advised on the choice of counsel: Lyttelton ('who knew little about higher education but was tactful and also well known to the members of the Committee'), Sidney Webb, and Kemp ('my old friend . . . who was one of my "devils" at Lincoln's Inn in those days'). The hearing lasted for three days, from 17 to 19 December 1902. It resolved itself into a fight between Liverpool (for its independence) and Leeds (to preserve the integrity of the federal Victoria University) conducted on occasion with unseemly venom. Ripon gave evidence against Liverpool like 'a wild animal at bay' and Acland (also opposing Liverpool) lost his temper when cornered by 'mere' lawyers. Haldane, who had characteristically mastered all the details, was in his element; courteous, unruffled, and with an inexhaustible supply of facts and figures. The case was about a proposed university in Lancashire, not Yorkshire. But when it was necessary to confound the witnesses from Yorkshire who came to oppose Liverpool, Haldane said: '. . . I am not a Yorkshireman, and my knowledge of Yorkshire has been derived from visits there and a close study of calendars and materials; but I have studied this, I venture to think, more closely than some of the Yorkshire witnesses have themselves.' And a few minutes later he said, sweetly: 'I have got a statement which I have prepared and copies of which I will hand to my friend.' He then produced a list of institutions for higher education in Yorkshire towns with more than 20,000 inhabitants, and a second table setting out their functions. He then ran through them: Leeds, Sheffield, Bradford, Halifax . . . serving a population of three or four millions, until he reached his point: that far from opposing a dissolution of the federal Victoria University, Yorkshire ought to support it. Leeds could be the seat of another great university, surrounded by 'schools of the University' in other Yorkshire towns, with an effect 'the same as the effect is in London at the present time – a great co-ordination of every kind of education and a great stimulus in the teaching of these institutions.'

It was another opportunity to preach the gospel of regionalism for universities. And when taxed with the question: what could these three separate universities do which could not be done by the present Victoria

University? – Haldane's answer was again the case for regionalism. 'The Victoria University has an area of . . . 10,000 square miles. It ranges over a territory 100 miles in length, and the University resolves itself into nothing more than a degree-giving and examining board . . . .' And he went on to say that this was an obstruction to local participation in the affairs of the college where teaching is done, for 'by no amending of the charter can you give it that contact with the important local people . . .which would make it the real, living, permeating force that a body with co-ordinate functions, and within a convenient area would be.' 'You attach', he was asked, 'the greatest weight to the limitation of the sphere of influence of which you spoke yesterday?' 'The very greatest weight' was Haldane's reply.

In due course Haldane had to deal with the fear that to multiply degree-giving bodies would be to lower standards; an early version of the 'more means worse' argument. 'Can you suggest to us', asked Sir Edward Fry, any way to prevent a cheapening of the degree, 'supposing small Universities become prevalent in this country. You have thought of the subject more than most people?' Haldane was ready for this. External examiners would maintain the parity of degrees, and they would have to be selected so that they could not be over-ruled by the *in situ* professor.

Throughout Haldane's evidence there are glimpses of educational horizons far beyond the limited enquiry of the privy council committee. In advocating university status for the colleges in Liverpool, Manchester and Leeds, Haldane was looking as an ultimate objective to a regional university which incorporated technical institutes and polytechnics, some of them wealthier than the universities because they were financed by local authorities. And at one point he hinted at a still wider jurisdiction for universities: the colleges of the Victoria University, he said, were 'too little autonomous in so far as they have not got the powers necessary to enable them to organise education *from top to toe* [our italics] in their district'.

Haldane's *Case* to the privy council committee is a veritable manifesto for his beliefs about higher education, matured after a dozen years of thought:

I desire to see the extension of University education in England to a very large class of persons who cannot at present obtain it . . . all those who are about to follow any profession or occupation which requires knowledge, reflection and judgement. . . . The more of these persons who get a University education the better.... I regard higher education as an end in itself.... The changing conditions of the world in the twentieth century make higher instruction more necessary than formerly. In many spheres of life where natural capacity and special qualities of character, such as energy and courage, may have sufficed in the past, the possession of special knowledge, the application of trained intelligence, is now absolutely necessary for success.

He then went on to describe the importance of universities for the nation's industrial life (putting in some propaganda, of course, for the Charlottenburg concept), 'and the encouragement of research because it appeals specially to the great commercial classes of this country....' But this, he wrote, 'is one aspect only of the effect of applying intelligence, knowledge and thoroughness to the whole conduct of life....'

The opponents struggled to prevent a verdict. To grant Liverpool's petition, said Acland, 'prejudging the settlement of the whole of this enormously important question of supplying a University education to this great country, and this great empire' after consideration of only 12–15 hours, would be disastrous. And Ripon: '... the whole of this discussion raises most forcibly the general question of University education in this country ... it is a question which ought not to be decided upon the individual application of any of the Colleges....' But the privy councillors were not impressed; indeed Rosebery – even if he had no preconceived opinions about the issue – certainly had preconceived opinions about two of the witnesses. His hostility toward Acland and Ripon was frankly a legacy of his unhappy relations with them in his cabinet of 1894–5. In reply to a jocular inquiry from Balfour of Burleigh over lunch, Rosebery made the enigmatic response that his association with Acland had been 'like that of the three colleges whose federal ties we are asked to dissolve'; and when Acland and Ripon concluded their evidence, he flung a piece of paper over to the chairman (the duke of Devonshire) with the comment: 'Ripon and Acland were the two most taciturn members of my Cabinet, so now you understand what I suffered.' Fitzroy, indeed, formed the impression that the 'violence of the line taken by Lord Ripon and Acland has had a very marked effect on Lord Rosebery's attitude towards the question; as the Duke says, "his principal object has been to make them look ridiculous".' And it was surely Acland who inspired Rosebery's comment about one of the experts who had replied to a single question of counsel in a lengthy speech: that he was 'like the rock smitten by Moses.'

These were the actors, and these their prejudices, in a scene which made educational history in England. The privy councillors granted Liverpool's petition. On 16 February 1903 the king in council approved a report which recommended that the colleges at Liverpool and Manchester should receive charters as separate universities; but that before these charters were granted Leeds should be given the opportunity to make proposals for a university in Yorkshire; and that in framing these or similar charters 'the effect of the multiplication of such Universities should not be lost sight of' and due consideration be given to the points on which joint action was desirable.

All the parties, even Leeds, were satisfied with the outcome. Haldane wrote a flattering letter to Fitzroy, whose reaction was: 'I can, at any rate, claim to have succeeded so far as the two main objects for which I have striven are concerned: first, to get the subject dealt with by a Committee of the Privy Council instead of a Royal Commission, and secondly, to obtain from that Committee a decision in favour of University development on modern lines, in compliance with the exigencies of commerce and industry.'

Haldane himself was very proud of this victory for his views. 'The date of this Order in Council', he said, when, nine years later, he was installed as chancellor of the University of Bristol, 'is, I think, a memorable one. It gave State recognition to a new policy, but for which we might not have been assembled here tonight. The principle was accepted that the number of the English Universities was to be increased and their headquarters were to be in cities.' The campaign for civic universities had been won, but it was not in Haldane's nature to leave it at that. The gains had to be consolidated. So we find him still concerned in the affairs of Liverpool, and still acting as consultant to Fitzroy, when it came to settling the details of the charters for the new universities. The immediate problem was to define the exact nature of the joint action required of them. Fitzroy had anticipated trouble about this when the ruling was being considered: 'No doubt the scope and scheme of joint action will give rise to much discussion on points of detail', he had written to the duke on 14 January. 'Haldane for one is, I know, anxious that as free a hand as possible should be given to the universities to make their own arrangements. . . .' Later, when it transpired that Manchester and Leeds wanted obligatory consultation to cover even degree courses and subjects of examination, Haldane again pressed his view. 'I own', he wrote to Fitzroy at the beginning of April,

> that I think the Manchester and Leeds proposal a mischievous one. If you would like to know how heavily the four Scotch Universities are suffering from an analogous provision, Struthers [of the Scottish education department] . . . will give you the last information. The experience has been disastrous. The more progressive Scotch Universities have found themselves hampered. . . . I am very keen, therefore, that, if you can, you should let Liverpool shape its own Courses of instruction without being vetoed by Universities which may have other views of their work.

Ultimately a reconciling formula from the principal of Edinburgh, Sir William Turner, enabled this course to be taken. But it was not until Fitzroy had sounded Haldane on the formula that he ventured to act on it: 'Haldane came to see me about a clause I had drafted for insertion in the Charters of Liverpool and Manchester Universities, providing against science degrees being given for purely technological attainments', he recorded on 4 May. 'The suggestion came from Sir W. Turner, and I was glad to hear Haldane accept it with eagerness.' And in the explanatory memorandum he prepared for circulation to the committee, he backed his recommendation with the argument Haldane had supplied earlier: 'The experience of Scotland where an analogous provision has been in force since the Act of 1889, is, it is understood, of one voice as to its effect in hampering initiative and arresting enterprise, and it would surely be a pity when Liverpool is prepared to concede so much to the principle of co-operation to impose a condition which strains unanimity and may retard progress.'

This conflict of views was resolved but now a new one appeared. Sheffield was not content to remain a federated college attached to Leeds. Why not two universities in Yorkshire? The privy council did not put up much resistance, and by March 1905 a charter for a separate university at Sheffield was being negotiated. The draft ran into difficulties over mandatory consultation. If Sheffield had to submit its statutes and ordinances to Manchester, Liverpool, and Leeds, then these three universities should be obliged to submit theirs to Sheffield! To placate Sheffield, Fitzroy had to persuade the privy council committee to find another compromise. This compromise had to take note of the jealousy between Leeds and Sheffield. One way out (favoured by Rosebery) would be to oblige Sheffield to consult only the Lancashire universities. But this would cause umbrage in Leeds. In the end, a classical solution was reached: the tutelage of Sheffield should be subject to a time limit. On 3 April 1905 Fitzroy wrote to Rosebery:

> ... I had the opportunity of going into the matter with Haldane when he was here a few days ago. He quite agrees that a reciprocal arrangement, if practicable, would be best, but in the circumstances is content with what is proposed. Of course, as he says, if they had all started together, the case would have been different, but Sheffield comes in late and ought to be satisfied with obtaining its University on these terms: its objection to submit changes in its Statutes to Leeds ignores the position of the latter, as one of the constituents of the late Victoria University, and the rights that attach to it in consequence: rights which in his opinion it would be hard to ask it to surrender. He thinks a time limit, which you will observe has been introduced, ought to remove all Sheffield's objections as in seven, or, if they press for it, five years time we can say to the other Universities – either Sheffield shall go entirely free or be put on terms of complete reciprocity.

A draft charter for Sheffield was approved on 29 May 1905, 'thus bringing to an end a series of very responsible negotiations. . . . Few Committees of the Privy Council have been concerned with so large a task as bringing four Universities into being and prescribing all the conditions under which they should work in concert – a step which will have the most important consequences upon the development of university organisation.'

A drawback of the mole-technique is that the mole is rarely visible to the public. So it is not surprising that Haldane's claim to have played a large part in founding civic universities should have been challenged. That he did make this claim is not in doubt. When he was given an honorary degree at Liverpool he wrote to his mother: 'the degree . . . was conferred on me as the real founder of the University.' But this was no more than a pardonable indulgence in filial exaggeration, often to be found in Haldane's letters to his mother. In his autobiography he is more careful: 'one of the first of the new University movements on which I set to work was that in Liverpool, where my public-spirited friend, A. F. Warr, MP for one of the divisions . . . prepared the ground for me . . . . Liverpool presently made a splendid response.' Haldane did, nevertheless, expose himself to criticism from others who were instrumental in helping to create a university in Liverpool, and so to set a pattern for civic universities. Hopkinson, who as the first vice-chancellor of the newly-constituted University of Manchester, was in the middle of the negotiations, wrote that from the statement in Haldane's autobiography 'it appears that he had really not much knowledge of the subject . . . . On this question Haldane, in spite of his great ability and the interest he took in the subject is often quite mistaken.' And Muir, whose ideas played an important part in the early days of Liverpool, frankly instanced Haldane's account as an example of the readiness of people of importance to exaggerate their own achievement. According to Muir, Haldane's claim 'to be the real founder of the Liverpool University can certainly not be upheld', but except in the letter to his mother this is a claim he never made.

It is not difficult to reconcile these conflicting opinions. First, there was the mole-technique. It was Beatrice Webb who reflected that in the movement for new forms of universities at the beginning of the twentieth century 'Haldane will have played one of the principal *though unseen* parts' (our italics). Second, the whole style of Liverpool University owed much to the charismatic figure of Mackay, who was professor of history there; a Scot, steeped in the Scots tradition, with a passionate, almost mystical, vision of what a university should be, and a grim determination to create one in Liverpool. And Muir was Mackay's disciple. If vision alone were enough to create a university, Mackay could have done it. But before a university can be born, there has to be a midwife as well as a father. To be midwife was the essential part Haldane played; it was a part none of his critics could have played. The prospect of Mackay patiently negotiating with Fitzroy and the privy council would – from all accounts of Mackay's personality – have been ludicrous. On some details Haldane's recollections were at fault and in his enthusiasm for the new pattern of civic universities, Haldane did tend to overlook the fact that other people, too, were enthusiastic. These are fair targets for criticism. But his critics overlooked (or were ignorant of) the formidable difficulty of turning airy aspirations into the unexciting legalese of charters and statutes. No one can say that without Haldane it could not have been done. But it is pretty clear that without Haldane it would not have been done so quickly, so smoothly, and so wisely. Rhetoric may conceive an idea: it takes negotiation to deliver it.

On one detail Haldane's recollection was seriously at fault. In retrospect, proud of the part he had played in creating the civic universities, he wrote that after the Victoria University was reconstituted 'further new universities were set up with all possible speed. Besides Liverpool, Manchester, and Leeds, Birmingham, Bristol, and Sheffield received Charters.' In fact, the University of Birmingham received its charter three years before all this happened, in 1900, and its political midwife was Chamberlain.

Encounters between the two midwives led to some illuminating exchanges. In the summer of 1902 Haldane sent Chamberlain a copy of his essays, *Education and empire.* Chamberlain replied: 'I think that we agree in attaching chief importance now to the higher education.' Haldane, fresh from his success in launching the scheme for a London Charlottenburg now wanted Charlottenburgs to be attached to some of the regional universities.

> It seems to me [he wrote] that what would appeal most really to the public would be the proposition to add to the local Universities thoroughly equipped organisations for the development of the application of science to commerce and especially industry. This we might put forward as an entire policy. . . . We could point to a start made in London, & propose a second start for the Centre of England, to be localised in Birmingham University . . . . This once made a real & living institution the rest of the University would tend to grow, & it would be easier to get endowments for it. At least this is what I think as regards London & probably the same thing is true of Birmingham. The only effective way of getting the money is by private appeals to very rich men. I think that under your auspices I could manage something of this kind with regard to Birmingham, & I should be prepared most willingly to do my best . . . . Of course a thoroughly practical plan of the institution would have to be elaborated, with the special character of Midland industries in view. The Birmingham Charlottenburg should have its own special characteristics. So at least it strikes my mind.

This letter elicited a merited snub from Chamberlain: 'I think you can hardly be aware of any of the details of the Birmingham scheme which is much more advanced than you appear to suppose. We have laid out plans for a technical University, the buildings of which will cost a million when fully realised.' Later, when Chamberlain gave a speech at Leeds in 1903, he said: 'I heartily rejoice that Mr Haldane – by no means the first in the field, but still welcome, however late – (laughter) – should lend his influence and advocacy to the formation of Charlottenburg schools all over the country.' But at this stage Haldane and Chamberlain had fallen out over another matter, namely Chamberlain's enthusiasm for empire preference to encourage trade. Haldane regarded this policy as disastrous. His remedy for the ever increasing competition from abroad was not the imposition of imperial preference, but technological education in Britain, to improve the efficiency of British industry. However, as we record later in this chapter, Haldane was to become partner with Chamberlain's son a couple of years later, in 1905, when they were pressing for systematic grants to the new civic universities.

A committee of the privy council had set a pattern for higher education to which even the most recent universities in Britain conform. It is surprising how little publicity the episode received. Sidney Webb described (in an article in the *Cornhill* in April 1903) how in the middle of February 'a few of the London newspapers reported, briefly and obscurely enough, an official decision of no small moment to the future of English education. The other newspapers did not notice it at all and public opinion is still unaware that a decisive step in national policy has been taken. The decision was that of a special committee of the Privy Council. . . .' Taken in conjunction with the reorganisation of the University of London, the creation of the University of Birmingham, and the foundation of university colleges at Reading and Southampton, 'the simultaneous approval of the creation of three new universities in the northern counties may fairly be said to mark an epoch. We are actually engaged, on no small scale, in the business of making universities. We are evidently going, during the next few years, to endow each part of England with its own local university.'

Haldane noted the same indifference.

'It has always seemed to me that this decision of the Government as advised by the Privy Council in 1903 was a step of the first importance in the history of higher education. Little notice was, however, taken of it by the public or by writers about English education. The thick printed volumes containing the documents and the evidence repose undisturbed in the library of the Judicial Office in Downing Street.'

And again, in an article years afterwards:

'this question was brought to trial by the State before a very high tribunal, and a firm decision was given in favour of the principle. It is remarkable, as showing how slight has been the public interest in education, that the newspapers hardly noticed and did not report the proceedings\* which took place before the Special Committee of the Privy Council which conducted a semi-judicial inquiry into the subject in the end of 1902.'

Our portrait of Haldane at the turn of the century emerges from the causes he espoused: a teaching university in London, English Charlottenburgs, autonomous civic universities in four northern cities. But there was one cause which he declined to support, namely pressure for massive financial backing from the taxpayer. He was on record in Hansard (20 June 1889) as saying: 'nor do I think we are in great need of money in the Scotch Universities.' In 1898 he refused to support a plea that the University of London should be state-supported, as Strasbourg University was. In December 1895, December 1901 and February 1904, deputations waited on the chancellor of the exchequer to press for additional grants for higher education. Haldane did not take part in any of these deputations. And when Sir Norman Lockyer, addressing the British Association in 1903, declared that £24,000,000 was needed to bring British universities to the level of those in America and Germany, this sensational suggestion elicited no response whatever from Haldane.

It was not that Haldane disapproved of state aid to universities; indeed on appropriate occasions he advocated it. So we must seek other reasons for his lukewarmness. One reason is that he understood, as some of his naive contemporaries failed to understand, how a too willing generosity from the state can promote parsimony from private donors. Moreover his whole strategy for higher education rested on the belief that where your treasure is, there your heart is also: the local community which helped to finance its civic university would take pride in it and cherish it. '. . . I know of no better way', he said, 'of endowing and supporting a great seat of learning than through the munificence and liberality of the citizens of a great city. . . .' And on another occasion:

> That the State ought to do more than it does in the way of endowment, I agree . . . . But I am not sure that I wish to see the burden transferred to the State in the wholesale fashion that is sometimes

\* The proceedings were in fact reported in *The Times*, but without comment.

suggested. . . . Probably nothing conduces more to national efficiency than frugality in the use of national resources. The private donor should be encouraged and not left to expend his generosity in regions which do not concern the State directly. In writing this, I do not mean that the Government ought not to spend public money generously upon the Universities. I mean that it should not be spent unless and until a case for the necessity of such expenditure has been clearly made out.

Even over state support for the University of London, after its re-organisation in 1898, Haldane was strangely cautious. Following a deputation from the University of London to the treasury on 13 December 1900, the permanent secretary drew up proposals for a grant-in-aid. The chancellor of the exchequer (Hicks Beach) commented on the proposals:

I put this before the Lord President, who confidentially consulted Mr Haldane. The latter considers that your figures as to the help now given to the University are substantially accurate – and thinks that any Government help now to be given should be doled out in the most guarded & measured way: he does not wish those who now direct the Senate to be entrusted with more than you have suggested, but deprecates any announcement that the amount can never be exceeded.

Another reason for this muting of the financial consequences of his great schemes for the expansion of universities may have been purely political, a deliberate ploy on Haldane's part, so that he could retain the confidence of those in authority. It is significant that the chancellor's comment went on to say: 'The Lord President attaches much importance to Mr Haldane's opinion, with which he generally concurs. . . .' Finally, we must not exclude an ideological reason: the disciple of Green and Adam Smith would naturally not wish to allow educational institutions to become parasitic upon a central government.

At any rate, Haldane's views about state support for universities began to change soon after the turn of the century. In 1902 while still busy over Liverpool, he wrote to Chamberlain suggesting: 'I should like also to see a lump sum grant to each University which would raise locally as much more – say of £50,000 to be applied in strengthening the scientific & economic sides.' And Haldane had no misgivings about tapping rich men to support higher education.

'As you know, we have made a good start in London – where I am glad to say I now see my way to £330,000 out of £600,000 which we want at once. London ought to be made the Educational Capital of the Empire.' Despite their disagreement over other matters, Haldane and Chamberlain were eager to act as partners over higher education. 'There is one subject', Chamberlain wrote to Haldane, 'on which I fancy that you and I are nearer together than other men are on anything – I mean *Highest* Education.' But co-operation was to be with the son rather than the father. It was Austen Chamberlain, as chancellor of the exchequer, who invited Haldane in March 1904 to undertake a challenging task: to become chairman of a treasury committee to look into the distribution of state grants to university colleges in England.

Parliament had made its first grant-in-aid to the English university colleges in 1889. The annual sum to be distributed between them was £15,000. By 1903 it had risen to £27,000. In February 1904 a deputation from the university colleges waited on Austen Chamberlain to press for an increase. His response was to propose a doubling of the grant in 1904–5, with a possible further increase to £100,000 in 1905–6. Up to 1904 allocations were made by an *ad hoc* committee on a simple principle: they were roughly proportional to the annual cash income from other sources to the colleges, for work in arts and science of university standard, subject to a report on efficiency; no grant (save the one to Manchester) could exceed £3000 or one quarter of the local income; and colleges whose income was less than £4000 per annum were not eligible for grant.

Chamberlain coupled his proposal for a larger grant with a decision to set up a small independent committee to advise him on its apportionment. 'I shall endeavour', he told the deputation from the university colleges, 'to get gentlemen whose competence is recognised by all of you.' Haldane was to be chairman. His colleagues were Mowatt, Woods (formerly president of Trinity College, Oxford), and Cripps (an MP, and hardly perhaps a welcome choice for Haldane, because he had been leading counsel for the Yorkshire college against Liverpool in the famous privy council hearing). The secretary was a treasury man, Higgs. Continuity with past practice was assured because Woods had served on the quinquennial inspection committee in 1901–2 and Higgs had been secretary of that committee. The committee's terms of reference were to report how state aid to university teaching could be most effectively organised and applied. Their discretion was subject

o three conditions: that assistance be given only for instruction
ffording education of university standard in great centres of popula-
ion; that assistance be given with the object of stimulating local
enevolence; that existing requirements of a minimum local income
o qualify for grants be maintained. There were obvious defects in
he existing system. For one thing, there was no continuity. Since
889 no fewer than five *ad hoc* committees had been appointed to
istribute the grant; struggling and needy but promising institutions
vere excluded from grants; the subjects qualifying for grant were
imited to arts and science; the system of giving grants was too
mechanical, giving no consideration to special areas of weakness in the
olleges.

In eleven months the committee produced three reports. Only the
hird of these, issued on 23 February 1905, raised points of substance.
Beneath the surface of the committee's work Haldane took care to
keep up a running informal exchange of notes with Chamberlain
preserved in treasury records) so that Chamberlain could be well
nformed about the committee's intentions (and be softened up about
hem) in advance of publication. Some softening up was evidently
ecessary, for in December 1904 Chamberlain was expressing disquiet
bout the committee's intentions. Their exchange of letters is a revealing
xample of an early dispute about *dirigisme* attached to state grants
o universities.

I have been so busily engaged with my Constituents [wrote
Chamberlain on 21 December 1904] since I saw you on the subject
of Grants to University Colleges that I have had little time to
reflect upon the suggestions which you made. I confess, however,
that the more I think of them the more difficulties do they present
to my mind . . . . I cannot help fearing that the line which the
Committee contemplate taking will be met with very serious
criticism from the Colleges interested . . . . Your idea, as I understand
it, is, that, after making a small increase to the semi-permanent
Grants now given, the balance of the £100,000 available should be
preserved for distribution from year to year by a Committee to be
appointed by the Treasury according to their views of the urgency
of the cases presented to them by different Colleges. I think this
would tend to an interference with the independence of the Colleges
which would be regrettable. . . .

Haldane replied on the very same day, with a masterly defence of his proposals:

> I have your letter, & were I not compelled to leave town tomorrow for some days I should much prefer to ask you to let me come to see you to writing. The questions you raise have been under the close consideration of some of us for years past. . . . I quite agree that if you are dealing with a modern & thoroughly enlightened University College you may leave it to work out its own destiny. This is open under our recommendations. What we demur to is a stereotyped scheme applicable to all Colleges without discrimination . . . to distribute without laying down lines such as we indicate is to perpetuate what already exists to far too great an extent. . . . I would not write confidently had I not realised from personal observation both in England & Scotland the mischief of stagnation which the existing system has left to grow up unchecked. . . . If the Governing bodies only realised how little we contemplate interfering with the liberty of those that are efficient they would not question what we propose. But alas, they are not all efficient.

Haldane offered to call on Chamberlain early in January 1905 to discuss all this before the report was drafted. There is no record of their meeting but clearly Haldane's views prevailed, because they survived to inspire the final report.

This report shows unmistakable signs of its chairman's pen. (One wonders whether Haldane, like some other energetic chairmen of committees, left the secretary with little else to do but to keep records and arrange meetings.) For Haldane, the operation was one more stage in his master plan for an integrated educational system. The committee (so ran the report) considered that they should aim 'at devising such a scheme for the application of the new annual grant as may form a step in a policy for the development of the educational efficiency of the University Colleges'.

The main recommendations of the committee were:

   (i) The grants should be allocated partly according to the existing mechanical principle of 'payment by results' (i.e. in proportion to the colleges' incomes from other sources) and partly by a system of earmarked grants to remedy defects in three special areas: post-graduate research; books and equipment; salaries and superannuation.

(ii) Following the example of the Carnegie Trust for Scottish universities, the committee proposed that recipients of the grant should have direct access to an 'impartial authority', which they spelt out as a committee comprising representatives of the treasury and suitably qualified academics and 'possibly' the board of education. This committee, unlike its *ad hoc* forerunners, might also be the body which visited and inspected the colleges. Also, unlike its forerunners, the committee itself would receive the money hitherto sent direct to the colleges from the treasury and would distribute this and would submit an annual report to the treasury to be laid before parliament. Here was the genesis of the present University Grants Committee.

(iii) Consideration should be given (the wording is tentative: here was Haldane being careful not to fetter the discretion of the proposed committee) to enlarging the categories of work qualifying for grant, from the present restricted areas of arts and sciences, to include law, medicine, engineering and architecture.

These proposals, tame as they seem today, were considered to be too radical to be adopted by simple administrative action. Chamberlain presented them to his cabinet with the following comment:

This Committee [the Haldane committee] has now presented three Reports. . . . The third Report is a much more important document, since it proposes not only new conditions of distribution for the future but also the establishment of a permanent Committee to advise the Treasury on the subject. . . . The Report is a very valuable document, as was to be expected from the wide knowledge of the gentlemen who signed it and from the attention they have given to the subject for many years. I have directed that it shall be laid before both Houses and communicated to the Colleges concerned, so that we may have the benefit of the observations and criticisms of all those who are interested in University education before we finally decide on our course of action.

We do not know what the cabinet thought about the report. But the views of the colleges are well documented in the treasury records. On the whole the report was welcomed by academics. They liked the idea of a permanent committee to administer the grants, though there was a little nervousness as to whether this might not lead to 'irksome, and even injurious' government influence; and they commended the proposal that grants should be settled for five year periods and not annually. The reception was sufficiently encouraging for Murray of the treasury to suggest a course of action which was accepted without modification by Chamberlain, and after approval by Balfour, formed the basis for a treasury minute of 18 July 1905. By the terms of this minute the treasury readily accepted the proposal for a permanent committee which they undertook to 'endeavour . . . to constitute' in the following autumn; agreed to the double principle of allocation, although with some ninety per cent of the total grant being assigned on the existing basis for a period of not less than five years; and agreed that the balance of the grant should be reserved for books and equipment, post-graduate awards, and superannuation. But the treasury did not consider it prudent to put post-graduate students in direct relation with the proposed committee (this was a function of the department of scientific and industrial research twenty years later); also the treasury felt unable to sanction a special grant for supplementing teachers' salaries; and they insisted on strict adherence to a minimum local income before a college could qualify for treasury aid.

The treasury reason for turning down any supplementation of salaries was a frankly selfish one. Murray's memorandum on this point was: 'A very considerable rise in all these salaries is going on, as we find whenever anybody of the kind is wanted for a public Department; and I do not see any reason for making special efforts to raise the market against ourselves.' Against which Chamberlain commented: 'I entirely agree.'

Haldane's reaction to this emasculation of the committee's report is not known. It may well have contributed to the little bursts of criticism against the treasury which punctuated some of his speeches in the house of lords years later. The treasury, he said, speaking in 1915, 'looks at things in a penny wise and pound impotent fashion'. And again, in 1918: '. . . nothing is more likely to stultify and reduce to folly what we are endeavouring to do in the Bill than to introduce the Treasury as an expert in educational matters.' In the event, therefore, Haldane's committee made little immediate impact on the grant system, either by way of widening the discretion of the grant-giving committee (for the principle of earmarking had been reduced to a shadow of the original proposal mooted to Chamberlain toward the end of 1904) or by tack-

ling the major historical anomalies. But it did make an essential contribution in proposing a standing committee to deal with the grants in a
new way. Chamberlain did not in fact keep to the intention of appointing this committee in the autumn of 1905; it was left to the incoming
Liberal government, with assistance from Haldane himself in his ministerial capacity, to carry out the main proposal of the committee.

Intrigue, conspiracy, subterranean machinations: these were the
epithets which Haldane's enemies applied to his methods. If the words
are detached from their sinister implications they are fair comment.
Behind every tactical success in educational policy – for the University
of London, the consortium of colleges in South Kensington, the
northern universities, the apparatus for state support of higher education – lay not only Haldane's overt efforts, but also carefully contrived
dinner parties, confidential notes to ministers, a word in the ear of
*The Times* editorial staff, an evening hatching propaganda with the
Webbs, a critically important house guest at Cloan. If a portrait of
Haldane is to do justice to him, his motives for employing these
devious manoeuvres must be examined.

That personal ambition was not the motive is clear from an important episode which occurred in 1902. The days of the Conservative
government were numbered. The Opposition had hopes of a victory,
with cabinet office for their leading personalities. Some Liberals were
already dubious about Haldane's loyalty to the Liberal cause: on
educational issues he had worked closely with Conservative ministers
– Balfour, Devonshire, Hicks Beach, Chamberlain – and they trusted
him. The house of commons assumed that on issues of education
Haldane would be stubbornly bipartisan. After the episode in 1902
Haldane described himself as a 'pariah', a speech he had made in
parliament 'to which he entirely adhered' having 'excluded him from
the Tabernacle'. It came about in the following way.

In March 1902 the Conservative government introduced a bill
intended to lay the foundation of a national system of education. In
essence it was to abolish the school boards and to bring the board
schools, the voluntary schools, and further education, under the
authority of county or county borough councils. The bill roused
bitter hostility among dissenters, and largely on this account it was
opposed by a majority of Liberal MPs.

For Haldane the bill did not go far enough. He wanted education to
be reorganised under local control, but in localities much larger (and

more sophisticated) than county councils. His vision was of an England divided into educational provinces, each presided over by a council which would include experts on education, and under the 'permeating influence' (an expression he was constantly using at that time) of the local university. But the bill was a step in the right direction and Haldane – always conscious that in politics half a loaf is better than no bread – gave it strong, though critical, support at the first and second reading, in defiance of Liberal opinion. His two speeches, coming from a man so obviously disinterested in the party-political consequences of what he was saying, created a great impression. Despite its imperfections, he said, the bill presented a measure by which 'a real and substantial advance may be made in the only direction in which education could progress.' His ideal was that education should be treated as an organic whole 'in which you would have primary, secondary and tertiary education . . . linked together and permeated from the top with the intention of the university and not the spirit of the church.' Again, a glimpse of the grand regional plan: in Birmingham, he said, the university authorities had entered into an arrangement with the adjoining counties of Worcestershire and Staffordshire; in the same way Liverpool might cover one half of Lancashire and Manchester might cover the other half, 'and so on through the entire country.'

This idealistic vision threatened the denominational schools and many other vested interests. Lloyd George, vehemently defending the interests of the non-conformists, attacked Haldane: 'You cannot base any good system of education on an injustice to a large section of the community. . . . Politically speaking, my hon. friend seems always to be above the snow-line . . . . Let him descend from the region of eternal snow and come down to bare facts . . . .' (a reproach which, on a later occasion, drew from Haldane the riposte that the snow-line was 'a place from which a clear and wide prospect is sometimes to be had . . .'). Even the gentle Grey demurred: 'I venture to say that anyone who knows the penetrating zeal, the single-mindedness, the great knowledge, the hard work spent on education by my hon. and learned friend will differ from any course he takes on an educational matter with the greatest regret. . . .'

On 8 May 1902 the bill passed its second reading with a substantial government majority. But it was not yet safely on the statute book, and Haldane was anxious about the opposition to it. He turned, as he had on previous occasions, to the media – such as they were then – which might influence public opinion. On the day before the passage of the second reading, at Birmingham, he addressed the University on 'Our system of education' and subtly introduced *his* desired system: provincial councils, and the provincial university closely linked with the system administered by local authorities within its boundaries. In July he was with the Webbs conspiring with Sidney to create a literary 'demo': a symposium on the education bill to appear in the next issue of the *Nineteenth Century*, to strengthen the hand of the Conservatives. The symposium duly appeared in the October issue. There were further speeches, well reported in the daily press. Of a speech in North Berwick, *The Times* reported on 1 October: 'In regard to the powers of the Bill, he favoured the creation of larger areas and the policy of increasing the powers and responsibilities of municipal bodies. The system of devolution proposed by the Bill struck him as a step in the right direction.'

Two months later the bill cleared its final hurdles and reached the statute book on 20 December 1902. But this was not the end of the matter. The bill covered England and Wales but excluded London. Soon after its first introduction to parliament it became an open secret that a strong section of the cabinet wanted the education authority for London to be a joint committee of borough councils (almost certain to lack expertise in educational matters) instead of the London County Council. This, for Sidney Webb, who had achieved so much for London education through the technical education board, was a threat to the ark of the covenant. Haldane was drawn in to avert what seemed to Beatrice Webb 'a disaster of the first magnitude'. The partnership agreed upon an intense conspiracy. Even before the Education (London) bill (1903) appeared, the campaign against it was launched. On 20 July 1902 Haldane lunched with the Webbs; at the lunch Sidney was deputed to write a memorandum on the educational issues involved in London and Haldane undertook to convey it through Hugh Cecil to Balfour. The memorandum, running to fifty-five pages, was soon prepared. The copy preserved in the *Passfield papers* bears this pencilled note in Sidney's hand: 'Comments on the Education Bill for London projected by the Conservative Gov during 1902 – used to convince Conservatives, Churchmen & Educationalists in the autumn of 1902.'

The contents of this document belong to educational history and are not germane to our portrait; except for one point made by Webb which reveals how closely his ideas and Haldane's coincided. An authority formed out of the borough councils, Webb wrote, would have little sympathy with Higher Education, and would certainly be disinclined to do anything for the development of a Teaching University for the Metropolis . . . experience shows that all inexperienced administrators of education tend to begin by exaggerating the importance of the schooling given to the mass, and by undervaluing the training of the small minority who possess superior ability. . . . To supersede the experienced members of the School Board and Technical Education Board . . . by raw recruits from the Borough Councils . . . would be as regards all forms of higher education, to put back the clock by many years.

Haldane duly conveyed the memorandum to Hugh Cecil who acknowledged it (from Lucerne) on 29 September, saying that on his return to London he would have it copied. And he went on, 'I propose to send it to Arthur Balfour, Walter Long, Anson, & Londonderry, also to Whitmore & Freddy Smith. I shall say that it comes from you but emanates ultimately from a Progressive source. . . . I have long been in favour of the LCC having the control of London Education.' Throughout the autumn and winter of 1902–3 the conspirators continued to be busy. On 2 November Haldane arranged for the Webbs to meet the prime minister (Balfour) at a small dinner party. Two weeks later the dinner party was held, at which Beatrice 'seized every opportunity to insinuate [into Balfour] sound doctrine and information as to the position of London education.' At the beginning of January Haldane wrote to Beatrice from Cloan to say that 'things about London are still in the balance.' Balfour had been warned that he would break up the Unionist party in London if he favoured the LCC. 'I hope', added Haldane, 'Sidney has collared the Daily Mail. This is important.' A few days later, in a 'strictly secret' letter to Sidney, Haldane wrote, 'I felt so anxious about London that I went & saw Arthur Balfour on the subject. I put the case as strongly as was compatible with the moderation that was necessary.' During January 1903 Haldane brought *The Times* 'down on our side'. Sidney visited the *Daily Mail* offices nightly for a week to edit the educational material, and had interviews with *The Times*, *Telegraph*, and *Morning Post*. Haldane peppered Sidney with notes: on 16 February, that Mowatt had had a 'very satisfactory talk about the Bill' with the chancellor of the exchequer, and Haldane himself an equally satisfactory talk with the secretary of state for India. Two days later: 'Don't relax any effort. Great pressure is being put on the Government by the

London MPs or some of them. We will do all that can be done in the House. . . .' Again two days later: 'I hear that the London Members are coming round to the LCC idea. Hart Dyke, who is working for us, told me that Hayes Fisher had informed him that three quarters of the London Unionist members were *now* for the Bill on LCC lines. I am keeping our people quiet. . . .'

In March there was a set-back. On account of two by-elections the government had it in mind to postpone the bill altogether. This would not have suited the conspirators. Sidney, at Haldane's request, called on the prime minister's private secretary and on the Conservative Whip, to urge them to introduce the bill. In the event it was introduced by Anson on 3 April 1903. On the face of it, the bill was a defeat for Haldane and the Webbs: a compromise, with thirty-six LCC members, thirty-one borough council members, and twenty-five co-opted members. Haldane, writing from Ilmenau in Germany, was disappointed and declared he would vote against the bill unless it was remodelled. On 28 April, at the second reading of the bill, Haldane criticised it in a major speech, with (for him) unusual flights of rhetoric:

> London is the Metropolis of the Empire . . . the greatest city in the world . . . the place in this country to which we ought to be able to look for educational light and leading. . . . I, for one, shall never be satisfied until I see students from the distant parts of the Empire flocking to the universities in this country, and especially in London, for that higher education, that post-graduate training, in search of which they now go to the Continent or the United States. It is little short of a scandal that we should be able to provide so little education of that rank in the great Empire of which London is the Metropolis.

To entrust this high duty to borough councillors!

But there was room for compromise without loss of face. Provided the LCC could control co-option, there could be a majority (despite the borough councillors) on the side of the angels, and (more important) on the side of Haldane and the Webbs. So Haldane emphasised the necessity of getting really enlightened persons among the twenty-five to be co-opted. Haldane voted against the bill, but his 'brilliant suggestions' were noted by the bill's supporters. Following some amendments in committee the bill was passed in the early summer of 1903 in (Beatrice Webb reflected) 'almost exactly the shape Sidney would have given to it'. The conspirators had won.

# 5 At the Cabinet Table

In November 1905, nine years after Haldane had been invited by the students of Edinburgh to stand for the office of lord rector and had lost the election, he was invited again. For a second time the student magazine contained lyrical accounts of his eminence and virtues: 'On the question of education, Mr Haldane, as an expert, has no rival in the kingdom.' 'The best product of our Alma Mater ... "Brain of the Empire".' This time he was elected (though not solely on his own reputation: he swept in also on the wave of the incoming tide of Liberalism). He certainly lived up to specification, for the student magazine of January 1907, commenting on his year of office, called him 'the most popular Lord Rector of modern times'. His speech at the dinner to commemorate the opening of the Union shows how cleverly he could match himself to his audience. In *his* day as a student, he told them, they were very much under the professors. When the students left the lecture rooms they went on thinking about the lectures and the professors until they came back to the lecture room. Now, he said, all that was changed (which drew laughter and applause). Students now, after giving an ungrudging but strictly limited meed of admiration to their professors, betook themselves to the other side of university life. The university was a state of which the student was a citizen. No wonder he was popular at Edinburgh and could always command a good student audience there.

A month after the rectorial election there came a far more important Liberal victory. In December, after nine years in opposition, the Liberal party was back in power. Haldane, of course, had anticipated the victory for some time. Already in 1901 he was urging Sidney Webb to seek a place in parliament. He wrote about it to Beatrice: 'What a lot of work he could do at the L[ocal] G[overnment] Board or in the Education Office! ... Think over this seriously please.' For himself, even at that time, he contemplated the lord chancellorship.

The ensuing story of appointments to the new Liberal government is well known. Campbell-Bannerman became prime minister and refused to go to the house of lords to leave Asquith to lead in the commons. Haldane did not become lord chancellor. He was offered the attorney-generalship or the office of home secretary. He declined both. In his autobiography he explains why he did not want to be a law officer:

> I had had the best that the Bar itself could give me. But that was not the main reason for rejecting anything short of office in the Cabinet. My whole soul had been for years in the effort to bring about reform in higher education and in other departments of administration. To accept the Attorney-Generalship was to abandon influence which I had possessed even under the outgoing Unionist Government.

He became secretary of state for war, and, according to Beatrice Webb, was 'in a state of exuberant delight over his new task'. This was the decade of Haldane's great political ascendancy, when he created his place in history as a war minister and lord chancellor. But if these achievements were set aside, and if his work over these years were to be measured by nothing more than his 'spare time' activities in education, his place in history would still be distinguished. He was now in the full tide of his career, only in his fiftieth year, affluent (he said himself that he had to give up £15,000 to £20,000 a year at the bar in order to take office), influential, famous. Contemporaries often recalled his heavy build and massive head, contrasting with a cat-like tread and a thin piping voice. They remembered his invariably gentle, almost suave manner. Amery (perhaps a hostile critic) said 'there was something about him of the old-fashioned family butler.' But there was no doubt that he had a presence; Osbert Sitwell saw him, some years later: 'How well I can see him now, in my mind's eye, with his head bent, tortoise-like, a little to one side, entering the room with the air of a whole procession.' His time was divided between his comfortable house in Queen Anne's Gate and his estate at Cloan: a life-style, as Beatrice Webb observed, very remote from his concern for democratic institutions! His official preoccupation was the war office; but if he were seen – as he often was – walking across St James's Park with Fitzroy of the privy council, it could be assumed pretty reliably that they were discussing the future of the University College in Bristol, or the problems of higher education in London, or the pattern of state endowment of universities in Britain. It is only toward the middle of this phase of his career, in 1909, that his astonishing energy began to be eroded by illness. Nature, as he wrote, 'pulled me up rather suddenly' as a result of all night sittings in parliament and his work at the war office. His eyesight gave him trouble and it was found that he had diabetes, a disease which in pre-insulin days could be controlled only by an austere and troublesome diet. But the catalogue of his activities over these years showed no sign of thinning out. He was for ever pushing some imaginative educational plan and he used every academic engagement he could as a platform for propaganda.

There was no shortage of such engagements. Beside discharging the duties of the rectorship of Edinburgh University Haldane opened university buildings in Liverpool and Sheffield, and he received honorary degrees from Oxford, Cambridge, Manchester, Birmingham, Sheffield and Durham. Whenever he got the opportunity he expounded his philosophy of education. Those who aspired to found new university colleges came to regard Haldane as having a sort of academic Midas touch in negotiation: had he not negotiated reform in the University of London, the establishment of the Imperial College, and the creation of the idea of civic universities out of the federal Victoria University? We get a glimpse of the regard in which he was held from a letter written in 1913, when Haldane had become lord chancellor, by the newly appointed principal of Hartley College, Southampton, to Selby-Bigge, permanent secretary of the board of education:

When I had the pleasure of sitting next to you at the Clothworkers' Dinner . . . your description of Lord Haldane's zeal for the New University movement which he is championing raised in my mind the reflection that he might possibly like to be asked to lay the Foundation Stone of the New Buildings for this College. Southampton is the centre of a barren area. It is the proper place for the location of a University if Lord Haldane's scheme is to be complete. Will you kindly advise me as to whether my proposal to Lord Haldane would be likely to receive favourable consideration.

Haldane was duly approached by Selby-Bigge, and was obliged to return one of his rare refusals, characteristic in its courtesy:

I am reluctantly forced to say that there is no chance of my being able to lay the foundations of Hartley College Buildings this summer. The preparation of the address I have to deliver on the

1st September, and of two other addresses, coming on top of much other work, has driven me to annex every possible evening.

Nevertheless, a year later, Haldane was writing to Selby-Bigge: 'On Saturday, 20th, I go to Southampton to open the new Hartley College buildings. Could you get someone to send me some pabulum.' This was served up as 'The value of University training to democracy', in which he developed the theme – a novel one at that time – of the social function of a university.

Haldane's development of this theme at Southampton was interrupted by the war, which soon brought disaster to his own political career. But – to go back to the beginning of his tenure of cabinet office – one of his concerns outside the war office remained the promotion of a regional organisation of education.

There were now four northern universities, co-operating, through the Northern Universities joint matriculation board, to set a common examination for schools in the region. The examination had two functions: it gave schools in the region a scale against which to measure their achievement, and it guaranteed a minimum uniform standard for admission to the participating universities. This was a prototype of what some people were calling 'Haldane's scheme'. His next objective was to create a similar educational alliance in the south-west of England. University colleges (taking external London degrees) had been started in Reading and Southampton in 1902 and there had been a university college at Bristol since 1876. Westward of that there was an academic vacuum. Already in 1901, speaking at Liverpool, Haldane was asking why Bristol should not become an academic centre for the south-west of England. And he took up the same theme in a stirring address at the annual dinner of the University College Colston Society in Bristol in 1902. He was at first inclined to throw out the suggestion that Bristol, Reading and Southampton might affiliate into some sort of federal university. Enthusiasts in Bristol naturally wanted something much more individual than that. We have a charming glimpse of how one of them, M. W. Travers, a young science professor there, made his contribution to the campaign. It is to be found in an unpublished fragment of his autobiography. The date is January 1905.

At about 3 pm I was at Mr Haldane's chambers in New Court, Lincoln's Inn. I had sent him an abstract of my report to the College Senate and Council. . . . He told me that, as his party was not in office, he would not be directly concerned in any negotiations between the College and the Government, but as no party matter was involved, his advice would certainly be asked before any decision was taken. However, he could speak authoritatively as to the conditions which must be fulfilled before a Charter would be granted.

Speaking of the address in which he had recommended Bristol to consider affiliation with Southampton and Reading to form a University of the three University Colleges he said, – 'The day of composite Universities has gone by'. . . . Then speaking of my criticism of the somewhat complex constitution of modern universities he insisted that the Court could perform a real function in keeping the University in touch with a wide public. . . . He suggested that I should see Mr Walter Long . . . Sir Michael Hicks-Beach . . . and the Duke of Beaufort, and get them to form a committee external to both bodies,* and consisting mainly of Conservatives (this was interesting as coming from a Liberal statesman), to approach the two bodies, and to ask them to accept the principle of co-operation in the formation of a University.

Haldane invited Travers to keep in touch to report progress, although Travers himself had misgivings that his action 'might meet with more than criticism from high authority' because he was not acting on behalf of the College council at all. However he did keep in touch with Haldane and at the Royal Society soirée in June he met Haldane who said he 'was pleased with what we were doing'.

By December 1905 Haldane was in a key position to influence aspirations like these, for on 11 December a new standing committee of the privy council was set up to deal with matters concerning higher education which fell outside the scope of the privy council committees provided for under the Oxford and Cambridge Act of 1877 and the Universities (Scotland) Act of 1889; and Haldane was made a member. This committee was very influential in advising the government until its functions were gradually taken over, first by the treasury committee appointed in 1911 to administer state grants, and ultimately by the University Grants Committee. It is interesting, therefore, to put on record the genesis of the committee and to note the specific mention of Haldane's name in the memorandum. It was a memorandum from Fitzroy to the lord president of the council:

* i.e. the governing bodies of both the University College and the Merchant Venturers' Technical College; Haldane was insistent the University must include both.

Petitions for supplementary Charters to University Bodies and in connection with other matters touching the interests of Higher Education are often received and referred by the King in Council to a Committee of the Privy Council: it would be convenient to call into existence a standing Committee to deal with such petitions, when necessary, which with your approval I would propose should be constituted, unless otherwise ordained for any special purpose, as follows – the Lord President, the President of the Board of Education, and Mr Haldane, who I understand would always be glad to give his assistance.

This was the body which in 1908 was asked to consider a petition from the college at Bristol for university status. It was an occasion when Haldane's enthusiasm trapped him into one of his rare misjudgements.

There was no difficulty about a pattern for a charter; the charters recently granted to the four northern universities were perfectly satisfactory models for Bristol. But Fitzroy shared Haldane's desire to organise education by regions, under the *aegis* of regional universities, and to promote this he suggested that the universities of Wales and Birmingham might be approached to see whether they would cooperate with a new university at Bristol to form a joint matriculation board, to do for the west-country what the Northern joint board was doing for Lancashire and Yorkshire. 'It is conceded on all hands', wrote Fitzroy, 'that one of the most important functions of the new type of University is the influence it may exercise on secondary education within the area from which it draws its students, and the co-operation of Universities whose influence is felt over the same area tends to maintain a uniform standard which is of great value.' On 20 November 1908, Fitzroy recorded Haldane's prompt agreement with this proposal; but they had both, surprisingly, left out of account the sentiments of Welshmen, who did not want their university, barely fifteen years old, to become an integral part of the English system.*
It was the president of the board of education, Runciman, briefed by his officials, who saw this point and declared himself 'strongly opposed to the idea of a Joint Matriculation Board such as you suggest'. Fitzroy, with the authority of the lord president, advised Haldane to drop the

---

* By the time he became chairman of the royal commission on the University of Wales, Haldane had come to understand the sentiments of Welshmen over this!

idea and Haldane – never a man to permit his prejudices to prevail over
good evidence – wrote: 'I am impressed with what Mr Runciman says.
I concur in thinking that we must, at all events for the present, drop
the idea of a uniform matriculation test.'

Meanwhile Haldane was acting as *amicus curiae* on behalf of Bristol's
petition for a university; never conspicuously, never officially (it was
hardly the business of a secretary of state for war), putting in a timely
word in Whitehall or over cigars at a carefully contrived dinner party
in Queen Anne's Gate. We catch a moment of this in an exchange of
letters between J. W. Arrowsmith (a member of the Bristol University
College council) and Haldane, over the need to persuade the Bristol
Corporation to guarantee an annual subvention to the University.
'Dear Mr Haldane', he wrote on 15 March 1909:

> . . . The question now arises as to the Corporation grant and we
> want Mr Fitzroy to write a strong letter . . . pointing out that the
> Charter will be granted when the Privy Council are assured as to
> the amount which the Corporation are prepared to grant to the Uni-
> versity. If only I knew Mr Fitzroy well enough to write him a
> personal note I would not trouble you: perhaps this may be the last
> time I shall need to bother you but you have all through been so good
> to us amidst all your worry I am asking your help so far. . . .

A week later Haldane wrote to Fitzroy, 'Arrowsmith of Bristol
writes to me; he is a very good fellow, & I think he is probably right
in saying that a letter from you at this juncture would be of importance.
Perhaps you would communicate with him appropriately.' Four days
later a note went to the Bristol city council from the privy council.
The city council granted the proceeds of a penny rate to the aspiring
university college, and a charter was granted on 22 May 1909. Three
years later Haldane was installed as chancellor; it was at his installation
there that he made his moving confession of faith in the function and
future of civic universities.

The penny rate from the city of Bristol was more than a material
contribution to the University's income; it was a symbol of the civic
responsibility which Haldane believed was essential to sustain his system
of universities for the people. '. . . I appeal to all of you,' he said at his
installation as chancellor of Bristol, 'to workmen and employers, to the
man who can just manage to educate his children and to the wealthiest
alike, to concern yourselves in a great civic cause . . . . What is requisite

... is that the city should be proud of its University and should feel that it is its own child. ...'

Haldane had chosen his words very deliberately: 'workmen'; 'the man who can just manage to educate his children'. He was speaking in the wake of grave industrial strife, and, looking to education as the nostrum for social ailments, saw in these new civic universities an insurance for democracy. They would open the doors of Whitehall to working class boys who were clever enough to graduate and to gain entry to the civil service. Labour leaders, he told his audience in Bristol, were quite right in complaining that the prizes of state were far too much reserved for the upper classes. He enlarged on this theme at length earlier in the year, in April, when he gave evidence to the royal commission on the civil service (on which his sister sat as a member). The whole of his evidence is an exalted declaration of faith in the efficacy of education for responsible leadership. (One is reminded of Rashdall's verdict: that the great contribution made by universities in the middle ages was that they put the administration of human affairs in the hands of educated men.) There was a revealing exchange between Haldane and Philip Snowden (also a member of the commission). Snowden asked him:

> I take it, it is your view that we cannot devise a thoroughly demo-cratic system of entering into the Civil Service until we have very much widened the education ladder?

To which Haldane replied:

> That is exactly my view, and I should like to join hands with you, Mr Snowden, tomorrow in saying that the great mode of access to a democratic system in this country was to put other things aside and to deal with the education system from its foundation.

We have already noticed (p. 74) Haldane's cautious attitude toward parliamentary endowment for higher education. If universities were to flourish they must command the loyalty of the regional communities they served; they should be largely endowed, therefore, by local authorities and local industry. In Liverpool and Bristol, he exhorted the cities to finance their own institutions; this was at the root of the idea of a civic university. But in the decade in which we are now watching him at work it became evident to him that local sup-port would need to be powerfully augmented by the state if his aspirations for a democratic society were to be sustained. One reason for his change of view was his experience as chairman of the royal commission on the University of London; for he saw that University as the centre of learning for an empire, not merely for the London region. So the man who was unenthusiastic in 1903 about Norman Lockyer's inflated appeal for state support to British universities was, by 1914, concerned to secure machinery that would extract maximum support from the treasury. For the disbursement of public money on such a scale as this, it was essential to have machinery in which both the universities and parliament had confidence. The story of the construction of this machinery (the forerunner of the present University Grants Committee) is a veritable Whitehall comedy. The characters on the stage were ministers and officials in the board of education and the treasury. But hovering in the wings, and at times directing the play, was none other than the secretary of state for war.

Before the Conservative government resigned in 1905, Austen Chamberlain as chancellor of the exchequer had undertaken to appoint a standing committee to distribute the treasury grant-in-aid to universities and university colleges, as recommended by Haldane's *ad hoc* committee in 1904–5 (p. 80). But he left office without doing so. No sooner was Haldane in the new government than he assisted Asquith, the new chancellor, to repair this omission. 'I am very glad you have decided as you have done about the Advisory Committee', he wrote from Cloan on 28 December 1905. 'We will make some suggestions as regards names next week.' About six weeks later on 5 February 1906, the treasury announced the appointment of the committee.* The membership was unexceptionable, the terms of reference were clear; and at first everything ran smoothly. But, in its report published in July 1908, the advisory committee drew attention to the fact that university institutions were receiving parliamentary grants through three departments: the treasury, the board of education, and the board

---

* Two of the members, Woods (the chairman) and Sir Francis Mowatt, had served under Haldane on the committee which advised the previous government (p. 76). The new members were W. J. Collins, an MP; H. Jackson, a fellow of Trinity College, Cambridge; and the man who fourteen years later was to become the first chairman of the University Grants Committee: W. S. McCormick. McCormick had worked with Haldane on the Carnegie Trust for Universities in Scotland, and H. Frank Heath, in his biographical note of McCormick in the DNB, confirms that it was Haldane who secured his appointment to the treasury committee in 1906. It was one of the most fruitful appointments Haldane influenced.

of agriculture. Some co-ordination was desirable between these three sources of funds. The committee recommended that all state aid for university education should be brought under the review of a single authority. They suggested that after a transitional arrangement there should be introduced 'a Scheme that would comprise in a single vote the whole aid granted by Parliament to Universities and University Colleges for education of University character and standard.'

This raised the curtain on the comedy. Which department in Whitehall should be responsible for administering this consolidated vote? The advisory committee reported to the treasury. The treasury, in some puzzlement, sought advice from the board of education. They got advice; in sixteen typed folio pages from the incisive pen of Robert Morant, perhaps the most formidable permanent secretary the board ever had. Morant's reply was composed after extensive discussion with his minister, Runciman (just appointed to succeed Birrell), and Runciman (wrote Morant in a covering letter) 'has had a talk with Haldane . . . and tells me that Haldane is in strong agreement'. In brief, Morant's proposal was that the treasury advisory committee (consisting largely of its existing members) should 'for a period of (say) five years' act as an advisory committee to the board of education, and should ultimately be handed over to the board of education. It was a take-over bid.

Morant's letter was despatched to the treasury on 17 December 1908. The minute it provoked from a senior official there (T. L. Heath) was unambiguous: on 14 January 1909 he wrote:

This is an able letter from the B/Ed, but it is directed too exclusively and obviously to the one main object of getting the control over the £100,000 and its distribution under the B/Ed. . . . I think in fact that the B/Ed as at present administered is not qualified to take up the business without risk of friction . . . . I feel certain that the Board (as at present administered) would try to dictate to the Universities and University Colleges as they are now trying to do to Secondary Schools. . . .

There the matter rested until Sir P. Magnus, on 23 June 1910, asked a question in parliament about the consolidation of state grants to university institutions. Accordingly Runciman returned to the attack, supporting his case (that the board of education should take over responsibility for administering the grants) by saying that English universities, including the University of London, would welcome this arrangement. But the chancellor of the exchequer was Lloyd George, and he was not prepared to hand over the grants or the advisory committee; he played for time by saying he would await the outcome of a deputation from the University of London.

The next move was with Morant. By this time the royal commission on the University of London, under Haldane's chairmanship, had begun its sittings. So Morant proceeded to invoke Haldane's opinion: 'I think [he wrote in his brief for Runciman] that Haldane has quite reached the point of seeing the advisability of Unification of the Grants in this Board. He was much struck that the representative of Oxford University [in parliament] should have plumped for this board.' Armed with Morant's brief, Runciman sought the support of Asquith, who had become prime minister. There was a typically Asquithian response from No. 10 Downing Street: that the prime minister was disposed to think it well to let the question lie for a time 'as it seems to him to be full of diffties & not immediately urgent.'

The wrangle between the treasury and the board of education continued through 1910 and into 1911. Haldane did not appear on the stage at all, but it is clear that he was operating behind the scene. 'It is now being urged', wrote Morant in a warning message to his minister on 5 January 1911,

> by Mr McCormick and Sir Francis Mowatt [two members of the advisory committee] and is being apparently seriously considered by Sir George Murray and Mr Haldane, that the separate sets of Grants should be unified in the Treasury, removing from the Minister of Education responsibilities he at present holds in regard to University Colleges. . . . Is it not time something was done of a definite nature to indicate . . . that the problems they have been coolly discussing and the suggestions they have been working out are matters in the first place for the Minister of Education . . . .

And Morant went on to express his resentment that Mr Haldane should discuss these matters 'with two irresponsible outsiders whilst the Minister of Education is kept entirely in ignorance.' The fact is, concluded Morant, that 'the Treasury is in abysmal ignorance of the present state of affairs [in higher education] and has no conception of the close interrelation both of the work of individual University Colleges with that of Secondary Schools and Technical Institutions, and also of those Colleges with the various functions of this Board.'

Morant's tetchiness over Haldane's attitude was misconceived, for by now it was evident that Haldane's royal commission, and Haldane himself, had come round to the view that the minister of education *was* the proper person to administer state grants to university institutions. At this point Haldane himself briefly passed across the stage. We have the record in a memorandum from Frank Heath, who was in charge of the Universities branch at the board of education, written to Morant's successor a year later:

> ... Haldane had an important part in [the negotiations] and saw the P.M. about it because he is strongly of opinion that the funds necessary for the support of the modern Universities ... will never be forthcoming from the State until they form part of the Education budget placed before Parliament for Education. He has said this repeatedly and he strongly supported the transfer as the first step towards getting all the University money into a single pot in the control of the President of the Board.

Following Haldane's intervention with Asquith and a careful sounding of opinion in the university colleges, came the capitulation. 'The Prime Minister', Heath recalled, 'declared that any objections he feared as arising from the Universities were removed, and he informed Mr Runciman that if Mr Lloyd George would consent to the transference, he, the Prime Minister, would agree.' It was left to Runciman to negotiate the transfer direct with Lloyd George, but he was given an unambiguous clearance from Asquith. '... speak to him & don't write', ran the message from Murray at the treasury, '... and tell him that the Prime Minister is entirely in favour of the Scheme & that the Treasury will be very glad to get rid of the job.'

So Lloyd George was consulted by Runciman, and shown the proposed list of a new advisory committee, in a memorandum entitled 'Unification of University Grants under the Universities Branch of the Board of Education'. Runciman has left a precise record of this consultation (this is significant in view of what followed). Lloyd George imposed various conditions for consenting to the transfer, including an insistence that 'whoever is on the Committee ... Sir John Rhys *must* be a member of it'. (Rhys was principal of Jesus College, Oxford; a distinguished celtic scholar and a protagonist for education in Wales.)

Runciman agreed and on 17 June 1911 he issued a formal minute appointing a fresh standing committee, this time responsible to the

board of education.* It seemed as though the inter-departmental tussle
was now at an end, and the board of education, with the ready concurrence of the universities and colleges, had won the game. But
Runciman had reckoned without the unpredictability of the celtic
temperament. At a cabinet meeting on 11 August 1911 Lloyd George
pushed a note across the table to Runciman, reading:

> I observe you stated in the Hse the other day that the control of U.
> Grants had passed from the Try to the Board of Education. What
> on earth made you say this? I never even discussed the question with
> you. I must put this right in the Hse on Appropriation Bill. The
> Colleges are furious and Austen [Chamberlain] attacks it. D.Ll-G.

Runciman replied to this note reminding Lloyd George that he had
agreed to the transfer, that the treasury had agreed, and that far from
the colleges being furious, their heads had passed amiable resolutions.
Back came a second note from Lloyd George:

> I never even heard of it. Who did you correspond with? You never
> submitted the proposal to me. Why did you not do so? Austen was
> the first man to mention it to me. I cannot acquiesce in your state-
> ment. The Cabinet never even considered the matter. Was it men-
> tioned at all to the PM? D.Ll-G.

Runciman reminded him of his conversation concerning the committee and Sir John Rhys, to which he assented but said across the
table that that was the committee only. And then Runciman wrote to
him to say that the prime minister had twice fully discussed it, and that
the transfer of the committee was on the record in published official
documents. Lloyd George, wrote Runciman afterwards, 'had nothing
to add to this'.

What provoked this outburst? Simply that Austen Chamberlain had embarrassed Lloyd George on the issue, and there was uneasi-
ness among the Welsh. During September 1911 a formula of compromise was reached between the two ministers: the committee remained
attached to the board of education but the treasury was given a kind of
veto over its decisions and its membership. Morant protested to his

---

* It was, for the first time, exclusively composed of academics: McCormick
as chairman, Professor J. A. Ewing, Dr William Osler, Miss E. Penrose, Professor
Walter Raleigh, Sir John Rhys, and Sir Arthur Rucker; to advise the board of
education as to the distribution of exchequer grants available from the board for
university education in England and Wales.

chief over this compromise but Runciman silenced him, stating that the committee remained a board of education committee, and he anticipated no trouble over reappointments. But there was to be other trouble. Lloyd George would not consent to the vote for the University of Wales being transferred from the treasury. It now looked as though the grant system might be fragmented; the board of education aiding the University of London, the treasury aiding the University of Wales; and one or the other left to aid the remaining university institutions.

Meanwhile there had been changes in the cast on the stage. The querulous Morant had been replaced by the more urbane Selby-Bigge and Runciman had been replaced by J. A. Pease, a Quaker. In January 1912 (three years after the first exchange of correspondence between Morant and the treasury) Pease was being briefed to continue the wrangle and to secure a clean take-over. 'If the treasury', wrote Pease, 'raise any objection the matter will be one for cabinet decision & Haldane's help will then be valuable. . . .' Once more Haldane's virtuosity as negotiator was invoked, not formally at cabinet but in Haldane's preferred milieu: the unrecorded private conversation. Haldane, we are told, 'addressed Lloyd George forcibly on the subject'. We do not know what he said, but at 'the end of the talk Lloyd George said to Haldane that their conversation had completely altered his (George's) attitude on the matter and that he agreed with Haldane that the Grants should be on the Board of Education Votes.' But even Haldane could not predict Lloyd George's wiliness. For despite this change of heart the treasury still wanted to *appear* not to have capitulated. In a frankly disingenuous way (as Selby-Bigge reported in a very confidential note to his minister) the permanent secretary to the treasury (Chalmers) wanted the chancellor of the exchequer to be able to say to Austen Chamberlain that no change whatever had been made in the position, and that he and the treasury retained just as much control over university grants as formerly. But he also wanted the universities and the advisory committee to go on believing that the position of the treasury had changed, and the board of education, on the advice of its own committee, would decide how the sum was distributed.

Following a meeting on 2 February with Lloyd George. Pease recorded a fresh compromise: 'I have agreed to the vote remaining on Treasury & I have arranged with the Chancellor today that my department will be the only one for the Univ. Comtee to deal with.' And a second face-saver from the treasury embodied the final arrangement, on 21 February 1912:

> ... I am directed by the Lords Commissioners of H.M. Treasury to state that, as a result of the further consideration which has been given to the question of the Grants for Universities and Colleges, Great Britain, My Lords have come to the conclusion that it will be better that the actual provision for such grants should continue to be made upon that Vote (Class IV, vote 7). It would not be regular to make so considerable a change in the form of the estimates without consulting the Public Accounts Committee.

By the earlier compromise the 'substance' lay with the treasury and the 'letter' lay with the board of education. Now the compromise was reversed: the treasury would have formal control of the vote; the board of education actual control. This is substantially what Haldane wanted, but a diary entry which Austen Chamberlain made a few days later reveals Haldane's irrepressible tenacity. He still wanted to secure the letter as well as the substance. Whilst at Grillion's, Chamberlain wrote, Haldane had:

> sought me out to talk about the administration of the University Grants. He is trying to get them put under the Board of Education which he says has now been reorganized and has an admirable University branch, through which he urges they would obtain much larger grants than they do from the Treasury. Against him, he said, Lloyd George quoted me as being strongly opposed to the transfer of these grants from the Treasury to the Board of Education. This is quite true, for I have always feared that the Board of Education would seek to impose their views of what ought to be taught upon the Universities and would stereotype the University courses: whereas the Treasury, not being in this matter a department of specialists, was content merely to ascertain that the work carried on was of a University standard and that certain other necessary financial conditions were observed.

This passage from Chamberlain's diary is often taken to be the explanation for the decision taken in 1919 (when he was chancellor of the exchequer) to put the University Grants Committee under the treasury and not under the board of education. But in fact Chamberlain changed his mind and became reconciled to Haldane's view (p. 151). Safeguarding the autonomy of universities was an ancillary reason, but not the main one why the UGC was placed under the treasury.

The cares of the war office, the propagation of regional universities, the design of machinery for state aid to higher education: even all these were not enough to fill Haldane's diary. His heaviest educational commitment during this phase of his career was undoubtedly to the University of London. We have already seen him at work there, as far back as 1887, when he was conferring with Balfour over its problems, and we have depicted his vigorous co-conspiracy with Sidney Webb over the University of London Act 1898 and the creation of a London Charlottenburg.

It was in January 1906 that the departmental committee under Haldane had recommended the creation of a great institution for science and technology at South Kensington. But nineteen months passed before the College was created. No one questioned the need for higher technological education in London; the delicate negotiations to secure a site were well in hand; the sources for finance were assured. The delay was due solely to disputes about control. The tidy solution was to integrate the new College completely into the University of London. But this would have meant concessions from the other interested parties: the government (which owned the Royal College of Science), the LCC (with its responsibility for further education in the metropolis), the City and Guilds Institute (which owned part of the property and had pioneered technical education), the 1851 commissioners (who controlled the site), and the several rich men who had promised endowments to the new college. There were strong reasons against integration. The University had only just emerged from the most drastic reform it had ever undergone. There was still dissent within the University between those dedicated to its old function as an external examining board for the Empire, and those striving to re-create it as a teaching university. The University itself was ambivalent about accepting a new and unusual addition which might turn out to be a formidable cuckoo in its academic nest; but which, if refused, might become a rival university. And enthusiasts for the institution were apprehensive that its freedom would be constrained if it were not autonomous. 'Success in the work before the Institution', wrote Ogilvie of the board of education, who had served on the departmental committee, 'may demand action and relations of a kind quite foreign not only to existing University traditions but to any conception of the elasticity permissible within a University. . . .'

There is no doubt that Haldane's departmental committee, in recommending initial autonomy for the College, leading to possible ultimate integration with the University, had papered over the cracks which were bound to appear as soon as anyone began to draft a precise constitution. For months there were meetings and exchanges of memoranda between the board of education and the University. At times it seemed as though the University might modify its constitution in ways which (as Morant put it) would render it more fit to be 'suzerain' of the new Institution. At times it was feared that Haldane (invisible in these negotiations but still actively engaged in them) might 'hand the whole thing over straight to the University'. In fact although Haldane still favoured incorporation, and was determined in the end to get it, he was prepared to compromise for a quick solution. Over all the arguments lay the shadow (or, as some would put it, the hope) of a royal commission to enquire into the constitution of the University of London; and this was used as a justification for delaying any decision at all about the new College. Delay was the one thing Haldane did not want. Once more, he appeared at the critical moment to influence events. We know that in May 1906 a meeting was held in his room at the war office to try to get the various parties to agree. Haldane 'doesn't bark', wrote a civil servant (Sykes) who attended this meeting and reported it to Morant, 'He purrs. . . . But I hope & trust his scratch is being nipped in the bud so to speak.' For nearly nine months negotiations dragged on. But on 13 February 1907, the same civil servant was able to report to Morant that he had met Haldane at dinner; Haldane had said, 'Well, the new President [McKenna had just succeeded Birrell at the Board of Education] has a very simple course open to him . . . to get that Charter, which has been circulated, through as soon as possible.' The very same day McKenna wrote to Haldane as follows: 'On the lines of the Final Report of the Departmental Committee. . . . I can settle the matter at once and the Charter already circulated could be put through promptly. . . . On the merits I think the Report of the Departmental Committee is right, including as it does, a proposal for a Royal Commission to be subsequently appointed. . . .' McKenna straightway conveyed this decision to the University, adding that the senate should be informed that he would be prepared, 'say 12 months' after the institution at South Kensington had been established, to advise the appointment of a royal commission to consider its amalgamation with the University. 'I am glad', wrote Haldane to Morant, 'of the progress you have made in getting this troublesome matter settled. It is very satisfactory.' Indeed it was; it had all worked out as Haldane wished. In July 1907 a charter was granted to create the Imperial College. In December 1908 the University itself asked for a royal commission to secure the incorporation of the College. The commission was appointed on 24 February 1909, just as Haldane was approaching another turning point in his career. He was within sight of achieving what he wanted as secretary of state for war. Early in May 1908 the Webbs had found him confident of finishing his work at the war office in eighteen months. He was – despite the responsibilities of office – anxious to involve himself in educational problems again. He offered himself as chairman of the royal commission (the evidence for this is in a private and personal note from Morant to Buckle of *The Times* on 16 February 1909). His offer was accepted and he embarked on four years of intensive enquiry which in its concluding stages, somehow, he combined with the supreme office of lord high chancellor.

It was characteristic of Haldane that he took great pains to pick his team, though he did not get all his own way. Sidney Webb, who had worked for years to create a comprehensive system of higher education in London, plied Haldane with suggestions. But the days when the Webbs were Haldane's most trusted co-conspirators were over, and it seems likely that Morant had more influence than Webb on the choice of names. At any rate only one of Webb's suggestions (Lord Milner) was adopted.*

There was an entertaining exchange of notes about the inclusion of a woman on the commission. Webb, not surprisingly, suggested one: Mrs Bryant, and later, after consultation with Beatrice, came up with a list of six, with a preference for the formidable Jane Harrison of Newnham who 'smokes furiously & will not object to the Chairman's cigars, or to any masculine unconventionality in the way of ease & comfort'. Haldane, notwithstanding his predilection for women's rights, was lukewarm about having a woman at all on his commission; and Morant believed that the only point of having a woman on the

* Among Webb's other suggestions were Lord Avebury, Herbert Fisher, Bertrand Russell, and Gilbert Murray. It is difficult to imagine them working as a team. The final choice was: Lord Milner, Sir Robert Romer, Lawrence Currie, E. B. Sargant, Mrs L. Creighton, W. S. McCormick, and Morant himself, whose inclusion Haldane made a condition of his accepting the chairmanship.

commission was to deal 'with the details of Women's Education.'
Gregory Foster had advised Morant: 'I cannot think of any woman
who will be the slightest use on the Commission.' In the end Mrs
Creighton (about whom Haldane had expressed 'some personal
disinclination') was appointed; but Haldane had his way over one
essential appointment: John Kemp, who had helped him over the
Liverpool case and, more recently, in drafting legislation for the army,
was appointed as one of the secretaries.

In hindsight the composition of this commission was criticised.
There was, for instance, no medical man, and the commission made
far-reaching recommendations about medical education, though it
was not Haldane's intention to include this in his terms of reference.
It was added as an afterthought, on the prompting of the American
Abraham Flexner. The members were almost entirely graduates of
universities other than London; this, too, provoked some resentment.
But it was, by and large, the sort of body Haldane liked to work with:
'small and impartial, not representing interests, but rather of a judicial
and decisive nature.'

The terms of reference, to the annoyance of some members of the
senate, went far beyond the question of the incorporation of the
Imperial College of Science and Technology. 'Our task', asserted the
report, 'may, therefore, be shortly stated as follows: To examine the
existing provision for university education in London in the light of
what we think ought to exist, and to make practical recommendations
towards the realisation of the ideal.' Besides sittings to hear evidence,
the commission met seventy-two times to discuss its impressions and to
classify its opinions. It commissioned a historical report from Sir W.
Allchin. It devoured books, previous reports, and parliamentary papers.
And it sought evidence not only from witnesses in Britain, but from
Germany, France, Canada, and the United States. Its massive report
was published just over four years later.

A line by line analysis of the report would be a fruitful topic for the
historian of education, but it does not directly concern us here. In later
years Haldane protested that the report was a consensus of the whole
commission (as indeed it was) and ideas in it should not be attributed
to him alone. But his personality dominated the hearings. His educational philosophy permeated the theoretical passages in the report.
His capacity to design institutions consistent with his philosophy is
evident in many of the report's recommendations. And so the report
illuminates at many points our portrait of Haldane.

It illuminates, for instance, his courtesy with witnesses. Some of them must have been nervous at the prospect of submitting themselves to cross-examination by a famous barrister. But Haldane's manner was relaxed, urbane, disarming. He would never browbeat a witness; still less try to trap a witness into supporting opinions dear to his own heart. Repeatedly he told witnesses not to assume, from the slant of a question, that it disclosed the commission's views. 'I am not pronouncing on it,' he told one witness over the level of entry into the University, 'but I have a doubt in my mind.' When he was chairman of the commission on the University of Wales, a similar courtesy characterised his questions: 'Sometimes when we put suggestions I am afraid that people run off with the idea that we are putting preconceived views. We are of course only testing opinion and trying to bring out points which people have overlooked.' 'You must never assume that anything is in the mind of the Commission because we cross-examine witnesses severely on their proposals: our business is to elicit their views by questions or putting counterproposals?' Only occasionally do his convictions colour his comment. Thus on the London commission, speaking to Lord Justice Fletcher Moulton over external examinations, he allowed himself to say: 'As you know, the whole tendency of University education abroad is against you. . . .' (Haldane's colleagues on the commission were not always so cordial. Thus Morant questioned Sir A. Keogh: 'I want to get it clear. I keep putting it more crudely than you do in order to get your exact meaning.' To which Keogh replied: 'You certainly put it crudely.')

The report illuminates, too, Haldane's deductive approach to educational issues. He could have guided his colleagues into a pragmatic solution of the problem which had precipitated the commission – the future of the Imperial College – and then led them to propose some consequential readjustments in the organisation of the University. But he set to work quite differently: the commission first decided what were 'the essentials of a university in a great centre of population', and then discussed 'the application of the foregoing principles' to the specific problems of the University of London.

The specific problems arose from two notorious defects. First, as we describe on p. 27, for most of its history the University had comprised not students and teachers, but candidates and examiners. The external degree had won a worldwide reputation and brought benefits to thousands of graduates. So the graduates of the University, organised in convocation, were a powerful lobby defending the external degree and suspicious of any increase in power among the teaching staff. Second, the teaching institutions attached to the University as 'schools' were financially and educationally independent of it. They varied in quality and level of teaching from the excellent to the mediocre; and the University was unable to influence them through the power of the purse or the power to make appointments; its only effective influence was to prescribe a rigid syllabus and to pass or fail the candidates who sat the examinations. And this sole influence, as an examining board, had a paralysing effect upon the teacher, for he put his students at risk if he introduced any innovation into the curriculum. A consequence of both these defects was a persistent weakness in the government of the University. It was powerless to co-ordinate the institutions which taught for its degrees; and the teachers in these institutions were, for the most part, powerless to influence the examinations for which they prepared candidates.

Before prescribing the remedy for these defects, the commission set itself to describe the paradigm of a city university in the twentieth century; and it is this section of the report which is imbued with ideas upon which Haldane had reflected for years. In one passage after another we are back in Göttingen among the pupils of Lotze, but not in nostalgic retrospect. The commission discusses how to adapt the *spirit* of the German university, not its structure or its constitution, to the English civic university in a community which wants its graduates to work in commerce, industry, and government. 'Speaking generally', says the report, 'it may be said that in nearly every case the development of the modern English universities is the gradual evolution of a complete group of Faculties in institutions originally founded for the pursuit of science and technology.' And it goes on to make the point that this utilitarian bias is no obstacle to the achievement of a true academic attitude. (One recollects Samuel Alexander's famous epigram: 'Liberality in education is a spirit of pursuit, not a choice of subject.')

Over the spirit of pursuit, the commission is emphatic and clear. It is essential that students 'should be able to work in intimate and constant association with their fellow students . . . and also in close contact with their teachers. The University should be organised on this basis . . . students and teachers should be brought together in living intercourse in the daily work of the University. . . . The main business of a university is the training of its undergraduates . . . .' But the training of undergraduates must not be separated from post-graduate work and research: '. . . it is in the best interests of the University that the most distinguished of its professors should take part in the teaching of the undergraduates from the beginning of their university career . . . it is the personal influence of the man doing original work in his subject which inspires belief in it . . . .' And the commissioners quote Helmholtz: 'Anyone who has once come into contact with one or more men of the first rank must have had his whole mental standard altered for the rest of his life.' This is what a reformed University of London must offer to its students.

It was, of course, a frontal attack on the external degree. To abolish external degrees at that stage was, the commissioners knew, impracticable. But the report emphasises that they are a poor substitute for internal degrees, and that they cannot be taken as evidence that the graduate has been educated; only that he has acquired a certain level of knowledge. And the trend of policy in the University should be to make full-time education accessible to all who are qualified for it and who want it, so that external degrees become redundant. The one concession which the commissioners make to the obvious fact that such a trend as this will take a long time is to advocate the provision of university education for evening students, by teachers exempt from any teaching in the day time, appointed by the University, with qualifications as high, and salaries at the same level, as teachers in colleges catering for full-time students. And that was the stimulus for Birkbeck College, of which Haldane later became president.

The practical consequences of these convictions were obvious. A reformed University of London must have considerable control over the colleges which teach. The colleges must look to the University as both their paymaster and as the 'employer' of their professors. The control of finance and property and general policy would rest in a small executive composed of laymen and a few academics. But the academic power, over curricula, examinations, and the like, should be delegated to university-wide faculties, and boards of studies, cutting across the entrenched interests of individual colleges. Complementary to this concentration of influence from the periphery towards the centre, there should be a dispersal of influence from the centre to the periphery. If the University appoints the right professors, then it can devolve upon them responsibility for what they teach and how they examine, and the inexorable control of curricula and examinations from the centre can be relaxed, even to the extent that the degree would bear the title of the college where it was earned.

The identification of examinations with education was – indeed still is – a tenacious misconception in English education. It had troubled Haldane for years. Students at Scottish universities in the early nineteenth century commonly did not take degree examinations. They came to the university to 'get' education; they returned to farm and village with class certificates certifying that they had attended, but without a degree – which in any case they did not need. In English universities (except among affluent undergraduates at Oxford or Cambridge) the compulsion to take examinations and to get degrees was ineradicable. Not that Haldane objected to healthy competition, hard work, and the lustre of academic honours. What he objected to were examinations which distorted, and did not stimulate, education. In his opinion – and the commissioners shared it – the examinations organised by the University of London were a positive hindrance to good education. The commissioners were crystal clear on this issue, and there is no doubt whatever that their verdict embodied one of Haldane's most powerful convictions. The following passage from the report sums it up (though the style strikes us as more eloquent than Haldane's own drafting):

> We are convinced that both a detailed syllabus and an external examination are inconsistent with the true interests of university education, injurious to the students, degrading to the teachers, and ineffective for the attainment of the ends they are supposed to promote. . . . Even the so-called Internal examinations of the University of London are practically external, because of the large number of institutions involved, and the demands of the common syllabus. . . . The effect upon the students and the teachers is disastrous. . . . They cannot pursue knowledge both for its own sake and also for the sake of passing the test of an examination. . . . We shall make recommendations which will dispense with the necessity of the syllabus, by ensuring the appointment of teachers who can be trusted with the charge of university education.

And the report goes on to advocate what is now called 'continuous assessment':

> It appears to us only fair that due weight should be given to the whole record of the students' work in the University. If the academic freedom of the professors and the students is to be maintained . . . it is absolutely necessary that, subject to proper safeguards, the

degrees of the University should practically be the certificates given by the professors themselves, and that the students should have entire confidence that they may trust their academic fate to honest work under their instruction and direction.

The commissioners went on to apply these principles to the University of London in great detail, and – almost incidentally – proposed a solution for the specific problem of Imperial College, namely that it should be incorporated into the University and supervised by a special committee for technology, separate from the structure of the faculties. But the report covered much more than this, and Haldane's influence pervades many other passages. There is, for example, an interesting section on the status of students, where *Lernfreiheit* – the reverse face of the coin of *Lehrfreiheit* – is mentioned. (It is a noteworthy feature of the influence of Germany upon British higher education, that *Lehrfreiheit* luxuriated in British universities, but *Lernfreiheit* never took root.) So it is interesting to read the suggestion that students should be relieved of the 'rather onerous obligation' placed on internal students to attend a given amount of instruction as a condition of admission to its examinations. In its 'schools' the University, says the report, should confine itself to approving the curriculum, and not compel any student to take more than he desired. The excellence of the teaching should be relied upon to commend it to candidates for degrees. The only exceptions to this discretion should be in medicine and technology, where attendance has to be compulsory.

There are other suggestions to encourage *Lernfreiheit*. For example a medical student should be able to arrest his course in order to pursue further than is required of him 'any subject which fascinates his attention and appeals to his mind'. The commission considered, too, whether students should be free to migrate from one university to another during their undergraduate career, as they did in Germany; but this was rejected because not all British universities were organised in the same way.

The commissioners considered another question of great interest to Haldane, namely the contribution which the University could make to higher education in the colonies. They prescribed that external degree examination for colonial territories should be discontinued, and replaced by examinations planned in conjunction with the colonial office, adapted to local needs. Then, say the commissioners, the University 'would have abandoned once for all the pernicious theory underlying its present practice that the kind of education it thinks best for its own students must be the best for all peoples who own allegiance to the British flag'. A whole generation passed, until the Asquith report on higher education in the colonies (1945), before this warning was heeded.

Finally, we pick from the report one other interest to which Haldane returned toward the end of his life: its passages about adult education. The Workers' Educational Association (WEA) was flourishing at that time and it had acquired, through the work of Tawney and others, a reputation for the pursuit of knowledge (though predominantly knowledge about economics and political science) at a high standard and without distortion by examinations. To support the WEA tutorial classes was, the report said, a new and hopeful field 'for the spread of a pure love of learning – the main function of a University.' 'We think', concluded the commissioners, 'the University should consider the work it is doing for these men and women one of the most serious and important of its services to the metropolis. . . .'

To what extent was Haldane himself responsible for the great report on the University of London? His fellow members on the commission were themselves men of strong views and broad experience. But Haldane had been reflecting on the problems longer than any of his colleagues, and he certainly would not have put his signature to recommendations inconsistent with his principles. It is pretty clear from his correspondence (and from the style of parts of the report) that he gave a lot of attention to the drafting. And one only has to look back at Hansards as early as 1889 and to read some of his speeches, to find in embryo some of the considered recommendations of the commission. Bellot criticises Haldane's chairmanship as tendentious ('committed . . . to particular solutions of his own'). This, we think, is a misconceived criticism. Occasionally, as he questioned witnesses, Haldane's personal views did come to the surface. It would be undesirable, he suggested (in discussing Imperial College) to have more than one university in London. His preference for internal examinations and his dissatisfaction with external examinations were undisguised. He wanted polytechnics to remain places for sub-university work, not to ape Charlottenburg and so become unsuitable for workers; but as to higher technological education: 'we are rather anxious' to avoid a sharp line of demarcation, as in Germany, between universities and technological institutions. He reiterated his view that the quality of the university can be no better than the quality and personality of its teachers. He revealed his own conviction in his question: 'Is not the tendency of our time in all educational spheres and notably in the Universities to look to the record [of students' work] more and more' in assessing candidates for degrees? He responded in a lively way to any witness who favoured teaching by seminars: the romantic picture of the *Gelehrter* surrounded by his disciples. And – consistent with his sentiments since he supported the student petition from Edinburgh in 1888 – he made sure that the report gave due attention to student representation (on the court), student organisations, and amenities for student life. But to call this 'committed . . . to particular solutions of his own' is surely to exaggerate.

The report was signed at the end of March 1913 and published in April. Its publication (Haldane told his mother) caused a 'great stir'. It was welcomed by the press. The *Times Educational Supplement* called it a 'frankly revolutionary document'. Indeed for London it was, for if it had been adopted the University would have become faculty-controlled, the external degree would have been phased out, member colleges of the University would have been free to diversify their curricula and their procedures for awarding degrees, and student *Lernfreiheit* would have secured a foothold in English higher education. And there were other sweeping recommendations, e.g. to reorganise medical and legal education and to bring hospitals and inns of court into the sphere of influence of the University. But it was obviously going to be controversial, and editorials appealed to individual institutions in the University to sink their interests for the good of the whole. 'Let us have criticism and plenty of it', wrote *The Times*, but ' . . . let there be also the larger view, the wider outlook of its authors.' For anyone familiar with the University's history this was expecting too much. By May the council of the University of London Graduates' Association had lodged an emphatic protest against recommendations for the external work. Convocation, more judicially, appointed six subcommittees to examine the commission's recommendations on six fields of study. Asquith wisely staved off a request in parliament for a discussion of the report, but response at the official level was prompt and favourable. On 14 August the board of education appointed a departmental committee under Sir George Murray (now retired from the treasury) to recommend 'specific arrangements and provisions' required to give effect to the scheme of the report. The committee included in its membership Selby-Bigge, McCormick, and Kemp, with Heath as secretary. It met on 14 October and thereafter regularly until the third week in July 1914. It entered into what must have been tedious negotiations with all the parties concerned: convocation, the medical schools, Imperial College, Bedford College, and of course the militant 'externals'. In April 1914 the committee was able to produce an interim and confidential report. It endorsed the recommendation to concentrate the headquarters of the University and (as far as possible) its main teaching units in Bloomsbury. This was conditional upon King's College moving from the Strand to the Bloomsbury site and it is noteworthy, in view of later criticism (p. 160), that King's was represented as 'quite willing' to consider this. Even the 'externals' indicated a willingness to compromise on a formula proposed by Sidney Webb in a private letter to Haldane which is preserved in the records of the board of education. By July 1914 Fletcher Moulton was hopeful that he could secure the approval of the 'externals' to the compromise. Meanwhile negotiations with the medical schools were going quite well. The only implacably intransigent institution was the Imperial College, which had precipitated the whole enquiry.

So by July 1914 Haldane had little reason to be disappointed at the outcome of the mammoth task to which he had given so much time. It was indeed remarkable that a 'frankly revolutionary document' should have been flexible enough to have promoted the first moves, at any rate, in what might have been a sustained and profound evolutionary change in the University.

Although the affairs of universities took up most of the time and energy Haldane could put aside for work on education, he returned repeatedly in his speeches to the concept of a unified, articulated state system of education, a ladder from primary school to university, and beyond to adult education, with no rungs missing. The prospect at the turn of the century that the Liberals might return to power was the opportunity to refurbish and present to the public this grand scheme. Haldane made this the theme of many of his speeches. He knew that politicians could remain in office only so long as they responded to what the public demanded; and over education Haldane made it his business to create demand through public speaking, and then to devise response through private conspiracy. And so we watch him in 1901, addressing his audience in Dumfries: '. . . what I feel to be the great problem today is the welding of the educational system of this country into one complete whole, in which elementary education, secondary education, and the university shall all be indissoluble parts of one system. . . . The universities must be not merely detachable super-structures, but the brain and intelligence which permeate the whole system.' Again, at the Colston Society in Bristol in 1902: 'For my part I do not believe any system of education will ever be satisfactory which does not link together the primary, the secondary, and tertiary system, and make the tertiary the head, with a University dominating the whole edifice with what the Germans call *Geist* – a spirit of intelligence.' And in 1903, at St Andrews, he was saying that education must be put under popular control. As an election drew closer, he reminded his audience, at Ealing in 1904, that the Liberal party's programme for social reform, including national education, would have to depend on the 'voice of the country'. (But in fact the Liberals did not wait for the voice of the country before laying their plans for a national system of education; even before the general election of January 1906 had confirmed the new government in power, with an unexpectedly large majority, a cabinet committee including Lord Crewe and Haldane was already at work, and Haldane was grasping the nettle of sectarian education by giving Crewe the quite ruthless advice that voluntary schools should be controlled by a popularly elected majority of managers: 'no popular control, no rate aid, would thus be the principle.') He realised where the opposition lay, though he under-estimated its virulence: 'To confine the functions of the State to purely secular teaching would avert many difficulties and is what I should personally prefer. But public opinion has not yet been driven to acceptance of this. . . .' Soon after the Liberals took office Birrell did in 1906 introduce a mild bill to amend the Education acts of 1902–3 by prescribing full public control of rate-aided schools and appointment of teachers without reference to religious belief. The bill passed the commons but was thrown out by the lords. Haldane, then busy at the war office, realised that he couldn't stir his colleagues to 'a large policy' about education. Public interest in educational reform was too small; the vested interests of the churches were too great. He is not on record as having pursued the idea of a comprehensive educational system again until 1913. By the winter of 1912 the end was in sight of his labours on the London royal commission. The office of lord chancellor – although on his own admission it was an excessively onerous one – did not fill his life. He began another campaign for reform of the infra-structure of education. 'When I was at the War Office', he told the 'Eighty' Club in April 1913, 'I was appalled to find that of the recruits we took something like 13 per cent could not read or write. . . . Surely that shows something wrong with our national system? . . . The State will never be in a sound position until you have redressed the situation of today.' And in Manchester, in the same year: 'I have been for four years chairman of a Royal Commission on university education, which has been a great education to me because I have learned how utterly chaotic and backward is the state of education – elementary, secondary, and higher – in this country.'

These were strong words from a man so little given to exaggeration and rhetoric. This time he did stimulate support from his colleagues. Early in December 1912 it was agreed that Haldane should become chairman of a hybrid committee of ministers, officials, and educational experts, to work out a comprehensive scheme of reform. Once more it brought him into conflict with Lloyd George, though their association began amicably enough; for Lloyd George was a member of his committee* and – as chancellor of the exchequer – a key member. Moreover Lloyd George was thinking on what were (for Haldane) the 'right' lines. For he told Haldane that he would be reluctant to find any large sum except for a scheme which would strike the imagination and could fairly be represented as a stage towards the establishment of a national system of education regardless of denominational squabbles. This, from Lloyd George who was under perpetual pressure from the nonconformists, was an encouraging start. But nonconformists were not the only ones who would have to be appeased if Haldane's concept was to be approved; for it was on too big a scale to be entrusted to the existing machinery of local government. Local authorities would have to surrender some of their present powers to larger areas; and this would certainly raise great opposition. Furthermore, any coherent educational system would require universities to submit themselves to surveillance by the board of education. Haldane was vague about this last consequence. It was 'somehow or other connected with the idea that the status of the Board of Education should be improved and that it should be in some way extended or glorified so as to really fit it to deal with University Education.'

---

* The other members included Pease, president of the board of education; Runciman, formerly president of the board, and now translated to agriculture; Selby-Bigge and Struthers, permanent secretaries respectively of the board of education and the Scottish education department, and A. H. D. Acland, a member of the board's consultative committee.

So wrote the board's secretary, Selby-Bigge to his president, Pease.

The climax came early in 1913. On 10 January Haldane wrote to his mother: 'I am off to Manchester to speak there tonight & to make an important pronouncement on Education by desire of the P.M. and Ll.G. I have worked out our new Education plans & have been given charge of the business.'

It was indeed an important pronouncement. Haldane announced to the Manchester Reform Club that the government had decided that education was 'the next and most urgent of the great social problems to be taken up'; that: 'Until we have given democracy that equality of educational opportunity, the democracy will always be restless.' He told them that a national and unified education system was needed, working from the top downwards, through the agency of the new university machinery; and that to secure this end, administrative areas larger than counties would be needed – possibly counties could be grouped in areas in which the university interest might provide a centre for secondary schools and the training of teachers.

Haldane left no doubt that he was making an official pronouncement: 'what I am now going to say to you, I say not casually or with any light sense of responsibility, but after consultation with the Prime Minister and with the Chancellor of the Exchequer.' But this was not the view of the chancellor of the exchequer! Just as Lloyd George had repudiated Runciman's announcement about the source of university finance eighteen months earlier (p. 98), so he now repudiated what he called Haldane's 'magniloquent speech' in Manchester. No, said Lloyd George: land, not education, was to be the next great subject to be taken up by the government. And as for Haldane's consultations with Asquith, Pease, and himself, Lloyd George admitted that they had occurred, but Haldane 'had spoken quite vaguely to each, representing to each in turn that he had fully consulted the other two and had their sanction for his proposals. . . .' (This indictment has the ring of truth; it was Haldane's style.) The cabinet, said Lloyd George, had not been consulted at all. Lloyd George in any case took a poor view of the speech. 'Interminable verbiage' was his description of it to the editor of the *Manchester Guardian*: 'and he added something more scathing about "a barrel of tallow" – a picturesque description of Haldane's physical peculiarities – which, when set fire to could indeed produce "any amount of smoke but no flame". . . .'

Haldane, however, got his own way. The king's speech at the

opening of parliament on 10 March 1913 announced: 'Proposals will be submitted to you for the development of a national system of education'; and, as lord chancellor, Haldane had the satisfaction of reading the speech to the lords himself! He wrote to his mother: 'The King's Speech has got the Education policy in, & that will count for more than Crowns and Swords of State, and robes. . . .'

Thereafter the hybrid committee continued to meet and make progress. Asquith on 17 March confirmed that the bill would be introduced in that session. And Haldane, intent on making audible 'the voice of the country', threw himself again into a circuit of speeches: to the National Union of Teachers on 25 March, to secondary and technical school teachers on 29 March, to the 'Eighty' Club on 4 April. It was no set speech. He cleverly adapted himself to each audience. To the elementary school teachers he is said to have spoken for ninety minutes (after the ejection of half a dozen heckling women at the beginning). He assured the teachers that he did not have in mind a central bureaucracy; there would be local devolution to take advantage of local enthusiasm, and he emphasised the importance and status of the teacher and hinted at the need to introduce a four-year training course, bringing them into the university atmosphere. To the secondary school teachers he stressed the need to relieve universities of the burden of secondary school work (and so to raise the level of sixth forms) and the need to do away with the 'old fashioned' system of degrees by examinations in favour of the student's record. The *Times Educational Supplement* commented on both speeches under a headline: 'The promised land'; but made the pertinent point that most of what Haldane had said was not new. The important point was that 'no less a personage than the Lord High Chancellor of England' was saying it.

During the early months of 1913 the bill took shape. By April a first draft had been prepared. It contained twenty-six clauses which included provision for a comprehensive system of schooling, for continuation schools, and for provincial associations composed from local authorities: all objectives for which Haldane had been campaigning. At the beginning of May Selby-Bigge sent a copy of the bill to Haldane with a long covering letter, apologising for its length and adding: '. . . but I know your patience is inexhaustible.' Haldane replied with a characteristic note of encouragement:

Coming up from Durham in the train today I got time to dig into your Education Bill. I think it an excellent start off. . . . But the essence of it all is that the money must be promised with it. . . . As to this I will see my colleagues. The Bill if it passes with the money grant will lay the foundations of a great system, and will I think sustain the first and most difficult stones of the edifice.

There was a preliminary discussion at cabinet which (Haldane wrote) 'might have been worse', and, he added, '. . . I have had a good private talk with Lloyd George.' As an earnest that the bill was being taken seriously, the government issued a communiqué on 14 July – when it was clear that such an ambitious measure could not be dealt with before the session ended – announcing their intention to proceed instead with a one-clause bill which would form a not inappropriate peg (as they put it) on which to hang a statement of policy for a national system of education. On 22 July Pease, as president of the board of education, introduced this one-clause bill. The commons received the accompanying statement of policy with guarded approval; 'a very large overcoat on a very small peg', as one MP put it. And it did not go unnoticed that Lord Haldane had had a hand in the matter.

After the summer recess, work on the bill was resumed. By December 1913 a fresh draft was circulated to the cabinet. The king's speech at the opening of the new session again included the bill in the government's programme. Haldane concentrated on securing the money, which meant persuading Lloyd George to include it in the finance bill, and, of course, getting cabinet approval. He adopted his familiar strategy. 'Late tonight', he wrote to Selby-Bigge on 20 April 1914,

> I drove the PM to Downing Street after dinner & had a talk . . . . My talk was an excellent one. I think he will agree to £500,000 for 14–15, £3,500,000 (with a carry over) for 15–16 & £4,250,000 for 16–17. This last figure is a little over what you mentioned to me. But an inspiration came to me & I proposed to offer £20,000 a year apiece to Oxford and Cambridge for *Science*. This turned the scale . . . . I hope I have made a good start for you.

There is an undated fragment of another note from Haldane to Selby-Bigge, written shortly afterwards: 'It was satisfactory that the Cabinet passed our plans tonight so far as money goes. We have now to deal with Parliament.'

Haldane had, of course, to carry the chancellor of the exchequer with him, as well as the prime minister. This called for a different technique, including a barrage of blandishment. So, in briefing Lloyd George on what to say about educational reform in the house of commons, Haldane was not above recourse to flattery; he expressed the hope that Lloyd George would 'take the fullest credit for a great reform which the country will owe to your courage and imagination.' Lloyd George responded well. On 25 June the finance bill passed the house of commons.

The next evening there was a celebration at the National Liberal Club. Haldane described the budget as 'the greatest budget that my rt. hon. friend has yet introduced, and its inner purpose deserves well to be understood. . . . The inwardness of the present Budget is the purpose which is latent in it of a great reform which will put the chances of the coming generation on a footing such as we have not yet seen.' Lloyd George, not to be outdone in flattery, thanked the lord chancellor

> for his superb exposition . . . . I have never regretted more than I do tonight that the Lord Chancellor has left the House of Commons. . . . It was a great speech and it displayed not merely the great intellectual qualities of the Lord Chancellor but . . . his thoroughly kind heart. What he did not reveal to you was that he had a great part not merely in the construction of this Budget, but in its initiation and in its inspiration.

Once again it was too late in the session to put the education bill through parliament. On 7 July Asquith announced that it would be postponed again. This time it was swept out of sight by the tide of the German armies.

On the brink of fulfilment Haldane's hopes for education had been dashed. Only one item – and that an unexpected one – was salvaged. In the ministerial changes brought about by resignations at the outbreak of war, Christopher Addison became parliamentary secretary to Pease at the board of education. Addison already knew Haldane and fortunately he was a lively diarist. He records on 12 June, on the eve of the war: 'Pleasant hour with Haldane. Miss Haldane happily absent.' So his relationship with Haldane was evidently cordial, and it was natural that he should consult Haldane. He records (on 2 December 1914) 'Selby-Bigge seems inclined to fold his hands, resign himself to fate, and surrender without a struggle all the advances promised by the Budget.' Addison was determined that despite the war – or indeed because of it – the government should do something straight away about technical training. His chief, Pease, was inclined to limit proposals to trade schools, but authorised Addison to prepare something more ambitious. By 10 December he was already consulting Haldane about it. He got hearty encouragement, Haldane adding that 'we must link our application on to the war somehow or other.' With the help of officials Addison produced a plan. It was despatched from the board to the treasury in January and on 29 January Addison was summoned by Haldane for what was to become a historic interview. Haldane's greeting was: 'Addison, this document has compromise written all over it. Just tell me frankly what you would like to do if you had a free hand?' Addison expanded into a much more comprehensive scheme for assistance to science and technology for the benefit of industry. To his delight, Haldane's reaction was to say that he and Lloyd George, with Pease's full consent, wanted Addison to undertake the 'chairmanship of a small committee to work out a scheme whereby national assistance could be given to scientific and industrial research.' He suggested that Heath (of the Universities branch) should be one of the members and warned Addison to 'avoid axe grinders like poison.'

By 20 March Addison had a much fuller scheme ready. The draft was discussed at a lunch arranged by Pease 'in the little room off the main Dining Room' at the Carlton, with Haldane there, together with Lloyd George, McCormick and Addison. All went promisingly. 'Haldane charged me at the end to keep the ball rolling and placed on me the responsibility for carrying on the campaign.' The scheme envisaged the formation of a central committee of research, nation-wide in its scope. At first it was thought that this could be set up under the minister for education, even though the jurisdiction of the board was confined to England and Wales. Later, however, it was found necessary to resort to a constitutional device that was to inspire one of Haldane's most ambitious projects when he came to plan for post-war educational development: a two-tier structure under the auspices of the privy council, with an executive committee, served by an advisory council of experts.

The scheme was approved in May 1915. This month saw also the shattering climacteric of Haldane's career. He had already resigned himself to the inevitable postponement of his long-laid plans for the University of London, just as the Murray committee was about to recommend action upon them. He had secured the funds to launch a peaceful educational revolution, only to see the bill shelved until parliament could think about such things again. But in his political career he was, up to 1914, on the top of the wave; only fifty-nine years old and at the height of his influence. When he left the war office in 1912 to become lord chancellor, *The Times* showered encomium upon him: 'Everything, or almost everything, that Lord Haldane set out to do when he took office he has accomplished . . . by sheer force of character, by invincible good humour, and by an imperturbability which has seldom been equalled by any public man. . . .'

The wave was to dash him on a cruel shore. He now had to eat the bitter fruit of his long and profound affection for German culture. As hostility toward Germany became more feverish, criticism of his pro-German proclivities began to spread. Then came twisted rumours about his notorious secret mission to Germany, shortly before the war. News of his visit had of course leaked (though he tried to throw reporters off the scent by pretending he was there on educational matters) and it was interpreted as an attempt to parley with the enemy. Frequently Haldane pleaded with the government to clear his name by releasing a statement about the mission, but his pleas were refused.★ The mystery about this visit, coupled with Haldane's frequent, and sometimes too fulsome, allusions to the superiority of German education, industry, and culture, prompted a mean and virulent press campaign against him. In September 1914 he felt obliged to offer his resignation from the office of lord chancellor. It was refused and in January 1915 he was given a place in the war council. But Asquith could not, or would not, withstand the storm of censure. On 26 May 1915 he jettisoned Haldane. It was a bitter shock, second only to the far off catastrophe of his broken engagement, twenty-five years away. Some of his parliamentary colleagues (but not all) turned their backs on him. He was actually assaulted in the streets, his life was threatened and, even a couple of years later, he was still having to be shadowed, for his safety, by detectives.

★ Beneath his composure there was a deep resentment about this. In 1915 he did unburden himself about it to Lord Mersey, saying: 'my life is uncertain and I should like to feel that I had told the story to someone who could in case of need repeat it.'

# 6 On the Periphery of Power

When Haldane attended the palace to surrender his seals of office the king invested him with the order of merit, but that was cold comfort. Just what loss of office meant to him is vividly caught by Fitzroy, in a rare glimpse of Haldane with his defences down, on a farewell visit to the privy council immediately after his surrender of the great seal:

> May 26 [1915] . . . Haldane, who had just left the King and been invested with the Order of Merit, came in. He had all the air of the fallen Minister, and I could not help recalling the fate which had overtaken another philosophic Chancellor [Francis Bacon] three hundred years ago . . . . He seemed thoroughly broken, and said goodbye to us with undisguised emotion. 'There has been', he said 'a lot of mud flung, and I must try to give myself a coat of whitewash'.

Haldane's love affair with German philosophy, inspired by that far-away student sojourn in Göttingen, was, in a way, the cause of this disaster to his political career. But at the same time it equipped him to meet adversity. Over his broken engagement he had told Webb that he was never so much himself 'as when hope goes & black misfortune crowds round.' He endured this mutilation of his influence with a noble stoicism and without a trace of self pity. C.P. Scott records having had lunch with him on 27 January 1917, when 'Haldane spoke quite dispassionately of the extraordinary persecution to which he had been subjected.' And Marie Belloc Lowndes, a close neighbour of Haldane, recollects:

> I saw him constantly . . . when it can truly be said hundreds of thousands of English men and women believed him to be very little better than a traitor. He took his astounding fall . . . not only with great dignity but with a kind of magnanimity which I thought moving . . . . He always walked from his house in Queen Anne's Gate to the House of Lords and he was such a singular-looking

being that he was often accosted by people who knew him from pictures which appeared in the press. Sometimes these passers by would fling violent abuse at him. Occasionally strangers would tell him they were sorry his work for his country . . . seemed to be forgotten.

In this second purgatory Haldane again found consolation from the Webbs. Beatrice had written to him on 4 June: 'Sidney & I have been very much perturbed by the events of the last weeks – more especially by the scandalous attack on you. We admire – more than we can express – your splendid & silent self-sacrifice. . . .' He dined with the Webbs on 14 June; it was the beginning of a new chapter in benign co-conspiracy, to help reconstruct the post-war society of England.

For Haldane's response to adversity was to work for the future, not to brood over the past. As ex-lord chancellor there was judicial work for him to do in the appeal courts. Two weeks after he relinquished office he wrote to Rosebery: 'I am now full of judicial work. . . . I have also educational work on hand that much wants pushing on.' Two months later he had set his compass for the future. He wrote on 29 August to Beatrice Webb (paraphrasing his mentor, Goethe): 'I have decided that he who would accomplish anything at all must limit himself & that I must concentrate on National Education.' It is a sign of his magnanimity that he accepted two invitations from Asquith: one to visit France to investigate the débacle of the battle of Loos; another, to join the privy council committee on scientific and industrial research. (Asquith, too, was being as generous as he could politically afford to be. In a note from the secretary of the board of education to Fitzroy at the privy council it is on record: 'As regards the composition of the Committee of Council, I understand that the Prime Minister was particularly anxious to associate Lord Haldane with the scheme . . . .') By the end of 1915 he was sitting regularly in the house of lords, making education his platform; and by April 1916 even the wounds which Lloyd George had inflicted on him less than a year before were healed: after dining together on 4 April 1916, their somewhat uneasy alliance was resumed.

Let us stand back from this portrait of Haldane for a moment. We see a man with astonishing resilience and unquenchable faith in the future. He could, in his sixtieth year, have lived on his lord chancellor's pension and discharged his obligation by sitting in the appeal courts. There was little encouragement to think about post-war England, for 1916 was the year of the Somme when (as A. J. P. Taylor put it) 'Kitchener's army found its graveyard. . . . Not only men perished. There perished also the zest and idealism with which nearly three million Englishmen had marched forth to war.' This defeat, even more than his private adversity, must have been a terrible burden for the man who had been responsible for the army. Yet in 1916 Haldane added to his legal work and his privy council committee at least four other tasks: the chairmanship of committees on air power and coal conservation, membership of the education subcommittee of Asquith's Reconstruction committee, and the chairmanship of another royal commission, to examine university education in Wales.

In December 1916 Asquith's government fell and Lloyd George, with a small war cabinet, assumed personal control: 'the nearest thing England has known to a Napoleon. . . .' Haldane wrote to Asquith: 'The old machine, by means of which I used to try to work, is now destroyed, and I do not see any prospect of another coming into existence, which would either take me on or which I could take on.' Lloyd George did in fact flirt with him: on 17 April 1917 Haldane told his mother that Lloyd George wanted him to come back ('all difficulties must be put aside for the nation wants your brains badly'). Nothing came of this, though Haldane did accept the chairmanship of another – and as it turned out very important – enquiry into the machinery of government. But educational reform remained the focus for his enthusiasm. Once the war was over, he told C. P. Scott, he would be able to devote himself entirely to education. Meanwhile he had committed himself, in April 1916, before Asquith's downfall, to a project after his own heart: chairmanship of the royal commission on university education in Wales.

Haldane was not the government's first choice as chairman. The original membership, proposed after discussion with Lloyd George and McKenna, is to be found in a letter from the board of education to the treasury on 25 February 1916. Viscount Bryce was to be chairman. We do not know why or how the switch was made. Bryce, who was in his seventy-eighth year, may have declined the task. Haldane's name was an obvious alternative, and it is likely that Sir Henry Jones, whose name also appeared on the proposed list of members and who was a close friend of Haldane and of Lloyd George, had a hand in the decision to invite Haldane. In these circumstances it can be assumed that Haldane had no part in drawing up the terms of reference or in picking the team he was to work with. It was an interesting team. In contrast to the membership of the London commission, there were no Olympian figures such as Milner or Romer. The commissioners were scholars or administrators in fields of special interest to Wales: literature, philosophy, music, science, medicine, agriculture.* Two of the members (Jones and Edwards) were Welsh by birth and up-bringing and prominent in the Welsh renaissance at the end of the nineteenth century, and Bruce was the son of Lord Aberdare, whose report on Welsh education in 1881 was regarded as the educational charter of modern Wales. The commissioners were charged to make a full scale examination of the organisation of university education in Wales, although the circumstances which precipitated their appoint-ment were interestingly similar to those which precipitated the royal commission on the University of London. In London the problem was how to associate the Imperial College with the University; in Wales it was how to associate the proposed medical school at Cardiff with the University. But in Wales, as in London, the explicit reason for the commission was a side issue. The Welsh colleges wanted (and needed) more money from the treasury. The advisory committee for university grants, after visiting the colleges in 1913, recommended an increase in grant but coupled their recommendation with misgivings about the lack of an adequate co-ordinating authority which could be entrusted with the allocation of grants among the three colleges, at Bangor, Aberystwyth, and Cardiff. Meanwhile a committee of enquiry set up by the board of education to examine proposals for a national medical school in Wales also recommended financial support but with similar misgivings. So, in February 1915, the treasury issued a minute declining to sanction grants recommended by either committee unless the University and the colleges could agree on reforms in their constitution. They failed to agree, whereupon the treasury announced a decision that grants would be increased on condition that the University and its colleges asked for the immediate appointment of a royal commission. To this *dirigiste* demand the University capitulated, perhaps more willingly than might have been expected, for there was – as the commission subsequently discovered – a growing sense of 'discomfort, dissatisfaction and disappointment'

---

* The members were: Viscount Haldane (chairman), W. N. Bruce, Sir William Osler, Sir H. Jones, Sir Owen Morgan Edwards, Professor W. H. Bragg (who did not attend any of the meetings at which evidence was taken), W. H. Hadow, A. D. Hall, and Miss Emily Penrose.

in the federal structure of a university which had no physical presence except through its three independent colleges.

The commission was announced on 12 April 1916, with Haldane as chairman. His appointment was well received. For one thing he was not an Englishman – the Scots could be expected to approach Welsh problems with more sympathy. Also he had frequently spoken with enthusiasm about educational progress in Wales (even saying in parliament in 1899 that Scotland had everything to learn from Wales in higher education!). In Aberystwyth he was remembered as having made a memorable address to students in 1910, telling them that the Welsh, like the Scots, were idealists but – unlike the Scots – imaginative rather than reflective and therefore capable of important innovations in education and religion. So when the *Times Educational Supplement* commented on the commissioners, it must have gratified Haldane to read in the correspondence columns afterwards a letter from a Welsh MP, E. T. John: '. . . the assistance of a statesman of genius so outstanding, of such conspicuous erudition so entirely sympathetic and appreciative as Lord Haldane is warmly welcomed. The catholicity of his temperament, with all its Continental implications arouses no prejudice in the Principality, while his intimate knowledge of Scottish conditions and his study of the problems of university administration peculiarly commend his appointment to the people of Wales.'

Haldane plunged into the work of the commission with energy and enthusiasm. Here again was the familiar technique. He led the commissioners through a meticulous study of the state of the University and its history, followed by thirty-one sessions at which witnesses were examined (there were only four occasions which he did not attend at all). Then came another thirty-six deliberative sessions before the report was signed on 6 February 1918. The meetings were held in London but of course Haldane realised how important it was, if the report was to be credible, to appear on the spot. So in June 1916 the commissioners took the road and visited Cardiff Swansea, Aberystwyth, and Bangor. 'The Welsh Expedition', he wrote to his friend Gosse, 'was a success', and afterwards he often spoke warmly of his visit. 'We became very much moved', he told the house of lords in a debate on the Education bill two years later, 'by what we found there. We found that part of the country – the Principality – moved and permeated by the spirit of education. . . . It has the advantage of a democracy permeated by ideas.' The visit evidently made a good impression. William George wrote to his brother, Lloyd George: 'I had the pleasure of meeting your friend Lord Haldane today. He was very suave & cordial and appears to be very keen on making a good job of it.'

Haldane examined witnesses with the familiar disarming approach. On 15 December 1916 (for instance) three students appeared before the commission. Included in their case was a request that students should be represented on the senate (the body which would have responsibility for academic affairs) rather than the council (the executive body) or the court (a very large and ineffective body). This request, in the context of English and Scottish universities, was an innovation. Haldane listened patiently. 'The Senate particularly?', he asked. 'Yes' was the reply. 'I see', he said, 'you have fixed your mind upon the Senate. But, no doubt, you are not averse to our considering the other bodies in addition or alternatively, as the case may be. We have spoken of representation upon some of the governing bodies of the University, it may be the Senate or the Court or both, but can you point out in any concrete fashion the utility of that? Do not imagine that in putting the question I am doubting it, but I just want to get your reasons?' Haldane exercised, too, a firm control over his fellow commissioners. When Osler ventured to assure the town clerk of Swansea, on the question of the technical college there, that there would be no difficulty about a technical college of the first rank becoming a constituent college, Haldane interposed: 'This is really a matter for the Commission to debate. I think that we had better keep this for our own discussion?'

The detailed recommendations of the Welsh royal commission, as of the London one, are relevant to our portrait of Haldane only in so far as they illuminate his character and his ideas. But this is just what some of the recommendations do, for they are (to use Haldane's favourite word at that time) permeated with his philosophical concepts about universities, and are couched in language which reveals his deepening conviction that democracy would not survive without an educated citizenry. Above all, the report on Wales, like the report on London, has a powerful theme running through it to which all minor issues were harmonised. For London, the theme was a university fit for the metropolis of the Empire. For Wales, the theme was a university as a national expression of the spirit of the Welsh people. It was a theme consistent with many of Haldane's cherished beliefs. His dedication to *Lehrfreiheit* was easily translated into the need to cultivate a university in Wales free to develop its own peculiarly

Welsh identity, uninhibited by the proximity of England.* His insistence on the importance of introducing technical education took on a new meaning in Wales, for the colleges there began as liberal arts colleges to which technology had to be added, whereas in England many of the civic universities began as technical colleges which had to be humanised. His popular theme, that higher education should permeate the whole society, was peculiarly relevant to Wales, where the university colleges had been endowed – as it was commonly said – 'from the pence of the people'. Many passages in the commission's report and, more significantly, many references in Haldane's speeches afterwards, indicate that he was really excited by the potentialities for higher education in Wales; it lifted his speeches to unaccustomed levels of eloquence. 'You have an opportunity', he told the court of the University at its first meeting after it was reconstituted, 'which no other university in the kingdom has. Will you use it? Will you make the most of it? If you do, then I venture to say that you will not only have profited yourselves, but you will have set an example to the rest of the United Kingdom. . . .'

We can suppose that Haldane left recommendations on some issues to his colleagues: Osler for medicine, Hadow for music, Hall for agriculture. But three issues discussed in the report deserve special mention because they were certainly greatly influenced by Haldane himself and he often referred to them in his speeches afterwards. The first is a beautifully lucid exposition of the differences between a university which is a federation of colleges and a university in which there is a devolution of authority and responsibility to colleges. In Wales there was the weakness of London over again: a university which stifled initiative in its constituent colleges by controlling examinations and curricula but which was powerless to control the quality of teaching or the allocation of public finance. It was an arrangement which produced 'unprogressive uniformity' but which was unable to prevent wasteful duplication among the colleges. The remedy was similar to that proposed for London: give the University control over the treasury grant by making the grant to the University for distribution among the colleges, and give the University control over the appointment of professors and heads of departments in the colleges; but leave to the colleges a maximum of autonomy in the design of

---

* 'You are a very quick people although you have been terribly downtrodden by English examiners', he told the University College at Swansea.

courses and the setting and marking of examinations. 'The principle
is not federalism but devolution. . . .'

The second issue which clearly caught Haldane's imagination was
a proposal from Caernarvon county council to involve a cross section
of the public in the policies of the University. According to the
constitution of the English civic universities and the University of
Wales, *de facto* government was by a small body called the council
(which delegated academic affairs to the senate); but the council was
the executive for a very large body called the court, which might
contain between 100 and 200 members, representing local authorities,
graduates, learned societies, educational bodies, and so on. If those
who drafted this pattern ever expected much from the courts, they
were disappointed; in most universities their meetings were little
more than annual parties which listen to an address, transact a little
formal business, and have tea. The Caernarvon county council proposed to put life into the court of the University of Wales. Their
submission ran:

> The University Court should be peripatetic and should sit for a
> number of days at the visited centre when conferences with members
> of the local education authorities and teachers would be held,
> public lectures on educational questions given, and public meetings
> held at which awards and honours gained by local students would
> be announced – following the precedent of the Eisteddfod and its
> conferences and sectional meetings.

The commission fixed on this imaginative idea with enthusiasm.
Listen to Haldane pursuing it in an exchange with Lloyd George's
brother during one of the hearings: it would, said Mr W. George,
make a meeting of the university court an 'Eisteddfod' of its own,
a 'real high festival for education . . . something really fine'.

'A great occasion?' asked Haldane. 'Yes.'

'And possibly it might sit in public so that the people might hear?'
And George supplied the crescendo: 'And men of outstanding eminence
coming there to lecture, and everything of that sort giving pomp
and circumstance to the gathering.'

'A couple of days' meeting?' 'At least a couple of days . . . .'

'Which should focus the attention of Wales?' 'Yes and guide the
policy of Wales in educational matters for the coming year and be
an inspiration and guidance for the people. . . .'

When the commission framed their recommendations they gave prominence to this idea. 'Our conception of the University Court', they wrote, 'is that of a Parliament of higher education. . . .' They enlarged the court to 200 or more and greatly increased the representation of local authorities (though not to give them at least fifty per cent, which was what Denbigh and Caernarvon wanted).* And the commissioners' euphoric proposal was that the court 'should not hurry through its formal agenda in one day with its attention divided between the business and the clock or railway-guide, but should set out deliberately to spend four or five or six days on the discussion of both the practical affairs and the broader aims of higher education. . . . Great projects of reform and development might be discussed. . . .' That Haldane himself was captivated by the idea is evident from his address to the court when it held its first meeting under the new constitution: '. . . the scheme was that the Parliament of the University . . . should discuss these great matters. We did not contemplate that it should discuss after the easy-going fashion of such University Courts as exist in more strictly Saxon countries.' Great principles, he went on to say, would be discussed at the court on behalf of the people of Wales. The purpose 'is to recognise the very highest education – education of the university type – as part of the national life . . . . That is the new principle, a principle which has not been applied to any other University in the United Kingdom. . . .'

The third issue to which Haldane was personally committed, and which filled his interests for the last phase of his life, was the obligation of the University to undertake extra-mural work. The Welsh people did not need any prompting about this. Their adult education movement was already vigorous. Indeed at one point in the hearings Haldane had to caution the representatives of the Workers' Education Association (WEA) against making too great a call upon the resources of the University: 'Do not pour out your treasure over too wide an area, otherwise it will be lost. The content of a university is like a precious liquid – there is not too much of it.' The significance of Haldane's interest in adult education at this time is that he was beginning to see in this the solution to a dilemma: the dilemma (as he put it to students in London a few years later) of how to bring what is

---

* Other new elements in the court included representatives of the students, MPs for Wales and Monmouthshire, tutorial classes, the National Library of Wales, the National Museum of Wales, the Welsh Agricultural Society, and the Hon. Society of Cymmrodorion.

really higher education to bear upon the democracy. On one hand he stood uncompromisingly for quality in higher education. In this sense he was an elitist and said so, though he wanted everyone capable of joining the elite to have the opportunity to do so. On the other hand he wanted the whole of British society to be permeated by the influence of the universities. 'Until you get an enlightened democracy', he told the people of Swansea, 'you will not get an inspired democracy.' The solution was not to bring the people indiscriminately into the universities (he would have opposed mass higher education as it is talked about today); it was to take the universities to the people. Hence, for Haldane, the great political importance of the extra-mural departments of universities and his pleasure at the enthusiasm for this activity in Wales.

The report met with general and spontaneous acclaim.

> The people of Wales have every reason to congratulate themselves and to be grateful for the findings and recommendations of the Royal Commission, for the proposals of the Commission are at once sane and imaginative . . . the final adoption, rejection, elucidation or development of the more important proposals [submitted to the commission] has been almost invariably influenced by an appreciation of the spirit which animates the Welsh renascence of today. . . . Throughout the report there run, as golden threads, notes of intimacy and sincerity. . . .

The University welcomed it and the Colleges too, though perhaps with some apprehension that devolution might give them less freedom than federation. What mattered most was the response of the government. Lloyd George was by this time prime minister.* He and Fisher (now president of the board of education) received a deputation from the University on 14 August 1918, and Lloyd George made a most welcome statement. Provided the recommendations of the royal commission were in the main adopted, he said, the government would give financial backing:

> The Report is one of the most important documents, I think, in the history not merely of education in Wales, but of Wales itself; it is a very able document and its conclusions seem to be, in the

---

* His opinion of the Welsh colleges had not been flattering. He is on record as saying that 'in order to get a proper reorganisation of the Welsh University, the first thing would be to hire somebody to anaesthetise the three Principals.'

main, very practical and very sensible. . . . What I propose is this:
We should give £1 for £1. If you raise a penny rate, we will
give the equivalent of it.

This was just what the commissioners hoped for, because the idea
of a rating levy throughout Wales was the brain-child of Sir H. Jones,
which initially had run the gauntlet of Haldane's scepticism (he had
turned it down when he first heard about it, in the garden of a hotel
on the Menai Straits) but which was ultimately included as one of the
recommendations.

Not everything went according to plan. The medical school, in
particular, remained a problem until it received a special charter in
1931. But by May 1919 the University had prepared its submissions
for reform. A petition and draft charter were lodged with the privy
council on 17 June 1920 and on 13 August 1920 the supplementary
charter was approved by the king in council. Haldane had little to
do with these negotiations, but he gave an impressive welcome to
the reorganised University in the two memorable addresses from which
we have already quoted. It was typical of him not to reminisce about
the past but to turn the attention of his audience to the future: 'The
business of the Royal Commission', he told the academics of Cardiff,
'has been to dig. It is the business of Wales to plant and water.'

Another task in the cause of higher education was completed. Not
all the commission's hopes were realised. In particular the court never
measured up to the ambitious role offered to it. It was hard to believe
(wrote the historian of the University thirty-five years afterwards) that
the proposal, 'attractive though Lord Haldane had found it, was ever
more than a pleasing fantasy'. But the other recommendations were
so sound and practicable that it was not until 1960 that another commission was needed to re-examine the University of Wales. The
indecisiveness of its report (published in 1964) is in striking contrast
to the solidity of the structure Haldane and his colleagues built in
1916.

Haldane was now ready for the next task. There could be no more
telling postscript to the task he had completed in Wales than his
laconic note to Gosse, written on 25 November 1920: 'I leave for
Wales this morning – to open the University. I return by sleeping
car through the night. Tomorrow night I start again for Cloan. . . .'

We must now take the reader back to 1916, for Haldane, in the years after his downfall, had other educational interests beside the University of Wales. It was true, as he frequently said, that he had lived for universities. But he came more and more to regard the successive stages of education as indivisible. It was only the outbreak of war which held up the first wave of legislation to reform the school system which Haldane and Lloyd George (neither of them with any formal responsibility for education) had inspired. As secretary of state for war Haldane had been shocked at the amount of illiteracy among recruits. To reconcile his lofty views about universities and his liberal ideals of democracy, he had to accept a logic which made it plain that even in a perfect society not every boy or girl could aspire to become a bachelor of arts. There must be honourable and satisfying alternatives to higher education. So, having witnessed (as he told the house of lords) the establishment of ten new universities in the country* and having acted as midwife to some of them, Haldane turned his attention more and more to other levels of education.

So, back to 7 April 1916, when Beatrice Webb wrote in her diary:

> We dined with Haldane last night – for one of our periodical talks. He was looking very well & is in good form in spite of his political retreat. He has been seeing something of his former colleagues – even Lloyd George & has been trying to persuade him to take up a great scheme of technical ½-time education 14–18 after the War. 'Tho' I have not been heard of' he said somewhat pathetically, 'I have been very busy – I have a room in the Ed. department'.

His mind, wrote Beatrice, was 'running much more on raising the standard of education of the whole population than in [the] old days.' A fortnight before this dinner party Haldane had given the foundation oration at University College, London. His conversation with the Webbs doubtless ran on the same theme. For Haldane got preoccupations – it would be exaggerating to call them obsessions – and his preoccupation was now with vocational training. 'But you, after all', he told his audience of students, 'can never be more than a nucleus. The vast majority of our working countrymen are wage earners, belonging to the industrial classes. Do the interests of the nation

---

* Haldane was exaggerating a little! His list included London (which was not formerly a teaching university), Birmingham, Liverpool, Manchester (*pace* the Victoria University), Leeds, Sheffield, Bristol, Armstrong College attached to Durham, and two universities in Ireland.

require that they too should be infused with the reflective habit which is born of knowledge? My answer is an emphatic yes.' He did not shirk the issue by devious speech: 'You cannot in practice give complete equality in educational opportunity to all classes.' Few children of the working class can really get on to the educational ladder. But the problem is not insoluble: 'the greatest educational discovery of the most recent years appears to me to be that of the latent possibilities of what is called vocational training.' Haldane's formula was modest enough on modern standards: compulsory education to fourteen; then a bifurcation at which the middle and upper class and those of the working class so exceptional as to be able to tread the narrow ladder would go to secondary schools; and the great mass of elementary pupils would go into jobs. But for these there should be compulsory continuation classes such as Germany (Haldane had the courage to mention this) had so successfully developed. The day-release classes (as we now call them) were to be no mere craft-training: they were to have intellectual content and (he did not specify what he meant) 'physical and spiritual content' as well. The old faith in the efficacy of education was as strong as ever. For a quarter of a century, he told his audience, he had represented a Scottish constituency where farm labourers were of the very highest quality. And why? They 'had been educated in Scottish schools as hardly an English farm labourer in the Southern Counties is ever educated.'

How were these aspirations to be turned into legislation? Already part of Haldane's message had got across to the public. People were realising that Britain's unpreparedness to fight Germany was as much educational as military; that the defeat of Germany would buy time to equip Britain's educational system to compete with the post-war world. Buy time, but no more: so that even with guns blazing across the Channel and train-loads of wounded arriving at Charing Cross and Victoria, plans had to be laid to improve education. The *Times Educational Supplement* carried, from October 1915 to May 1916 a string of articles pressing for a royal commission on education. Haldane, recollecting that dust was accumulating on his royal commission report on London, opposed this pressure. A royal commission, he told the house of lords, 'simply means an opiate to send restless people to sleep, the putting of things off and nothing being done for four or five years. We cannot wait for four or five years.' The best way to push things forward would be to have an inconspicuous and discreet committee to review sketch plans already on the drawing board and to advise parliament how to proceed next session. With his astonishing pertinacity, Haldane now saw an opportunity to revive the draft bill of 1914. The thinking had already been put into it; the political atmosphere then had been brought to the right temperature. The operation abandoned in July 1914 (when Asquith announced that the bill could not be introduced in that session of parliament) could simply be resumed.

Haldane's campaign in the ensuing months of 1916 to reach this objective makes breathless reading. Some circumstances were in his favour. He was installed, unofficially, in the board of education. He had Asquith's somewhat remorseful support. He had no public office to fill his days with routine. But the smear still stuck. Even in 1917 Mr Pemberton Billing, in the house of commons, questioned the government on Haldane's membership of various committees and added: 'Is the right hon. Gentleman aware that Lord Haldane is universally distrusted by the people and that the action of the Government is looked upon as an affront to them?' There were cries of 'no'; but it was a sharp reminder that Haldane was an embarrassment to any government.

On 4 April Lloyd George came to dine at Queen Anne's Gate. At the dinner were McCormick, Blair (chief education officer of the LCC), Struthers and Heath. Haldane wrote to his sister afterwards that they had made out a plan which Lloyd George had undertaken to try to put through. 'He and I have made an alliance on Edn once more', he added. He also sent a note to Lloyd George: 'After you left I found this in today's Times published in the Educational Supplement. It shows how people are moving towards the ideas we were speaking of & I send it to you. Tonight's talk was a very useful one. You may accomplish more than you can easily realise.' The enclosure was a cutting calling on the government to respond promptly to the demand for investigation and action in the cause of educational reform, without a prolonged enquiry. Haldane was keen to restore the educational alliance with Lloyd George, and on 10 May wrote to him to say that he had spoken to the prime minister about 'our plan for a small private Committee of Educational experts to consider principles & policy' and that Asquith had been quite agreeable. 'The Committee', he went on, 'need not be announced, & should be as private & informal as possible. I saw Vaughan Nash [secretary of the Reconstruction committee set up by Asquith in March 1916] who agrees that it will not interfere with the Reconstruction Committee.'

This Reconstruction committee had been set up to prepare what Haldane, when speaking in the house of lords in December 1915, had called a Peace Book; and by the beginning of May, Vaughan Nash was already in touch with Selby-Bigge about the planning that was needed for post-war development in education. At the end of the month, Selby-Bigge submitted a case for appointing a reviewing committee on the lines of the earlier one presided over by Haldane in 1913, and on 23 June, the Reconstruction committee endorsed this proposal, resolving, however, that the decision should be kept secret, and that 'if any question arises concerning the necessity of reviewing the education system of the country as a whole, it should be stated that the Reconstruction Committee has taken up the matter.' This disposed of the call for a royal commission, and on 30 June Crewe took the opportunity to announce that the government had decided not to have one.

Haldane, meanwhile, had been working away on his own: on one hand pursuing his notion of a private committee of experts, and on the other preparing to launch a public campaign with a major speech in the house of lords. Towards the end of May he wrote to his mother that he was ready 'with full material' for the opening of the campaign; but in view of the controversy surrounding him, he was more than ever sensitive to the need for careful timing, and it was not till July that he judged it safe to put his motion in the lords.

The house of lords speech, delivered on 12 July, was a master-piece of close argument, perhaps the greatest education speech of his career. The notice was: 'To call attention to the training of the nation and to the necessity of preparing for the future.' Haldane began with some striking facts. Ninety per cent of young persons got no further education after the age of fourteen. 'I have often wondered how many Watts's, Kelvins, and Darwins have been lost in the vast mass of untrained talent which the children of the working classes afford.' Then came a plea for continuation schools. Of 5·85 million young persons between the ages of sixteen and twenty-five in England and Wales, 5·35 million got no education at all. He reminded their lordships that plans to remedy this deplorable state of things were worked out long ago and in 1913 and 1914 were included in the king's speech; all that was needed now was to revive these plans. Education was, to the British public, a 'tiresome' word, and Haldane (he was inconsistent on this principle) concluded that 'the only way is for the leaders to take a definite decision without waiting for any particular mandate . . . .'

Somewhat unwisely perhaps, and certainly gratuitously, for it was not an integral part of his argument, Haldane criticised the education given by Oxford and Cambridge, not on its quality (which he admitted was excellent) but on its lack of relevance to the art and science of administration in public affairs. Perhaps he did this in order to provoke debate and to draw their lordships' fire away from the issue he really cared for. If this was his purpose he succeeded. Some of the lords plunged into a spirited defence of the classics (employing the common fallacious argument – which Haldane did not fail to notice – that because some classicists are superb administrators, the classics are a good educational training for administration). Curzon, in particular, castigated Haldane on this part of his speech. All this ensured good press coverage, and the debate went on for three days.

The most searching criticism of Haldane's speech came from outside the House, from Sadler, writing to *The Times*. ' . . .the fear haunts one', wrote Sadler, 'that the fundamental issues of the business have not yet been thought out . . .' and he instanced five 'cardinal points upon which, so far as I know, no agreement has yet been reached throughout English inquiries into our educational needs'. These included the career prospects for teachers, the attitude of employers to continuation classes, the financing of private schools, and the very perplexing question: 'What spiritual authority shall decide the content of the religious training given in schools under public management . . .?'

It was a letter from a man who knew as much about the education system as Haldane did, and they were real (if scarcely 'cardinal') points that he raised. But the letter was coloured by dislike and (probably) jealousy of Haldane. For Sadler had set his heart on becoming president of the board of education (in which he was disappointed) and he suspected Haldane of working behind the scenes in ways which (among other things) might deprive him of this opportunity. Two days after this correspondence, Sadler wrote in a private letter: 'Lord Haldane has written me an angry letter. I have replied quietly at length. He is really plotting, & resents being found out & hindered.'

Haldane was indeed plotting. Shortly afterwards – or so it seems, for it is not possible to determine the exact date – he ventured to bring a plan of his own to official notice by means of a memorandum which has been preserved amongst the records of the Reconstruction committee. The first surviving version of this memorandum is type-

— his 'penguin-like gesture' —

written, and not only unsigned and unaddressed, but undated and unheaded. But a slightly amended copy bears the pencilled heading: 'Mem: by Lord Haldane. Reviewing Sub Comm:' and both style and content strongly confirm this provenance. The purpose of the memorandum was to draw attention to the need for new administrative machinery to meet the growing demand for an expansion in the national system of education: a need represented as all the more pressing in view of the recent establishment, on a nation-wide basis, of the privy council committee to deal with the application of science to industry. 'What is wanted is a Body which, while not unduly meddlesome in details, should work out great principles, and on this Body the representatives of both England and Scotland would have to sit.' It was proposed that 'the Lord President of the Council, Lord Crewe, should preside – just as he does already in the case of the application of Science to Industry – over a special Committee of the Privy Council containing Cabinet and ex Cabinet Ministers, and that under this Committee should work a Committee of experts responsible to it, whose business it would be to prepare and work out plans and keep the machinery moving.' The memorandum then went on to discuss membership. For the main committee, the names which 'occur[red]' were Crewe, Balfour, and Chamberlain, together with Tennant for Scotland and the president of the English board of education. '*To these might be added* [our italics] the name of Lord Haldane.' For the subcommittee, Selby-Bigge, Struthers, McCormick and Blair were mentioned. There remained the question of the presidency of this body, and this was easily solved: 'The suggestion made by the expert members is that they would welcome Lord Haldane as Chairman of this Committee, and there is reason to think that Lord Haldane has no objection to serving on both, and indeed would prefer to serve on the Sub Committee and would be able to find the time for the purpose.'

Then came the disclosure of Haldane's long-term goal (not of course for himself, but for the country). 'It would be quite sufficient to set up the new Committees by a minute, without saying whether or not they were to be permanent, but it is to be hoped that they would grow into a permanent organization for the supervision of National Education.' It is interesting to reflect on the different course which our educational system might have taken if this permanent organisation had materialised. It might have been a parallel development to the department of scientific and industrial research (which did materialise from the other committee to which Haldane referred in his memorandum). It would presumably have had surveillance over all education, from the nursery school to the university and beyond. But matters did not end that way. Haldane's proposal for a committee of the privy council served by an expert subcommittee was dovetailed into the government's own plan for a reviewing subcommittee of the Reconstruction committee. The decision to appoint a reviewing committee, reached by the Reconstruction committee in June, had been announced in the house of commons on 18 July; a formal memorandum, with proposed terms of reference and composition, was submitted to Asquith on 25 July; and on the 26th, the last day of the debate in the house of lords, Crewe reiterated the government's pledge to proceed with the appointment of the committee, a pledge which drew from Haldane renewed protest against the needless delay of a further general enquiry. Since the second day's debate on the 19th, he had been up to Cloan. Before leaving for Scotland on the 20th, he had written to Gosse of his fear that Crewe would prove 'dilatory' on the final day of the debate. 'Immediate & vigorous action is what is wanted.' A period of repose at Cloan was apt to clear his mind, and it seems likely that he drafted the memorandum during his stay there and launched it on his return – shortly before, or immediately after, the conclusion of the debate. However this may have been, the original reference to a committee of the privy council, made in the first surviving draft of the memorandum was amended in pencil to read 'Reviewing Committee', and formal invitations to serve on such a body were duly despatched from the Reconstruction committee on 8 August. Haldane was amongst those invited, and it was explained that the chairmanship would be taken by Crewe who proposed 'to delegate a considerable amount of work to a Sub Committee of experts'. It was also announced that a preliminary meeting of the committee would be held at the privy council office on 11 August. This was its one and only meeting; but it made the decision Haldane wanted. He was asked 'to prepare in association with a group of English and Scottish educational experts a memorandum outlining the questions which required consideration'. That same day he wrote to Gosse: 'We met today – the Cabinet Committee – & I was unanimously placed in a position of great responsibility for plans & power to mould them. All were most cordial. We resolved on secrecy, so it will be difficult for the "Times" to hear anything definite. And as my plan has been adopted & put through it can hardly now be upset.' The experts he gathered round him were Selby-Bigge, Blair, Heath, McCormick and Struthers: all tried collaborators, four out of six of them Scottish. It was the membership he had in mind when discussing the proposal with Lloyd George.

Haldane lost no time in complying with the Reviewing committee's request. By 17 August he had drafted a memorandum for his colleagues to consider. It began with the characteristic deductive approach: 'Agreement in general principles is the foundation of progress in agreement on details' – and he set out eleven propositions which appeared 'to emerge from discussion'. Continuation schools and educational provinces subsuming local authorities were of course included, and one of his older motifs was there: the award of certificates at secondary schools, which should be the normal passport to the university, based more on the school record than on a mere examination. He put as his priorities the reorganisation of the final year at elementary schools, raising the leaving age to fourteen, a system of continuation schools, and more secondary education.

In August 1916 the president of the board of education, Henderson, became paymaster general. He was succeeded by Crewe, who adopted an attitude which evidently upset Haldane's plans. He wrote to Gosse on 27 August:

> As to Education what I am going to write is very private. After I left Crewe seemed to me to have yielded to the importunities of the old set. As a result of what I looked on as a breach of the spirit of our understanding, a breach the significance of which I don't think he realised, I sent him an ultimatum. I will not go on but will conduct an independent campaign unless I am given a sufficiently free hand. I await his reply, which may mean a breach. But this is a secret between you & me. It accounts for his reticence to you.

But the storm blew over. On 15 September he wrote again to Gosse: 'I had an excellent final interview with Crewe & Asquith this morning, & arranged my Education organisation. I only hope it will not be meddled with again.'

There was some complaint in parliament (on 8 August) and in *The Times* (on 11 August) about the secrecy surrounding the enquiries into education, but protest was stilled by an announcement made in the house of commons on 10 October. The government was evidently still on the defensive, for it had prepared an answer in anticipation of a supplementary question which was not in fact asked: 'The Committee is a Sub Committee of the Reconstruction Committee and is composed entirely of Ministers and ex-Ministers. I cannot undertake at the moment to give the names but I will consider the matter.'

During the autumn Haldane pressed on with his two-pronged attack: on some days, speeches to stimulate interest; on other days, meetings at his home in Queen Anne's Gate. At home his subcommittee met regularly. It is fascinating to watch how, during these years out of office, Haldane operated on the periphery of power by making his own home, as it were, a field headquarters. On one day the education subcommittee would meet in his upper smoking room. On another day the committee on the machinery of government (set up in 1917) would meet two floors below. 'We sit twice a week', wrote Beatrice Webb, 'over tea and muffins in Haldane's comfortable dining room discussing the theory and practice of government.'

The education subcommittee met almost weekly from 10 October to 27 November. On 15 November the first version of a report for the reviewing committee was drafted. It was headed 'Memorandum. Strictly confidential' and was signed by Heath, though it was written in the first person as from Haldane. It may be that this style was simply to conform with the wording of the resolution that Haldane should prepare the paper 'in association' with the experts. Or it may be that the paper went further than the experts were prepared to go; certainly one of them, Selby-Bigge, severely criticised it afterwards.

It was a tough document, in some ways (e.g. over continuation schools and the need for larger local education authority areas) going beyond the draft bill of 1914. It emphasised the time lag in educational reform: 'A nation gathers the full fruit of the education it has given some 20 years after the child is born, and the national plans for education like those for the navy must be drawn accordingly.' It condemned the existing fabric of education as being 'weak from bottom to top'. It pressed for compulsory continuation schools and an adequate supply of teachers: 'If we can lay these two girders well and truly we shall find the rest of our programme relatively easy and simple.' Then came advocacy for larger education authorities, 'to maintain a great service of teachers', to administer scholarships, and 'to facilitate other important reforms in higher education'. This is far from the neo-Hegelian *étatism* which some of Haldane's critics attributed to him. On the contrary (as Haldane pointed out) while there is much to be said for state action in matters of urgency and for limited periods, an undue extension of state action is likely to weaken local initiative; so his recommendation was devolution, but devolution to institutions strong enough to accept the responsibility.

Officials of the board of education did not care much for Haldane's report, and on 20 November one of the experts, Selby-Bigge, wrote to Nash that he was labouring on a separate memorandum from the board to the reviewing committee. Criticism in the office focussed mainly on the pivotal recommendation of larger areas and Selby-Bigge, in a departmental minute on a second draft of Haldane's document, put his finger on the essential weakness of the proposal. For once Haldane, the superb tactician, wanted to go too far too fast. For years he had been preaching Matthew Arnold's doctrine – that British education should be organised in provinces – but Haldane had never really faced up to the fiscal consequences of this policy. The provincial councils, he often said, should *control* the educational system, maintain the teaching service, administer the scholarships. To discharge these functions the councils would need the backing of financial authority. Without money they would be powerless. If they were to have money it would be at the cost of local government sovereignty. One civil servant in the board of education returned a minute to Selby-Bigge dismissing the proposal as 'quite out of touch with realities . . .' and went on: 'I therefore refrain from offering any comment on it'. Was this a sign that on the periphery of power Haldane had overlooked the necessity to carry civil servants with him when it came to propose political action?

Haldane's report was never considered by the reviewing committee, for in December the government fell and the committee and its sub-committee were among the casualties. It was an eclipse for Haldane too. He lost his privileged (if anomalous) position in the board of education. Lloyd George appointed Fisher to be the board's president and he set up a new Reconstruction committee. At Fisher's request the old reviewing committee was dissolved and replaced by a panel for education under the chairmanship of W. G. S. Adams. Haldane's name was not on the panel; nor was he needed as consultant at the board of education: for not only was Fisher himself a scholar and an ex-vice-chancellor; to replace Heath (who had been appointed secretary to the new D.S.I.R.) he brought in Gilbert Murray from Oxford. This permeation of the board by distinguished academics was exactly what Haldane (himself an academic manqué) had wanted. The success of Haldane's own policies made him superfluous. This happens to success-ful men, and it is a mortifying victory.

But there was a bright edge to the cloud. Fisher liked and respected Haldane (Fisher had been one of the first to write a note of sympathy when Haldane lost office in 1915). Although he did not bring Haldane officially into his machine, the two men had many talks about education. Fisher (Haldane wrote to his sister) 'is very sympathetic to my programme. . . . There seems to be a real prospect of getting something done. He is putting nursery schools, continuation schools, improved secondary education and physical training in his programme.' And Fisher, in his autobiography, acknowledges Haldane's influence in both speeches and 'private consultations with the officers to the Board of Education'.

From January 1917 until Fisher's Education bill was passed in August 1918, Haldane campaigned and conspired unsparingly to support Fisher's reforms. He addressed meetings up and down the country. He spoke in the house of lords. He lobbied colleagues. He conferred with civil servants. Wherever he could make a move on the chessboard of politics toward winning the game – which was to put his 1914 reforms, brought up to date, on the statute book – he made the move. He was content, apart from occasional nostalgic references to his own earlier endeavours, to give all the credit to Fisher. His eyes were never off the game, and Fisher was generous in allowing Haldane to watch it from close by. We get a glimpse of this generosity on 20 February, when a preliminary memorandum for a comprehensive scheme of reform was agreed in principle by the war cabinet after half an hour's discussion. Fisher must have told Haldane of the good news straight away, for on 22 February Haldane was already writing to Lloyd George: 'It was with very great pleasure that I learned confidentially from Fisher that you had given your approval to his plans for educational reform. They are admirable plans & this is a great step on. It has never before been taken & I hope to be of all the little use I can in furthering the new departure in Education which your Government has taken.'

But Haldane's current preoccupation was to press for provincial councils, although he must have known by now that his views were opposed by board of education officials, other experts like Sadler, and local authorities themselves. Here he went much further than Fisher was prepared to go. In practically every speech Haldane 'plugged' provincial councils as he had long ago conceived them, with a university at the head permeating the schools and other educational institutions beneath. Thus at Perth on 6 January 1917: 'it was inevitable that we should have larger areas and more powerful authorities.' And at Huddersfield, a few days later, he was reported as saying: 'Why should they not take the West Riding, London, and Lancashire, and make them into educational provinces . . .?'

Criticism of these views continued but they seemed to make no impression on Haldane. Fisher himself was sufficiently moved to try the idea out in a deliberately vague way, when he made his first major speech in the house of commons on 19 April. There was a need, he said, 'that the county authorities, either separately or combined together in provincial committees, should make complete and progressive schemes for education in their respective areas. . . .'

Haldane's speeches, now laced with compliments on Fisher's 'brilliant performance', continued to press for provincial councils – authorities which would 'control their university, continuation schools, scholarships, and the supply of teachers'. On 9 May he launched a spring offensive in the house of lords, which led to a full debate on the issue. All the arguments were redeployed: provincial regions in which things could be worked out according to the *genius loci;* the analogy of the successful devolution of education to one province already: Scotland; the idea extended to the rest of the kingdom, with seven or eight provinces for England and Wales.

(It is interesting to reflect that this concept of devolution to large provinces is in fact about to happen in England and Wales over the management of rivers. There are to be ten great regional water authorities, with powers to raise money by precepts on the rates and to control water resources in their regions.)

But their lordships were not prepared to welcome the idea of educational provinces. Crewe must have expressed the view of many even of Haldane's friends when he suggested in the debate that Haldane had under-estimated the difficulty of grouping local authority areas and that he seemed to be approaching 'extremist' views on the subject; and there were murmurings that the French educational system might provide a better model for England than the German system.

When Fisher moved the first reading of the Education bill on 10 August 1917, he used Haldane's proposals as a backcloth for his own. There *could,* he said, be eight or nine provincial councils, with wide powers, including the power to levy a rate.

That, I understand, is the scheme advocated by Lord Haldane, who, of course, speaks on all educational questions with great authority. Or the Board might be empowered by Statute to provide for the establishment of provincial associations after consultation with the authorities concerned, the local education authorities being empowered to delegate administrative and educational functions to these associations .... The Bill follows the second of these paths.

But Fisher had misunderstood Haldane.* The bill provided just the sort of 'start off' he wanted; it also provided, as firmly as he could have wished, for continuation schools. After reading Fisher's speech, Haldane sent him a generous note of congratulation.

It was only a first reading of the bill and much remained to be done. The house of commons rose on 21 August without the bill having been given a second reading. 'My chief concern', wrote Haldane to Gosse, 'is to help to stir up a current which will carry Fisher's Bill into law. For the Philistines will obstruct him presently if we do not work....' So, after his summer holiday at Cloan, Haldane took the road again to campaign for Fisher's bill: Edinburgh on 28 September, then Dundee, then Glasgow, then Chelmsford (where he vigorously protested at the government's suggestion that they might not be able to include the bill in the coming session). But some of Haldane's speeches at that time may have been what is now called 'counter-productive'; for whilst he was hammering away at the need for provincial councils, Fisher and officials at the board of education were preparing to bow to the storm of opposition from local education authorities directed against the administrative provisions of the bill, and especially the clause about provincial associations.

Instead of pressing forward with the existing bill during the remainder of the session, the government decided to introduce an amended bill to take account of the local opposition at an early stage

* Haldane repudiated the assumption that his scheme for provincial authorities or councils included power to levy a rate. In his congratulatory note to Fisher, written on 13 August, he protested: '. . . I have never wished to do more than develope (sic) these much as you propose, & in particular I have always repudiated the idea of giving to Provincial Authorities rating powers independent of those of the L.E.A.s. The control of State Grants through properly devised and approved schemes by the Provincial Authorities is another matter.' That Haldane was misunderstood over this, was partly his own fault, for although he pointed to the Scottish Education Fund as an example of the way provincial councils might be financed, he was deliberately reticent about the details of such an arrangement, claiming indeed, that the government would be far better at devising a viable scheme than he would!

in the following session. This was presented for a first reading in the house of commons on 14 January 1918, and although as Fisher explained the new bill was substantially the same as the previous one, certain changes had been made in the administrative provisions. Thus the earlier clause, proposing no more than voluntary provincial associations, was withdrawn; and all that was left of Haldane's 'preoccupation' was a weak substitute (clause 6) facilitating the federation of local education authorities for certain purposes. The bill went its way smoothly, and on completion of the committee stage Haldane wrote to Fisher: 'A line of warm congratulation. You have taken a great Bill through Committee, & you have also established a very high & valuable parliamentary reputation. It was a great thing for the country when [you] accepted office as Minister of Education.' In the house of lords Haldane warmly (and selflessly) acclaimed Fisher's achievement, and even mildly rebuked Lord Gainford (who was Pease, a former president of the board of education, who had been responsible for drafting the bill of 1914) when Gainford could not resist a 'friendly charge . . . of plagiarism', and quoted clauses from the 1914 bill to show that Fisher's bill was not original. 'It is', said Haldane magnanimously, 'the largeness of spirit of the Bill and the way in which it is welded into an organic whole with a new spirit that distinguishes it from previous attempts in education.' But Haldane himself could not resist striking one more blow for provincial councils: '. . . when I look at Clause 6 I find that it is not in as good a form as the original clause in the original Bill . . . . I want to see these local education authorities federating and taking into counsel the teachers of the universities in their localities for much larger educational purposes.'* (Was this an early symptom of the futile obstinacy of an ageing man?) On 8 August the bill received the royal assent. For Haldane another campaign was over – one which had been conducted by remote control, as it were, from the dining room table and the smoking room of 28 Queen Anne's Gate.

All credit for the new reforms went to Fisher. Even Lloyd George (who was in a position to know better) makes no mention of Haldane's part when he praises Fisher's work in the *War memoirs*. But there were people who realised that the successful passing of the Education act was only the last move in a long and sometimes frustrating political

---

* Although – and this is significant in view of a speech he made nine years later (p. 166t.) – Haldane went on to say: 'I certainly shall not move any Amendment in committee on this subject but shall be thankful for what I have got.'

negotiation in which Haldane had made the opening moves and which he had loyally supported after he had been deprived of the final laurels. One of these people was Selby-Bigge. After the first reading of the bill in 1917, Haldane had written to congratulate him, as the permanent secretary of the board of education. Here is Bigge's reply. It is a fitting verdict on the whole campaign:

Dear Lord Haldane,

Many thanks for your letter of the 17th. I am glad you like our Bill. Much of it is of course familiar to you, and if not its actual parent you certainly are a blood relation, and you are entitled at all events to a share in the congratulations on its birth. You have also done yeoman service in preparing the way for it in the Country .... If we can get the Bill on the Statute Book and get on the Estimates a pair of millions which will by a natural process breed other millions, we shall have done something for a better England.

# 7 Ebb-tide

Beatrice Webb's assessment of Haldane, if one makes allowance for her monstrous egotism, is more penetrating than that of any of his contemporaries. But she was deplorably sanctimonious about some of Haldane's indulgences and this, we believe, led her to misjudge his attitude to success. The food he ate, the cigars he smoked, and the company he kept, all came in for her censorious and feline comment. Haldane, she wrote in her diary, had 'a childish liking, mingled with personal vanity, in being "in the know" with, I will not say a finger, but a whole hand in the pie'. 'His foible has been to be in with all those who were wielding world power and to let the other side know it. He has always delighted in power and the appearance of power. . . .' And again: 'He is, in short, a *power* worshipper.'

People who accept great responsibility and do so willingly (even eagerly, as Haldane did) are commonly thought to worship power. Some do. But many do not; they regard it as an inevitable component of responsibility, to be valued only because access to power makes it possible to discharge responsibility well. In our portrait of Haldane we do not discern a relish of power for its own sake. What we do discern is a sweeping gusto for the techniques of politics: to be in possession of all the necessary facts, to know all the right people, to have fore-warning for trends of opinion and intuition for timing – not to enhance power, but to persuade a whole nation to take another step toward what Haldane believed to be the good society. This is not a worship of power; it is a pride in responsibility.

Beatrice Webb misjudged also Haldane's vanity. Satisfaction over his achievements he undoubtedly enjoyed, though he did not boast about them except to his mother. But did he really enjoy flattery? Beatrice Webb wrote that 'self seekers and promoters of causes . . . habitually and often grossly kowtow to him – for it is only too obvious that he likes it.' Doubtless people did flatter him, for he had great influence, but it is a false conclusion to assume that he liked flattery. He probably decided, as other influential men have, that it saved time not to expostulate; better to put up with it in silence. One suspects that Beatrice Webb, when she wrote about Haldane, was sometimes holding a mirror to herself. On 28 March 1926, for instance, Haldane reviewed, in the *Observer*, Beatrice's *My apprenticeship*. The review was judicious, restrained, and in places gently critical ('Her rejection of the contributions made by politicians', Haldane wrote, 'seems excessive in its emphasis'). Beatrice, in her diary, bridled at this criticism. Haldane was hurt, she concluded, because she had not written enough, or appreciatively enough, about him in her book! She excuses herself: the omission was due to absent-mindedness. She rationalises the omission: '. . . Haldane is exactly one of the personages who will come off unduly badly in memoirs. . . .' And she ends with the condescending comment: 'All of which makes me more regretful that I did not give him his due; he shall get it in the following volume.' And then Beatrice's essential compassion breaks through: 'But alas! he is not likely to be there to read it.'

It is surely obvious that Beatrice Webb's assessment of Haldane is tangled up with Beatrice Webb's assessment of herself. '. . . now and again', she wrote, 'our diverse scales of values have obviously clashed and then we have become for a time antagonistic or indifferent to each other. There has even been not a little mutual contempt.'

So, when it comes to putting into our portrait Haldane's attitude to power, we prefer to observe Haldane rather than to listen to Beatrice. The test of whether a successful man has succumbed to the temptations of power comes in his old age. Retirement from office affects successful men in diverse ways. Some feel envy and hostility toward those who supplant them and although they may try to conceal it, it shows in pathetic gestures to prolong influence and to deplore change. Others give a benevolent welcome to their successors and may even be inclined to praise their efforts uncritically. Haldane was generous toward those who supplanted him. Of course, after retirement, it is natural for a man who has made history to want to remain close to where history is being made. A cynic might label his kindness and approval of his juniors as ingratiation, so that he may remain admired by them. Whether Haldane used his charm consciously or unconsciously to keep the confidence of Fisher and Selby-Bigge, Fitzroy and McCormick, we do not know; but throughout this ebbing tide of his influence Haldane never repined. Of course he liked to be consulted, and often he was not. Of course his vanity was stirred (e.g. by his reception when he went to Bristol as chancellor

– the University 'looks on me as its father' – and when he laid the foundation stone for the University College of Nottingham – 'The reception was wonderful'), but a little vanity is a harmless indulgence to which an old man is entitled, provided he does not use it to bore his friends. Above all, he never sulked when he saw great things happening to education without his help, he was never bitter, he never obstructed. And when he was once more invited into office to help the first Labour government, he was firm about the conditions under which he would do it but he accepted without condescension.

At the end of world war I Haldane was already a sick man. For nearly ten years he had suffered from diabetes and there was some permanent damage from the eye trouble he had in 1909. It was diabetes which again laid him low in 1918. Dean Inge visited him in September and recorded: 'Then we went to Cloan.... I had some prayers with old Mrs Haldane, who seems quite unchanged, but Lord Haldane is now an old man....' And a similar report was made to Mrs Inge in the previous summer: '... Lord Haldane is not the man he was; he is ageing in every way.' But there was no self-pity and no surrender to bodily ailments. Haldane drove himself relentlessly to continue his educational evangelisation. He still spun his web across Whitehall. Thus, in May 1919, when there were rumours that Fisher might be leaving the board of education, Haldane wrote to T. Jones in the war cabinet offices: 'I am concerned about the persistent rumours that Fisher may be moved from the Board of Education. Probably these rumours are quite premature, but I am certain that to move him from his present office would be a profound mistake. He has magnificent work in front of him, which he alone can do .... I think the P.M. knows this, but it is very desirable that it should be present to his mind.' Through his contacts in the house of lords and through Fisher and Selby-Bigge, Fitzroy and McCormick, Haldane was able to watch closely the changes in the educational scene during the post-war years. Three changes particularly interested him: the financing of universities, the re-organisation of Oxford and Cambridge, and the creation of new civic universities. Let us turn from Haldane's portrait for a few pages to sketch this scene.

First, the financing of universities. On pp. 99–101 we describe the petty wrangle between the treasury and the board of education in 1912 over which of these departments should distribute parliamentary grants among the universities and university colleges. The final outcome was that the grants were largely controlled by the board of education, but were divided between the treasury and the board's votes as follows (the figures are for 1918–19): treasury votes of £22,000 for English universities as degree-giving bodies, and £149,000 for arts and science work in English universities and colleges; and board of education votes of £65,000 for work in technology and medicine, and £32,000 for the Imperial College of Science and Technology. The £149,000 from the treasury was transferred in quarterly instalments to a deposit account of the board of education and paid out on the recommendation of an advisory committee (presided over by McCormick) appointed by and responsible to the board of education. But – it is an echo from the time of Lloyd George at the treasury – the treasury retained control of the grant for higher education in Wales (£36,500), and there were separate arrangements for the universities of Scotland and Ireland. It was an anomalous and untidy arrangement. On 19 December 1918 Fisher broached the matter with the chancellor of the exchequer (Bonar Law): 'The existing division of University Grants between the Votes of the Treasury and the Board of Education is inconvenient, and difficult to justify on any principle. The distinction indeed is only a formal one as regards England, because the main part of the Treasury grant (the £149,000) is transferred in quarterly instalments . . . and actually paid out by the Board.' And he went on to cite (slightly inaccurately) the recommendation of the royal commission on the University of Wales, which was that payments to the Welsh colleges should in future be entrusted to the board of education. The treasury was disposed to acquiesce. An official minuted: 'Mr Fisher's . . . proposal that the State grants in aid of University work should be borne on the Vote for the Board of Education can be agreed to . . . .' And on 18 January the chancellor of the exchequer (now Austen Chamberlain) wrote: '(i) I agree as to the transfer of votes from Try to M/E.'

It seemed that the principle for which Haldane had been contending – that education, and therefore finance for education, should be regarded as one organic whole – was on the eve of acceptance. But four days later Austen Chamberlain countermanded the decision, directing 'that in view of the conversation with Mr Fisher yesterday the decision on point (i) must be held up for the time being.' For six months the two departments exchanged notes and negotiated. The outcome was the exact opposite of the solution for which Haldane had been working. Virtually all grants in aid of university education in the United Kingdom were put on the treasury vote, and their distribution was to be by the treasury on the advice of a committee appointed by them, to be known as the University Grants Committee.

It is commonly supposed that the deciding factor in this turnabout was an argument suggested by Austen Chamberlain seven years earlier, and subsequently attributed to Fisher, namely that 'the Board of Education would seek to impose their views' upon the universities and that the autonomy of universities would be better safeguarded if grants came from the treasury. This supposition is wrong. The deciding factor is clear in a letter from T. L. Heath at the treasury to Fisher, on 3 May 1919. Since the committee to administer the grants was to be one for the whole United Kingdom, it had to be appointed by one authority with jurisdiction for the three kingdoms. The writ of the board of education ran only in England and Wales. Therefore, it had to be the treasury which appointed the committee, after consultation with the board of education, the secretary for Scotland and the chief secretary of Ireland. In his autobiography Fisher refers to the safeguarding of autonomy as a *consequential* advantage, but makes it clear that the prime reason for the decision was that the jurisdiction of the board of education did not extend over Scotland.

Throughout these negotiations Haldane was only an observer. There is no evidence that he was consulted by ministers or officials. Nor – and this is consistent with our portrait of him – is there any evidence that he attempted to influence the outcome although it went against one of his strongly held principles. On the contrary: in a speech in the house of lords a year later (on 21 July 1920) he complimented the government on setting up the UGC and said that the whole system had been 'put on a better footing'. In the 1930s another attempt to transfer the grant to the board of education was contemplated. The president of the board drafted a letter: 'I should like you to consider whether the UGC should not become responsible to the Board of Education rather than the Treasury. I do not imagine that there is another European country where the universities are considered to be outside the province of the Ministry of Education.' But the letter was not sent. Only in the 1960s – amid querulous misgivings among some academics – was Haldane's wish fulfilled.

The second change in the educational scene was the incorporation of Oxford and Cambridge into the system of treasury grants. This had to be preceded by a royal commission on these two universities. Asquith was chosen as chairman. It was, even Asquith's sympathetic biographer admits, 'a bad appointment'. The report was dull and unadventurous. Sir Charles Firth had written to Haldane: 'Several people here have expressed a wish that you were its chairman instead of Asquith. My impression is that Asquith's views on higher education are those prevalent at Balliol in 1870, and that he has learnt nothing about it since.' Nevertheless when the Oxford and Cambridge bill was introduced into the house of lords on 19 April 1923, Haldane praised the report, and the nearest he came to criticism was to say: 'It did its work in a conservative fashion, and in University matters that is sometimes not undesirable.'

The third change in the educational scene was in an area much closer to Haldane's affections: in the civic universities. Since 1905 he had been on the standing committee of the privy council for the modern universities of England and Wales, and we have already described its important activities in the early years of the century and the part which Haldane played in them. The committee was still in existence but it was consulted less and less as time went on. The treasury grants committee, under McCormick, had since 1911 given advice on the sort of problems which had previously been referred to the privy council committee. After the committee was metamorphosed into the UGC, under the same chairman, in 1919, this privy council committee was replaced in 1923 by a fresh privy council committee for all universities in England and Wales. Haldane was not appointed to this, though he continued to serve occasionally on the corresponding committee for Scottish universities and assisted at a hearing in 1923 about the entry requirements for the universities of Scotland.

For good economic reasons the board of education and the UGC did not share Haldane's enthusiasm for additions to a network of regional universities in England. But the pressure to add universities was kept up. Haldane's interest was, for instance, enlisted in 1918 by the proponents for a federal university of the south-west, to embrace the college at Exeter and three other colleges in Devon and Cornwall. He was quoted as having been 'rather impressed'. But Fisher and McCormick firmly turned the proposal down. It was as well; it would have been federalism in its most enervating form. Two years later, in 1920, there was a petition for a charter to raise the college at Reading to university status. That, too, was turned down for the time being. Fifteen years earlier a decision of this kind would have rested, virtually, with Haldane and Fitzroy at the privy council. But this petition was dealt with as petitions still are today. Fitzroy, as clerk to the privy council, sent it to McCormick, as chairman of the UGC. There is no evidence that Fitzroy turned to Haldane at any stage for advice. They were in touch over university affairs in Scotland, and in 1923 there was one last flicker of their long partnership. As Fitzroy was about to retire, he noted in his diary:

> In compliance with Haldane's wishes, I wrote two letters on matters he wanted taken up before I retired: (1) [here came a request to have something done about the inferior food supplied by the contractor to the judges in the privy council!]; (2) the present position of the movement to establish a University at Reading, which in 1921 was held up for the collection of sufficient funds.

It was as gently as this that the ebb-tide of Haldane's influence in Whitehall ran out in the years immediately after the war; and for a reason which was – though he never put it this way himself – a great compliment to his work. What he had done, since the turn of the century, was to help establish a machinery for the planning and financing of education which superseded his personal influence, or that of any other single official.

It is a further testimony to the way Haldane confronted old age that this eclipse cast no shadow over his enthusiasm, nor did his poor health deter him from taking on exhausting work in the cause of education. He had proselytised for Fisher. He was now proselytising for adult education. In 1920–1 he addressed fifty or sixty meetings up and down the country. Hardly a year went by, up to 1927, without a major speech from him in the house of lords. He wrote letters to the press. In 1921, and again in 1922, he went to Germany and (an example of his dogged integrity) he had the courage to tell an English audience, in a speech at Wigan, 'I went to find out things for myself. . . . They are seeking to educate their democracy . . . unless we make the advance of our education as great as theirs, we shall presently be in a position of peril. . . .' His home in Queen Anne's Gate remained a centre for educational dialogue. He happily accepted ornamental offices, such as the presidency of Birkbeck. And, as we describe later, he threw the whole of his remaining energy into the last preoccupation of his life: adult education.

But in 1922 there was a more urgent, short term, preoccupation. The post-war boom had burst. Lloyd George's government had to make drastic economies. They appointed, under Sir Eric Geddes, a committee to recommend cuts in government expenditure. The report (the Geddes axe) came out in February 1922. It threatened to emasculate the Education act of 1918 and it put the universities, bulging with post-war students, on starvation rations. On 8 February 1922, just before the Geddes report was released, Haldane spoke eloquently in the house of lords, to try to dispel the apathy of their lordships over education. It was a plea for discrimination in the use of the axe – for everyone knew that savage cuts were inevitable. 'Germany', he said, 'is spending more liberally by a great deal than we are here on education, although her people are very poor.' We shall lose our competitive position with America and Germany, he warned them, unless we spend money on the education of our people. His warning was prophetic, but it made little impression on his colleagues on either side of the House. Then (in a surprising flash which disclosed his astonishing powers of political adaptation) he went on to warn their lordships that interest in education was becoming a 'monopoly of the Labour Party. I do not rejoice over that. I am not a member of the Labour Party, although I have great sympathy with it as being the only Party that is really keen about education. I have spoken for it and supported it on that ground, and on that ground alone.' The government, he told the coalition, 'has not been a reflective government'. It was the debate on the king's speech, and Haldane moved an amendment to underline his warning. It was simply to ask ministers to lay down principles (the deductive method again) for discrimination over the economies to be made. The response was depressing. Viscount Peel (a member of the government) declared: 'I would frankly say to the noble Viscount that if he and those who are interested in these subjects are going to constitute little zarebas of their own and to establish certain areas of administration within which profane people must not venture, then the chances of any economy must be very much reduced.' One feels that the old man was no longer getting from the lords the respect due to him after a lifetime of service. The amendment was negatived. The axe fell, and Haldane's most cherished clause in the 1918 act – the provision for continuation schools – was assassinated. The decision to raise the leaving age to fourteen was not cancelled but the extra supply of teachers needed for this measure was not forthcoming; it is on record that in 1922 a quarter of the classes had more than sixty pupils.

There were, however, moments of sunshine for Haldane in this cold economic climate. In 1920 he had a tumultuous welcome in Bristol, as chancellor of the University. His car broke down and students hauled him through the streets in a cab chanting: 'Who saved

England? . . . Haldane.' And in June 1922, when he laid the foundation stone for another regional university, in Nottingham, he was drawn into the hall by students on an improvised throne. He spoke for an hour, back on his old theme: the Nottingham University as a centre for the East Midlands. Then, in 1924, came the brief Indian summer of his political life. We have quoted how, two years earlier, he had declared in the house of lords his sympathies with Labour. There were signs of his inclination even before that. Speaking to the students in Swansea in 1921 he had said: 'I know what I would do if I were leader of the Labour movement. I would put every ordinary item of the programme in the second place, and I would say, whatever the merits of all these items, the first way to accomplish them is to educate your people.' In January 1922 he disclosed publicly to Asquith his disenchantment with the Liberals, by declining to attend a meeting of Asquith Liberals in the Central Hall, Westminster. Explaining, at some length, to Asquith: 'My public life has for long been bound up with the cause of Education, more than anything else', he reaffirmed his sympathy 'with the great spirit and tradition of Liberalism' and then set out the conclusion which must have been a very painful one for him to reach:

It was for this reason that three years ago I decided for the future to work with whatever party was most in earnest with Education in the widest sense. . . .

I observed then, as I observe now, the almost complete lack of harmony between my strong conviction on this subject and the programme of official Liberalism. . . . In the official programme, and even in your own speeches, I can find no response about the thing I care for before any other at this moment, and regard as the key to reform generally.

The election of December 1923 foreshadowed the defeat of the Conservative government, and at the end of the month, Ramsay MacDonald went to Cloan to discuss what part Haldane would be prepared to play in the formation of a Labour administration. Haldane declined the presidency of the board of education, explaining that what education now needed was money, not reform. 'I said', he told Beatrice Webb later, 'I would willingly join & help in any way I could, subject to certain conditions. I must lead in the Lords as Lord Chancellor. . . . To this he [MacDonald] agreed after a night's sleep at Cloan.' It was no surprise that he turned down the portfolio of education. No more legislation was needed at that time, and he saw that he would be in a more influential position to determine the flow of public money as lord chancellor with a seat in the cabinet than in a lesser office.

Parliament resumed on 12 February 1924, after the change of government. Haldane's first speech on that day plunged straight into the need for more education in science. In this he was on firm ground. The concept of science-based industry was beginning to take root; the use of scientists in war had proved how profitable their work might be in peace. On other educational themes, however, Haldane was by now becoming quite unrealistic. Strikes and industrial disputes had bedevilled three previous governments. Haldane still nursed the illusion that education of the masses would 'tranquillise' them; once they understood both sides of the tensions between capital and labour they would go back to their mines and railways and factories content. It was a quixotic notion, which could have been dispelled by conversation with any Marxist. Hence the irony of Haldane's last preoccupation. Adult education was – it still is – a great and worthy cause, but not for one of the major reasons which Haldane supposed.

This last preoccupation we come back to later. But before that we turn aside again from our protrait of Haldane to examine the background. For there was an undischarged invoice in Haldane's educational transactions; the great report of the royal commission on the University of London. We have described (p. 111f.) how a departmental committee worked on the report up to the outbreak of war. Haldane took no part in this, nor did he defend the report against the criticisms it received when discussion of it was revived after the war. But some (though by no means all) of the criticism was misconceived and we believe that our portrait should include discussion of the fate (and vicarious influence) of the report.

Even before the end of the war Fisher initiated a move. In a confidential print to the cabinet on 5 February 1917, containing an outline of changes necessary for a complete and satisfactory scheme of educational reform, Fisher included 'provision of a sum to enable the recommendations of the Royal Commission on the London University to be carried into effect'. On 24 November, at Fisher's request, Sir George Murray submitted a report on the progress his committee had made up to the outbreak of war. Consideration of the matter was suspended in the early part of 1918, presumably while the Education bill was being put through parliament, but on 31 July a memorandum was completed and circulated on 1 August to the cabinet

committee for home affairs. The purpose of the memorandum was to
seek cabinet approval for a resumption of work by the Murray committee with a view to legislation, as an agreed measure, on the basis
of the Haldane report. In enumerating arguments for this approval
it is significant (in view of later criticism) that Fisher put first: 'The
present constitution of the London University is admittedly bad and
cumbrous.* The Report of the Royal Commission suggests a form of
constitution *more effective, more respectable, and more conducive to the
educational autonomy and development of the constituent colleges*' (the italics
are ours). Austen Chamberlain challenged the proposed expenditure
on the University of London on the ground that it would be dispro-
portionate to that on other universities. This elicited from Fisher a
further note (this time a secret one for the war cabinet) defending his
proposals, and asking again for a 'general concurrence to the scheme
for a reformed and invigorated University for London, which is set
out in the [royal commission's] report'.

By January 1919 arrangements had been made for Fisher to meet the
'externals', and later in the year draft legislation was actually drawn
up in the board of education. There is no evidence that Haldane took
part in any of these negotiations (though he and Fisher were seeing
something of one another, and Haldane was known to be involved
in the acquisition of the Bloomsbury site). In May 1920 it was publicly
announced that the site was on offer to the University, but a condition was that King's College should transfer to the site; and this
King's refused to do. So at the end of 1920 there was stalemate again.

The next attempt to break the stalemate was made by Charles
Trevelyan, who was president of the board of education in the short-
lived Labour government of 1924. On 30 July he submitted the
following memorandum to the cabinet:

Proposed Departmental Committee on London University.

I am anxious to be in a position to introduce legislation to put the
government of the University of London upon a satisfactory
footing. . . . A strong Royal Commission, appointed in 1909 and
presided over by the present Lord Chancellor, reported in 1913. . . .

* In Fisher's earlier draft of this memorandum (23 July 1918) this sentence had
continued:
    'and the meetings of the Senate present a scene of Polish anarchy which
    involves the whole University in discredit.'

I have reviewed the present position and have consulted with a selection of the most important academic authorities. There is a strong desire for reform in many quarters, but there is also a general feeling that some of the findings of the Haldane Commission require reconsideration in view of the long period that has elapsed. I therefore wish for the approval of the Cabinet to the appointment of a Departmental Committee.... I should propose that the Reference should be as follows: 'To consider the Final Report of the Royal Commission on University Education in London ... and ... to indicate what are the principal changes now most needed in the existing constitution of the University of London....'

On 5 August the cabinet (with Haldane present) agreed to appoint the committee. The chairman was to be Lord Ernle; but he had to resign on grounds of health after the first few meetings and an MP, E. Hilton Young, was appointed in his place. The committee reported in March 1926. A bill based on the report was introduced in June and received the royal assent in December.

Over the fundamental need – that the University should exercise an effective central control through the power of the purse – the new act achieved Haldane's main objective. But in other measures the committee, and the act based on its report, diverged from the pattern of organisation devised by the royal commission. The commission wanted a university organised as departments of study; the committee wanted to preserve a university of semi-independent institutions. The commission wanted *de facto* academic sovereignty to be devolved upon the faculties; the committee wanted to retain a strong academic council. The commission wanted to subordinate the external side of the University; the committee rejected this and recommended that for reasons of policy as well as of history, the external side should remain. But behind the facade of contrasting detail, the implicit philosophy in the two reports was similar; so much so, in fact, that when the bill was debated in the house of commons (at the second reading in November) the main opponent of the bill (Dr Graham Little, MP for the University and representative of the 'externals') rested his opposition on the assertion that the departmental committee's report was the 'lineal descendant of the Haldane Commission Report', whereas the main champion of the bill (Hilton Young himself) rested his advocacy for the bill on the assertion that it was 'almost directly contrary' to the recommendations of the commission.

These exchanges illustrate the difficulty of giving the report of the commission its rightful place in history; and the difficulty is compounded by the inflamed rhetoric which was aimed at it by some of its critics. Perhaps the most hysterical verdict is Hearnshaw's:

> The Haldane Commission was dominated and controlled by a small group of able and resolute men who were filled with that admiration and envy of Germany (mingled with fear of her) which prevailed in high places in the days before the war. They believed in bureaucracy; they worshipped organisation; they loved system and consistency; they longed for centralisation and co-ordination . . . they were inspired by the confidence that comes from philosophic doubtlessness and they were prepared for the ruthlessness which the enforcement of rigid principle requires.

The outburst ends: 'In particular· they lacked sympathy with King's and were ready to sacrifice her on the altar of organisation.' The author was the historian of King's, so his excesses may have been due to a surfeit of loyalty; but they carry one revealing message. The crude smear on Haldane and his Germanophil tendencies prompts one to ask whether some of the condemnation of the royal commission report may not have been mixed up – as Haldane himself believed – with prejudice against Haldane himself: a residue of the antipathies of 1914-16. More moderate, but hardly more judicious, was the verdict of Bellot: that the schemes of both Haldane and Webb for the University of London were highly doctrinaire and neither paid much heed to history.

Whether the commission's plan for a super-civic university in London, with devolution rather than federalism among the colleges, would have been a failure is arguable. Logan thinks it would have failed. But what, in justice to Haldane, has to be remembered is that in 1909-13 the key witnesses who came before the commission did not think so. The commission's provisions for incorporation were backed by Hill (the vice-chancellor), Miers and Rucker (the principal and past principal of the University) and a majority of the academic council. The proposals for faculty organisation were backed by Hill (though with reservations), Miers, Rucker, the whole of the academic council, and the professorial board of University College, not to mention such men as Foster and Ramsay. Over the 'civic' type of government there was some division on the academic council but a majority in favour, with support from Roscoe. The small non-representative senate was supported by Roscoe, Hill, and Foster.

Of course since 1909–13 circumstances had changed and this doubtless accounted for the volte-face which some of the witnesses to the Haldane commission (including Miers) deftly performed when as members of the Hilton Young committee they put their signatures to its report. The UGC had appeared on the scene; the colleges had become stronger and more prosperous; the jealousy between the external and internal sides of the University had abated; experience of incorporation had been disappointing. But there must still have been a lot of misunderstanding or merely ignorance about the commission's report. For instance the commission, far from proposing the suppression of college autonomy, specifically reserved for the colleges what matters most: devolution over courses and examinations. That Haldane himself was committed to academic autonomy in the colleges is clear from an address he gave to the Old Students' Association of the Royal College of Science in 1920. He asserted then that the colleges of the University 'should teach for their own degrees and examine for degrees which they should control . . . with only such supervision as was required on the part of the University to see that they did not lower the level of what was entrusted to them'; a principle, he went on to say, of 'devolution and complete autonomy'. We confess that we do not find these sentiments consistent with Hearnshaw's charge that the commission 'longed for centralisation and co-ordination'; nor with the suggestion that Logan makes, that Haldane thought the schools of the University 'had to be destroyed so that the new University could rise, phoenix-like, from their ashes'.

It has been remarked that Haldane was surprisingly reticent in his autobiography about the London royal commission, considering that it was, in some ways, the most massive assignment he had undertaken in educational work. It has been suggested that this reticence was due to Haldane's perplexity at the ultimate rejection of his report. We doubt whether this is the explanation, for he made frank and revealing comments about it in the debate on the second reading of the University of London bill in the house of lords in June 1926. He gave no impression then that the solution to the problems of the University had eluded him. A more likely explanation is that he was writing his autobiography in 1926 at a time when the whole question of the future of the University was still *sub judice*. To have indulged in polemics about the issues at such a time would have been totally out of keeping with Haldane's character; and to have introduced controversy into the book would have been inconsistent with its reflective theme – he was writing with 'all passion spent'.

Haldane's lifelong commitment to education was dominated by three major preoccupations: first, a network of regional universities; second, educational provinces, permeated by the provincial university, to provide improved primary and secondary education and continuation classes for the masses; third, adult education. Of course this was not the working out of a deliberate life-programme. But it is not imposing too rigid a logic on his career to suggest that there was an inner coherence about it; each preoccupation fell in place naturally from what Haldane had learnt from the previous preoccupation. It was the young Scottish graduate who saw the need for a more democratic higher education in England. It was the 'midwife' of civic universities who realised that if their quality was to be maintained there would have to be alternatives for the 'masses', and who campaigned for continuation schools and for the permeation of all schooling in a region by its local university. It was the chairman of royal commissions on London and Wales, and the missionary for the 1918 Education act, who heard the call to carry the evangel of knowledge through adult education to those who had been born too early to benefit from these reforms, in the mines and factories and farms. It was the successful war minister who saw that 'General Staff Work' was as urgently needed for the whole educational system as it was for the armed forces.

On the whole his preoccupations were reinforced by a shrewd and pragmatic judgement. His advocacy could not be faulted when he asserted that education at school and university was not only good for its own sake: it was demonstrably important for the British economy in peace and war. But Haldane's faith in the social efficacy of education rested on less secure foundations. 'Educate your people', he told the Scottish teachers at Dumfries, way back in 1901, 'and you have reduced to comparatively insignificant dimensions the problems of temperance, of housing, and of raising the condition of your masses.' A lifetime in the ruthless game of politics did nothing to dispel this cloudy illusion. Twenty-one years later he was telling the (surely sceptical) house of lords:

... I will venture to say to your Lordships that if that larger frame of mind [expanded by education] had been more diffused among the working classes to-day you would have avoided a great many strikes and contests . . . . I can only say again . . . that the effect of any movement of that kind [he was speaking about adult education] is more tranquillising, more calculated to avoid violent unrest, more calculated to allay jealousies than anything else that I see.

As far back as 1881 Haldane had lectured at the Working Mens' College and he must have been familiar with the university extension classes organised by Oxford and Cambridge since the 1870s. These were too dilettante to be regarded seriously as education, but the tutorial classes organised under the Workers' Educational Association (WEA) with the cooperation of the universities were otherwise. They were the first effective revival of sustained adult education for workers since the days of the Mechanics' Institutes. At their best (they often fell short of it) they took the form of year-long seminars,· at which the students were expected to submit written· work, and this, under the inspiration of men like Tawney, reached 'university standard'. Albert Mansbridge, one of the pioneers in this movement, recalls how Haldane became interested when he helped to organise a series of lectures in 1907–9, in Westminster Abbey and the royal gallery of the house of lords. (In 1909 Haldane took the chair at one of these lectures, given by Masterman, on democracy, and was pestered by suffragettes.) So adult education was a lifelong interest for Haldane, but it did not begin to become one of his preoccupations until he had listened to witnesses before the royal commissions on London and on Wales. What he heard there so appealed to his philosophical proclivities that he began to invest the WEA tutorial class (which was commonly a down-to-earth study of economics and political science) with an almost sacramental significance; an affair (as he called it) 'of the spirit'. Listen to extracts from his questions to representatives of the WEA at the Welsh commission: 'I want to get from you first a conception of the WEA' – and Haldane went on to outline it himself: not technical education, not school education, 'but the higher forms of education . . .?' The witness agreed. '. . . to suggest the great ideas connected with the search after truth which is the peculiar province of the University?' The witness agreed again. '. . . for that purpose', Haldane went on, 'it is one of your objects to bring in contact with the worker the man who is full of the university spirit and comes straight to the worker from its atmosphere, and communicates the flavour of the university teaching in its distinctive form?' This, replied the witness, was one of the justifications for the title *University* tutorial classes.

'Just as the well-to-do man who has been through the University takes up his book of poetry, philosophy or science in the evening, so you want your workers trained and encouraged to do that?' The witness, perhaps a little perplexed at the drift of the questioning, suggested that the practical worker might have something to contribute to the knowledge of the teacher too! The witness expressed a desire that some tutorial classes should be taken by professors. 'You are, I think', replied Haldane, 'right in your desire for that . . . the personality of a distinguished professor counts for a good deal.' Then Haldane went a stage farther: 'When you do discover first rate students you would like the scholarship system [to enter the university] made available to them?' And it was only when the WEA representatives wanted to reproduce in Wales the pattern of a land grant university (Wisconsin) in the United States that they got beyond the bounds of Haldane's enthusiasm and he had to warn them (as we quoted on p. 129) not to put too great a strain upon the University's resources.

The fruits of this experience on both royal commissions were strong recommendations to support extra-mural education, and Haldane's addresses and speeches in the house of lords afterwards show how deeply he identified himself with these recommendations. (Unlike Asquith, the chairman of the commission on Oxford and Cambridge, for whom – so his daughter said – the term extra-mural education was one which 'made my father wince'.)

Haldane was not included in the subcommittee on adult education set up by Lloyd George's Reconstruction committee in 1917 under the chairmanship of the master of Balliol, A. L. Smith, but he enthusiastically endorsed the committee's excellent report. By 1920 the cause of adult education had risen high enough among Haldane's priorities to be included in a house of lords speech. In 1870, he told the House, the government provided for the education of youth; now it was their duty to provide for the education of adults deprived of intra-mural university education. He commended the work of Mansbridge and the WEA and emphasised (as a political point) the tranquillising value of WEA classes for those who did not have the good fortune to be among the elite admitted to universities. The speech does disclose how Haldane was (as Beatrice Webb often accused him of being) a very patrician sort of radical. 'I am not suggesting', he said,

that you should contemplate the time when the working man will enter the walls of the university. He will do so, I hope, but he cannot do so in more than small numbers. I am contemplating the time when if Mahomet does not come to the mountain, the mountain will go to Mahomet. I am looking forward to the universities, through extra-mural work, reaching every district that requires it, training a new class of university tutor and, armed with that organisation, extending their beneficent work to the colliery district, the pottery districts, and the factory districts all over the country. Until you do that you will not have completed your system of giving educational opportunities, nor will you have laid the foundations of that tranquillity which you can only attain when you have got rid of class consciousness.

The speech made some impression. Crewe slipped in a brief reference to the 'very interesting suggestions' which Haldane had made 'on the possibility of universities stretching out tentacles, so to speak, all over the country'.

By the autumn of 1920 adult education had become Haldane's chief preoccupation. He was again busy at his familiar technique: a double-pronged campaign; at one time round the fireside at Queen Anne's Gate, plotting with Mansbridge, Tawney, Laski and others; at other times evangelising at public meetings to create a climate of opinion conducive to the raising of public money to support the movement. It was his last major service to education and it fell into the pattern of so much else which he had done. He did not create a new idea, others had done that a long time ago. He did not (though he tried to do this) succeed in lifting the idea to a higher philosophical (in his old age he would have called it 'spiritual') level. What he did do with the idea was to help to encase it in an institution. Haldane, drawing on his past experience with the army, saw the value of an organisation 'on something like a General Staff principle'. To institutionalise adult education would be to protect it, to confer status upon it, to give a sense of coherence to its practitioners. And so, in Queen Anne's Gate, the British Institute of Adult Education was founded in 1921. Haldane became its first president, and every year until 1927, even in the year when he was lord chancellor, he attended the annual conference and delivered an address. His value to the adult education movement was immense, not because of what he said (the addresses contain little that was both new and practicable) but because of the publicity given to his speeches. At that time he and Archbishop Temple were the two great public figures whose espousal of the movement kept it in the public eye. This publicity was essential, for Haldane's romantic vision of working class people 'who preferred to read Plato and Wordsworth to amusing themselves on the football field' while true of a tiny minority was, of course, a mirage as an aspiration for British society. The adult education movement remained a minority one, albeit a very significant minority, and minority movements need sponsors in high places. It was too much, perhaps, to hope that in the transient tenure of the Labour government much could be done for adult education. Under Trevelyan at the board of education the first complete code of regulations for the administration of grants for adult education was drawn up; but Haldane was disappointed: 'Trevelyan made vigorous efforts,' he wrote, 'but the importance of adult education was not fully taken in, although the principle was accepted.'

In 1925 Haldane was once again out of office, in his seventieth year, and far from well. But he threw his energy into the work of adult education. We know that he held a private conference with some university vice-chancellors, presumably to encourage them to cherish extra-mural work; and in the house of lords he appealed again to the government (in March 1925) to give a lead to the nation in promoting adult education in the 'University spirit', supporting his plea by assuring the House that he had 'gone about amongst' the working classes a good deal and he knew they would respond.

In this twilight of his life Haldane's faith in the efficacy of education never failed and he never missed an opportunity to reaffirm it. Thus, in what was his last address to students, when he opened the premises of the National Union of Students in 1925, he told the audience: 'the higher you go in education the more you find men and women . . . think in the main alike . . . .' But the twilight was growing deeper. Sometimes Haldane had to sit while giving an address. He was becoming a little deaf. On 19 November 1925 Beatrice Webb wrote:

Lunched today with Haldane (I wonder whether it is the last time?) The hand of death seemed to be moulding his features. To me it was inexpressibly sad watching him eating, drinking, and smoking away his life, though he looks so far gone that what he does matters little . . . there is a look of *vacancy* on his face which is new. . . . 'A death's head' said Sidney as we left the house.

A couple of years later his memory was playing tricks on him. On 9 March 1927 he said in the house of lords:

When the Education Bill of 1918 was before this House, I well remember moving a clause, which the Government accepted, enabling them to divide England for educational purposes into provinces which should be somewhat the size of Scotland. Wales would be one, Yorkshire would be one and Lancashire would be one, and it would be left to the provinces to work out their educational salvation in their own way. To me it is certain that half the questions we have been discussing today would have been solved long ago in these regions if that course had been taken . . . .

But our examination of the records shows that he never moved such a clause. He may have realised himself that his race was nearly run, for he wrote to Beatrice Webb from Cloan on 1 January 1927:

I reply on New Year's Day to your Christmas day letter. Not that the beginning of the year interests me much. Death may come during that year, & this may cause suffering to others. But for those who have to meet it, it comes to seem no more than an event implied by life. . . . I shall be here till just after the middle of January. Then I have appeals to hear. . . .

The race he had run was dedicated to the application of rational thought to the solution of political and social problems, and it was only in the last decade of his life that the rational regions of his mind succumbed to utopias. From adult education he expected far more than was good for the movement's own future. At first he welcomed WEA classes for the dubious reason that they offered – so he thought – the solution to his dilemma: how to preserve universities for the intellectual elite and yet to diffuse the university spirit through the masses. He assumed that intelligent manual workers would be content to study at night in tutorial classes and go back, still content, to their mines, dock, and looms. 'The idea of leisure', he said in a book of essays prepared by members of the British Institute of Adult Education, 'must change'. Leisure must be spent not in self-indulgence or mechanical amusement 'but in the liberation and development of the soul'. 'Spirit'; 'soul': gradually Hegelian terms, invested now with ecclesiastical connotations, drifted into his addresses. 'The work of diffusing higher education among the working classes is indeed a new missionary work,' he wrote in the same essay, and he suggested that in 'days when it is becoming more and more difficult for the Churches to attract students to the ministry, there is here thrown open a new missionary career, from which a spiritual side which may be very real is not excluded.' And in an article in the *Hibbert Journal* on 'The churches and higher education' he went further: whereas idealists, he explained, might be deterred from the profession of parish clergy by the existing route to the pulpit, they might be attracted to it if it were approached by a training designed in the first place for those wishing to undertake extra-mural teaching for universities. The prospect of teaching as well as preaching from the pulpit might provide a positive appeal. Thus might universities come to the aid of the church, and adult education acquire an added dimension.

This suggestion raises the whole question of whether the church should confuse what is Caesar's and what is God's. (Had not Lotze told him, over fifty years ago, that philosophy and Christianity belong to different spheres?) Fortunately Haldane was not drawn into controversy on this point. The speculations of his old age are really irrelevant to his contribution to adult education in the last decade of his life. Although most people engaged in adult education today have a much more modest conception of its role in society, they are deeply in Haldane's debt. He was the first major statesman to act as spokesman for the movement in parliament. He inspired the founders at a time when they were beset with frustrations. He helped to make adult education in England and Wales what it is today: incomparably the best of its kind in Europe.

# 8 Epilogue

Our portrait of Haldane must speak for itself. But having lived in his company, so to speak, for a couple of years, we find ourselves asking questions about the portrait we have drawn, and hazarding answers.

For us the most interesting question is this: to what extent did his education and his predisposition for philosophy affect what he said and did in politics? When *Vanity Fair* published a 'Spy' cartoon of Haldane in 1896, and labelled it 'A Hegelian politician', we may guess that Haldane was pleased with the title. But did the ideas of Hegel (or of English Hegelians like Green and Bosanquet) permeate (to use Haldane's word) his political platform?

We can put the question into a wider context. Intellectuals who enter public life can no longer practise the expertise they acquired as students. They have to be generalists, although if they have graduated from an English university, they are likely to have been trained as specialists, in classics, say, or law, or science. As public men, they are obliged to make speeches. In composing these they tend to go back to the indelible impressions of the one subject they mastered, and to take these as texts: the classicist, to Aristotle and Plato; the biologist, to Darwin and Mendel; the economist, to Mill and Keynes. Haldane's training was in philosophy and law. He had called philosophy his *Herz-studium*. Did his familiarity with Hegel and Schopenhauer and Goethe colour his public addresses and his political strategies?

His public addresses, yes. When Haldane was preparing some of these, especially if they were to be given to students, he drew heavily on his pre-political past; so much so that to understand these addresses it is essential to have some inkling of what Hegel meant by certain expressions which Haldane used. Rarely did academic audiences hear from him pragmatic advice from the practical statesman; what they heard was usually a distillate of philosophical ends rather than of political means. (It was this which elicited the witty rebuke from Bernard Shaw which we quote on p. 12f.) Hence the inscrutable phrases which obfuscate some of Haldane's most carefully composed speeches, phrases like 'the ethical life', 'the University spirit', the 'soul of a people'. He talked all round these terms but he did not define them. They were drawn from his rich store of nineteenth-century *Weltanschauung* and they undoubtedly meant much more to him than they did to his audiences.

The addresses include some strikingly Hegelian themes. 'The University', he told students at Edinburgh, 'is the handmaid of the State, of which it is the microcosm – a community in which also there are rulers and ruled, and in which the corporate life is a moulding influence.' And, a few minutes later in the same address: 'Such a University cannot be dependent in its spirit. It cannot live and thrive under the domination either of the Government or the Church . . . . It can recognise no authority except that which rests on the right of the Truth to command obedience.' A handmaid of the state independent of the state? The riddle is solved by Hegel. The state and all institutions within it – universities, associations, families – must live and have their being in rational thought. To be ethical is to accept the doctrine that the ultimate standard of truth and reality rests on an institutional rationality, an inner coherence of the state and all its parts (of which the university is one). The 'spirit' of a nation or of a university is measured by the degree to which it possesses this self-consistency. Morality (it is social morality which is meant) is living according to this faith in the rational, being obedient to it, doing one's duty (*Pflicht*) by it. It follows then that there should be no conflict between the state and its universities. The condition for *Freiheit* (freedom) is *Einheit* (unity, oneness). The framework of freedom within which the university operates is consensus about this doctrine. So Haldane is never heard to say (as we hear today) that universities must be independent of the state in order to be free to criticise the state. That, to Hegel, would have made no sense; the organs of the body do not criticise the body in which they function.

We have already described the problem which confronted Haldane when he preached on one hand democratic access to universities, and on the other, the need to preserve at all costs the university as the place where the 'highest' knowledge is pursued with an uncompromising passion for excellence. Many times he warned his audiences that the gates must be open for the working classes to enter but that in fact very few may expect to get in. Hegel had reflected on a somewhat similar problem. For him the prescription for *Einheit* in the state was an honoured bureaucracy of leaders in whom the masses, sufficiently enlightened to understand the purpose of the state, were prepared to put their trust. To oblige the masses to do this would not be compulsion. What may look like compulsion is only the process of persuading the masses to choose what they really want (which is what the state knows is best for them) instead of what they think they want. Haldane, of course, would not put it as crudely as this, but there is an echo of Hegel in his Edinburgh lecture: having told the students that 'the highest is also the most real' he went on to say that the highest should be made manifest by dispelling the mists of ignorance, and if that is done 'what is highest will in the main assert its authority with the majority.' And the purveyors of the highest: they are the leaders to be turned out by the universities. This Hegelian legacy is surely behind Haldane's ambivalent statements about the duty of politicians, to which we referred on pp. 13–14. When he addressed the 'Eighty' Club in Cambridge (an audience of potential leaders) he told them that politicians can only respond to public demand: they – the audience – must provide the ideas. But to his fellow parliamentarians, on more than one occasion, he took the opposite view: that governments must not wait for popular demand before acting for the public good; they must lead. And Haldane's frequent and exhausting circuits of public addresses: were these not consistent with Hegel's dictum, that to achieve *Einheit* it is essential to persuade the masses that what the state wants for them is for their own good?

When Haldane talked about the 'soul of a people', as he did to an enthusiastically receptive audience in Aberystwyth, he was again influenced by Hegel and perhaps Herder. Every nation has a *Volksgeist*, a soul of its own. Its language is the expression of its soul. All its institutions (including again the university) have to be in tune with the spirit of the nation; indeed, since the university is the nursery for leaders, it is the nation's prime channel for the expression of its soul, together with its literature and its art and music. So when Haldane came to preside over the royal commission on the University of Wales, his encouragement to the University to be distinctive, even un-English, was not just to curry favour for his recommendations for reform; it was consistent with all he had learnt in the Germany (euphoric from the triumph of 1870) of his younger days, about the philosophy of nationhood.

Haldane must often have been told how perplexing some of these concepts were to British audiences, and Webb took him gently to task for some of his views on democracy. The nearest he came to clarifying what he meant by such words as morality was also reminiscent of Hegel. He adjured his audience to cultivate hero-worship. 'Nothing is more stimulating to him who is striving to learn . . . so much as reverence . . . for the personality of a great intellectual and moral hero.' In other words the specification for a high morality and a noble soul is better not put into words, but seen in people. To understand what is meant by the 'soul' of ancient Greece, look with reverence at Socrates. Haldane drew his ethical principles not from the church but from the morality inherent in science and scholarship: a passionate dedication to accuracy as the approximation to truth; a consensus about truth which was truly cosmopolitan (he noticed this vividly after his mission to Germany in 1912); humility, earnestness in seeking knowledge. (He quoted with approval the words of Lessing: that if God were to offer him Truth in one hand and the Search for Truth in the other, he would choose the Search.)

And how do these noble sentiments correspond to Haldane's daily business in Westminster or at Queen Anne's Gate, conspiring, compromising where necessary, identifying himself (though not always very zealously) with party politics? Or at one of Lady Horner's weekend parties, in the high society which Beatrice Webb so heartily despised? Here Hegelian thought had to be reconciled with expediency; here Haldane's social conscience and compassion compelled him to search for the pragmatic, the opportune, solution. But this was not an attitude of hypocrisy.. Indeed it was a neo-Hegelian, Green, who taught that self-realisation cannot be attained except by serving society rather than self. The way to serve society, if one has the gifts, is to enter public life and, as Haldane had to explain to Beatrice Webb, this entailed familiarity with the whole spectrum of society, from country houses to crofters' cottages. Haldane's decision to go into politics was made in a spirit of altruism, not ambition. Having got into politics he had to discover how the philosopher-statesman can work within the system. It is a system hedged about with numerous constraints: the powerful drag of precedent, the massive stability of parliamentary procedure, the prejudices, the conventions. Even if he had wanted revolution, he had the sense to know that revolutions do not benefit society as much as progress through adaptation. So, like a poet who decides to write sonnets in classical form, Haldane set to work to master the techniques for effective political action within the constraints. This he did superbly, and in ways which would not have brought disapproval from his German mentors. For it was Hegel himself who, deeply preoccupied with the fallibility of political systems, saw the need to combine reason with passion in order to achieve political ends. And the ends Haldane sought would certainly have appealed to Hegel. That Haldane himself realised the necessity for compromise is evident from a passage in his appreciation of his old friend Fry. 'He had', Haldane wrote about Fry,

> an intense sense of the necessity of uprightness, and strong conviction that no result could be just in which morality and law appeared to become divorced. So strong was this sense in him that I think it would have actually stood in his way had he sought to exercise his powers in the arena of political life. In that field a certain giving is as essential to success as the most justifiable taking.

What did Haldane achieve? Our portrait, we hope, answers this question. But how much of his achievement is still visible? Our answer to that is that it lies in the foundations of our whole system of education. Without Haldane the University of London would undoubtedly have been reformed; civic universities (though possibly on a different and less flexible pattern) would have multiplied; the Charlottenburg idea or some variant of it would have been adopted; higher education would have been endowed by the state through some sort of University Grants Committee; adult education would have flourished; education by day-release would have appeared; the 1918 Education act would have been put on the statute book. But without Haldane, the style and tenor of all these would, we believe, have been the poorer; and – equally important – all of them would have been delayed. It was Haldane who, patiently over decades, created in the public mind and among politicians a consciousness of the need for quality and balance in education. With the monotonous persistence of the advertising patter on a commercial TV he propagated his beliefs until they became other peoples' beliefs; for example, the quintessence of the German concept of a university, so succinctly put by von Humboldt: that the teacher is not there for the sake of the student – both are there for the sake of knowledge ('beide sind für die Wissenschaft da'); that personal contact between teacher and student is the essence of a university; that students should study in order to *know*, not in order to pass examinations; that it was the duty of a democracy to offer equality of opportunity to learn, but not to appease the masses by any dilution of the criteria for excellence; that a democracy which is not permeated by education will be in danger. The very fact that we take these ideas for granted is evidence of the debt we owe to Haldane, for eighty years ago they were not taken for granted. He did not originate them, but through him they were institutionalised. And another testimony to the endurance of his achievement is that the institutions he helped to create, in order to preserve and promote educational ideals, now do what he, in the beginning, had to do single-handed. They have supplanted the dedicated individual.

And, last, we ask what was it in the man himself which enabled him to achieve so much? Haldane is, wrote Runciman to Churchill, our 'most industrious orator . . . if one may fairly call his formless and endless speeches oratory.' 'The smooth, persuasive voice inundates the House with a flood of words', wrote another observer. Even his ardent admirers, such as the students in Edinburgh, had to confess: 'Unfortunately he has a thin voice. He is no orator. His speeches are more enjoyable in the reading than in the hearing of them.' And as for his writing: 'I know I am a bad writer', he told his friend Gosse; and he told Asquith: 'beastly bad'. Beatrice Webb, always on the look-out for a penetrating generalisation, wrote: 'By common consent Haldane's writings are amateurish and undistinguished in substance and form; if they had not been the writings of a great public personage they would not be read.'

But Haldane was a great public personage, without the charismatic gifts of eloquence or an elegant style. Nor did he capture the imagination of the public through ostentation, like Disraeli, or through asceticism, like Ghandi. He lived well and comfortably as thousands of his contemporaries did. He was genial, generous, humorous, charming; but so were scores of other notables in British society whose names have been forgotten. He had a good mind and a first class memory; but so had many other Victorians who have faded out of the history books. He succumbed to harmless and amiable vanities. He struck some people (including Beatrice Webb when she was still Miss Potter) as pompous. His habit of looking on the bright side of things (*toujours bien, jamais mieux*) was mistaken by some people as complacency. His manner of working in politics – a word slipped in here, another there; an unsigned memorandum delivered on to a minister's desk at just the right moment; a dinner party at which the conversation was directed as inexorably as the moves in a game of chess: in the eyes of some people this was intrigue, all too devious to be trusted.

But Haldane was trusted. This was one ingredient of his success. Over a petition from a university college or an appeal to support adult education (and doubtless over hundreds of private and personal matters) the news that 'Mr Haldane is taking an interest in this' raised hopes and boosted morale. For if Haldane undertook to try to do something, his single-mindedness, his pertinacity, his capacity to mobilise all manner of resources, flattened out obstacles like a steam roller and, very often, left a smooth path which ordinary people could use to reach their goal. Once Haldane had seized upon one of his pre-occupations, no mole could be more persistent; anyone obstructing him knew he was in for a campaign not for a matter of weeks or months, but, if Haldane thought it necessary, for years.

His indefatigable resolution when he pursued a cause would not have been effective, of course, unless he had been a superb administra-'tor. Administration is the art of winning the willing co-operation of hundreds (sometimes thousands) of people to get something done which no individual could do alone. First, the administrator has to be clear in his own mind what he wants to get done. Second, he has to persuade other people that it is worth doing and that they want to help him do it (for successful adminstration depends on consent). Third, since great purposes cannot be achieved except through thousands of small steps, the administrator has to devise a strategy, to make sure that some steps are not taken prematurely (or the project will trip up), that some steps circumvent obstacles rather than try to climb over them, that progress is orderly and consolidated, and – very important – that those who are obliged to concentrate their energies on means never lose sight of the ends. Fourth, there is the supreme importance of timing. To take the right step at the wrong time can be fatal to the enterprise, and only a lively intuition can discern what is the right time. Finally, since the administrator is, as it were, conducting an orchestra in the performance of one of his own works, he must point to the players when he is applauded by the public; for without him they could play but without them he could not conduct. In other words the successful administrator must be self-effacing.

These were the elusive qualities which Haldane possessed in abundance. His sister recognised this; his mind, she wrote, was essentially an administrative one. And this brings us, full circle, to the early days when his personality was shaped by Goethe and Lotze and Hegel; for it has been truly said that administration is not a great strain on the intellect, but it is a very great strain on the character. The secret of

Haldane's achievement was that he understood himself, knew where his capacities lay, believed in everything he undertook to do and was unruffled by delays, serene in setbacks, steadfast in intention. His portrait speaks to us of a lifelong consistency of purpose; a compass set over books of philosophy and followed over forty years in politics. And the one thing that people knew about Haldane's purpose was that it never led him into conflict between personal ambition and the public good. For to work for the public good was his ambition. Elizabeth Haldane, writing to Beatrice Webb after her brother's death, told how so many of the people who had written to her 'speak of his character almost more than of his work as having influenced them'.

The Webbs had a profound influence on Haldane's opinions, for they were disinterested and frank critics, who criticised with genuine affection for him; and access to such criticism is very precious for public men. Their last letter to him is a touching epitaph. By the summer of 1928 his health was breaking up. On 14 August Beatrice wrote:

> . . . Sidney & I frequently talk and think about you and our long years of common effort (some would call it common intrigue!) for the public good. Your sister tells us that you are ordered to give up all sustained public work alike in the judicial & political sphere. That will be a great loss for those particular worlds, but from the point of view of advanced movements I think you are very much more needed as the 'great consultant'. . . .

On 18 August Elizabeth Haldane replied: 'I read a bit of your letter and summarized the rest. He said "Very good sense" & was pleased. But he is terribly weak and I really have no hope of recovery.' On 19 August 1928, Haldane died.

# References

Abbreviations
| | |
|---|---|
| *Autobiography* | R. B. Haldane, *An autobiography* (1929). |
| CAB | Cabinet records, public record office, London. |
| ED | Board of education records, public record office. |
| H.Pp. | Haldane papers, National Library of Scotland. |
| *Maurice* | Frederick Maurice, *Haldane*, 2 vols (1937, 1939). |
| PC | Privy council records, public record office. |
| P.Pp. | Passfield papers, British Library of Political and Economic Science. |
| RECO | Ministry of reconstruction records, public record office. |
| T | Treasury records, public record office. |

The bold figures preceding each source denote the pages, the light figures denote the lines of the text to which they refer.

Introduction

**xiii,** 16. *The nationalisation of universities* (1921) [Address to Old Students' Association, Royal College of Science, 9 Nov 1920].

17. *The ideal of the university* (1920) [Address to first meeting of the reconstructed court of the University of Wales, 25 Nov 1920].

21. *The Times*, 20 Aug 1928.

23. Albert Mansbridge, ibid, 21 Aug 1928.

24. H. Frank Heath, 'Lord Haldane: his influence on higher education and on administration', *Public Administration*, VI (1928) 350–60.

28. Alexander Morgan, 'Lord Haldane' in *Makers of Scottish education* (1929) 242–59.

**xiv,** 9. Frederick Maurice, *Haldane . . . the life of Viscount Haldane of Cloan*, 2 vols (1937, 1939).

15. J. F. Lockwood, 'Haldane and education', *Public Administration*, XXXV (1957) 232–44.

16. Douglas Logan, *Haldane and the University of London* (Haldane Memorial Lecture, 1960).

23. H. J. W. Hetherington, *Theory and practice* (Haldane Memorial Lecture, 1932).

25. J. Duff, *The scale and scope of British universities* (Haldane Memorial Lecture, 1961).

29. Alfred Hopkinson, *Penultima* (1930); J. R. B. Muir, *Ramsay Muir: an autobiography and some essays*, ed. S. Hodgson (1943).

30. F. J. C. Hearnshaw, *The centenary history of King's College, London, 1828–1928* (1929).

32. Ref. **xiv**, 16.
34. Michael Sadleir, *Michael Ernest Sadler* (1949).
38. H. Hale Bellot, *The University of London: a history* (1969).

**xv,** 2. H. J. W. Hetherington, *The life and letters of Sir Henry Jones* (1924).
12. Almeric Fitzroy, *Memoirs* (1925); H. A. L. Fisher, *An unfinished auto-biography* (1940).

Chapter 1: Appointment with Mr Haldane

**1,** 5. Violet Bonham Carter, 'Haldane of Cloan', *The Times*, 30 Jul 1956;
B. Webb, *Beatrice Webb's diaries, 1924–1932*, ed. M. Cole (1956) 31.
15. Austen Chamberlain, *Politics from inside* (1936) 325.
17. Edmund Gosse, quoted Dudley Sommer, *Haldane of Cloan* (1960) 154.
20. A. G. Gardiner, 'Robert [sic] Burdon Haldane' in *Prophets, priests and kings* (1908) 204–12.
24. B. Webb to E. S. Haldane, 14 Aug 1928, H.Pp., 5917; copy, P.Pp., II, 5.

**2,** 5. *Maurice*, I, 57.
9. Ref. **I**, 17; p. 218.
35. B. Webb, diary, 6 Jan 1927; P.Pp., I, 2, vol. 41.

**3,** 5. Ref. **I**, 20.
17. Ibid.
31. Christopher Addison, *Politics from within* (1924) I, 60.
33. John Buchan, 'Lord Haldane' in *Comments and characters*, ed. W. Forbes Gray (1940) 315–19.
n. Albert Mansbridge, *The trodden road* (1940) 149.

**4,** 6. H. G. Wells, *Experiment in autobiography* (1934) 766.
20. 4 Aug 1928; H.Pp., 6032; copy, P.Pp., II, 5.
33. *Autobiography*, p. 170.

**5,** 12. An aside, whilst taking evidence during a session of the royal commission on the University of London in March 1912: *Univ. educ. in London, R. com., appx. to final rept.*, q.15746; 1913 [Cd 6718] XL.
18. *Autobiography*, p. 5.
34. 'The conduct of life' in *The conduct of life and other addresses* (1914) 3–27 [Address to the associated societies of the University of Edinburgh on 14 Nov 1913].

**6,** 27. 27 Apr 1874, H.Pp., 5027; quoted *Maurice*, I, 18.
40. *Maurice*, I, 20.

**7,** 15. Ref. **6,** 27.
17. 30 Apr 1874; H.Pp., 5927.
35. *Maurice*, I, 18.

**8,** 9. Ibid., I, 20–1.
30. 'The soul of a people' in *Universities and national life* (1911) 1–32.

**9,** 8. *Maurice*, I, 23.
12. A. Seth Pringle-Pattison, 'Richard Burdon Haldane', *Proceedings of the British Academy*, XIV (1928) 410.
25. *Autobiography*, p. 8.

**10,** 10. Haldane to Asquith, 22 Jan 1923, 18 Oct 1926; Asquith Pp., 18.
31. Quoted Samuel Hynes, *The Edwardian turn of mind* (1968).

**11,** 4. Ibid.

  12. *Maurice,* I, 55.

  23. Ibid., I, 33; *Daily Herald,* 5 Feb 1920.

**12,** 4. *The future of democracy* (1918) [Address to WEA, Coventry branch, 13 Apr 1918].

  7. Cf. address to 'Eighty' Club at Cambridge in May 1904: *Constructive liberalism* (1904).

  8. Cf. speech in house of lords: *H. L. Debs,* 9 Dec 1924, col. 21.

  9. Cf. Haldane to Balfour, 16 Apr 1905: 'Thank God we are not all of one Party in the State – otherwise I should despair of the power to resist slumbrousness'; Balfour Pp., Add. MS. 49724.

  10. Cf. 'The dedicated life' in *Universities and national life* (1911) 65-110 [Rectorial address to University of Edinburgh, 10 Jan 1907].

**13,** 10. Quoted, R. F. W. Heuston, 'Lord Haldane' in *Lives of the lord chancellors, 1885-1940* (Oxford, 1964) 200.

  24. Address to 'Eighty' Club, May 1891: *Social problems* (1891).

  33. *Maurice,* I, 49-50.

  37. *H. L. Debs,* 24 Jul 1918, col. 1136.

**14,** 6. Ibid., 12 Jul 1916, col. 681.

**15,** 29. *Autobiography,* p. 115.

**16,** 32. Matthew Arnold, *Higher schools and universities in Germany* (1882).

**17,** 27. Ref. **15,** 29.

**18,** 17. Robert R. James, *Rosebery* (1963) 203.

  24. *Maurice,* I, 49-50.

  34. *Autobiography,* p. 107.

**19,** 4. B. Webb, *Our Partnership* (1948) 32.

  28. Kenneth Young, *Arthur James Balfour* (1963) 143.

**20,** 4. *Maurice,* I, 50.

  28. Kitty Muggeridge and Ruth Adams, *Beatrice Webb: a life, 1858-1943* (1967) 124.

  36. 25 Jul 1891, P.Pp., II, 1 (11) 218; 16 Jan 1898, II, 4a, 76.

**21,** 1. 27 Dec 1891, diary; P.Pp., I, 2, vol. 14.

  18. *Maurice,* I, 55.

  24. *Our partnership,* p. 98.

  30. John Simon, *Retrospect: the memoirs of the Rt Hon. Viscount Simon* (1952) 46.

Chapter 2: Apprenticeship

**22,** 8. J. I. Macpherson, *Twenty-one years of corporate life at Edinburgh University* (Edinburgh, 1905) 88; see also Eric Ashby and Mary Anderson, *The rise of the student estate in Britain* (1970) 32ff.

  32. *H. C. Debs,* 20 Jun 1889, col. 352.

**23,** 13. Ibid., cols 348-53.

**26,** 1. Ibid., 9 May 1892, cols 449-54.

**27,** 17. Janet Beveridge, *An epic of Clare Market* (1960) 11.

**29,** 26. Sir Charles Russell, at a meeting of the 'Eighty' Club in Cambridge in 1891; *Social problems* (1891).

  28. *The Student,* XI no. 3 (5 Nov 1896) 33-4.

**30,** 25. Ref. **29,** 26.

27. *Our partnership*, p. 98.

**31,** 7. 30 Apr 1891; H.Pp., 5903; P.Pp., II, 5.

11. 25 Jul 1891; ibid.

**33,** 33. *Maurice*, I, 78.

34. Ibid.

**34,** 2. 15 Jan 1897, Allchin Pp.; quoted, Douglas Logan, *Haldane and the University of London* (1960).

30. M. A. Hamilton, *Sidney and Beatrice Webb: a study in contemporary biography* (1932) 130.

**35,** 1. *Our partnership*, pp. 99–100.

7. Ibid., p. 102.

32. 3 Jul 1897; ED 24/5.

35. Ref. **35,** 7.

**36,** 12. Balfour Pp., Add. MS. 49724, quoted (without date) *Maurice*, I, 79.

29. H.Pp., 5904.

**37,** 8. *Autobiography*, p. 126.

27. *H. C. Debs*, 14 Jun 1898, cols 257–67.

37. *Autobiography*, p. 127.

**38,** 9. Henry Labouchere; *H. C. Debs*, 25 Jul 1898, col.1192.

38. Confidential print of memorandum by Haldane: 'The Irish question', 20 Oct 1898; Balfour Pp., Add. MS. 49724.

**39,** 12. 15 Oct 1898; H.Pp., 5960.

20. ED 24/5.

30. Haldane to Fitzroy, 9 Jul 1897, ED 24/5.

35. W. A. S. Hewins, *The apologia of an imperialist* (1929) I, 24.

**40,** 10. PC 8/510.

20. Haldane to Webb, 2 Nov 1903; P.Pp., II, 4a, 18.

25. *H. L. Debs*, 29 Jun 1926, col. 636.

28. *The nationalisation of universities* (1921).

Chapter 3: Co-conspirators

**42,** 30. 'Great Britain and Germany: a study in education' in *Education and empire* (1902) 1–38 [Address at Liverpool, Oct 1901].

**43,** 15. Matthew Arnold, *Higher schools and universities in Germany* (1882) 152.

25. *Autobiography*, p. 87.

32. Cf. his addresses at Liverpool and Dumfries in 1901, published in *Education and empire* (1902).

**44,** 25. 30 Dec 1902; H.Pp., 5905.

**45,** 4. Transcript of proceedings before the committee of council, 18 Dec 1902, q.238; PC 8/605/89731.

24. 'Universities and the schools in Scotland' in *Education and empire* (1902) 39–87; cf. ref. **42,** 30.

n. Friedrich Paulsen, *The German universities and university study*, Eng. ed. (1906) 113ff.

**46,** 36. 5 May 1902; H.Pp., 5905.

**47,** 5. 21 Jul 1902; ibid.

15. 1 Jun 1902; ibid.

25. *Maurice*, I, 112.
31. W. T. Stead, *The Right Hon. R. B. Haldane, K.C., M.P.* (Coming men on coming questions, VII, (1905)).
34. 10 May 1905; *Mining Journal*, 13 May 1905, ED 24/530.
**48,** 4. *Maurice*, I, 129.
18. P.Pp., II, 4b, 25.
22. Ibid., II, 4b, 28.
23. Haldane to Thursfield, 26 Sep 1901; H.Pp., 5905.
**49,** 22. 'Lord Rosebery's escape from Houndsditch', *Nineteenth Century*, L (1901) 366–86.
26. Cf. Haldane to B. Webb, 15 Sep 1901; P.Pp., II, 4b, 27.
40. 25 Apr 1902; *Our partnership*, p. 233.
**50,** 10. *Maurice*, I, 120.
**51,** 17. 9 May 1902; P.Pp., II, 4b, 36.
22. Ref. **50,** 10.
28. Diary, 28 May 1902; *Memoirs* (1925).
35. Fitzroy, diary, 25 June 1902; ibid.
**52,** 6. P.Pp., II, 4b, 63.
16. Lord Rosebery to Lord Monkswell, 27 Jun 1903, pubd in T. L. Humberstone, *University reform in London* (1926) appx I, pp. 167–71.
22. Minutes of LCC, 15 Jul 1903; ED 24/531.
26. B. Webb, *Our partnership*, p. 271.
**53,** 21. 'Memorandum on the proposed College of Technology'; ED 24/529. The printed copy preserved in the board of education bears a pencilled heading 'Mr Haldane's'.
**54,** 9. Morant to Mowatt, 25 Oct 1903, and to the president, 23 Jan 1904; ibid.
27. Ibid.
34. Lord Londonderry, at the annual dinner of the Institution of Mining and Metallurgy, 10 May 1905; ref. **47,** 34.
36. R. Coll, Sci., *Dept cttee prelim. rept;* 1905 [Cd 2610] LXI.
37. R. Coll. Sci., *Dept cttee final rept;* 1906 [Cd 2872] XXXI.
**55,** 14. *Univ. educ. in Ireland, appx to 2nd rept,* pp. 107–15 *passim*; 1902 [Cd 1900] XXXI.
**56,** 4. Uncorrected proof of minutes of conference between the departmental committee and representatives of the University of London, University College, and King's College, on 7 Jul 1905; ED 24/555.
8. ED 24/530.
10. Ibid.
15. Haldane to Morant, 26 Jun 1905; ED 24/530.
20. *Morning Post*, 3 Jul 1905; ED 24/530.
22. *The Times*, 3 Jul 1905.
**57,** 3. Ref. **56,** 4.
35. Ref. **54,** 37; paras 90–4.
**58,** 21. ED 24/530.
26. ED 24/529.

Chapter 4: Above the snow-line
**59,** 29. *H. C. Debs*, 16 Feb 1898, col.791.

**60,** 12. 20 Oct, 23 Dec 1898; Balfour Pp., Add. MS. 49724

15. *Autobiography*, pp. 132-3.

21. Ibid., pp. 133-4.

29. Ibid., p. 139.

**61,** 35. Matthew Arnold, *Higher schools and universities in Germany* (1882) 220.

40. *U.Cs Grants, Try cttee, rept by inspectors*, 31 Dec 1896; 1897 [245] LXX.

**62,** 7. H. C. Debs, 25 Jul 1898, col.1229.

10. 'Birmingham University', 23 Mar 1900; enclosure in memo to chancellor, 5 Dec 1900; T 1/9653B/3328/1901.

12. *Autobiography*, p. 139.

21. Petition of lord mayor of Birmingham and others, lodged with privy council, 24 Jun 1899; PC 8/516/82963.

26. Liverpool case, part 5; PC 8/605/89344.

**63,** 6. 'Great Britain and Germany' in *Education and empire* (1902) 32.

14. *The Times*, 23 Oct 1901.

n. Liverpool case, p. 77; ref. **62,** 26.

**64,** 14. *Maurice*, I, 140.

24. Confidential print, 12 Jul 1902; PC 8/605/88704.

37. Haldane to Chamberlain, 14 Aug 1902; Joseph Chamberlain Pp., JC 11/15/2.

**65,** 1. *Autobiography*, p. 141.

10. Ibid., p. 145.

16. Fitzroy, diary, 19 Dec 1902; *Memoirs*.

37. Transcript of shorthand notes of evidence, 17 Dec 1902, q.196; PC 8/605/89719.

**66,** 12. Ibid., 18 Dec 1902, qs 201, 202; PC 8/605/89731.

21. Ibid., q.208.

32. Ibid., q.216.

**67,** 8. Liverpool case, p. 75ff.; ref. **62,** 26.

19. Evidence, 19 Dec 1902, q.639.

22. Ibid., q.481.

30. Fitzroy, diary, 19 Dec 1902; *Memoirs*.

34. Ibid., 6 Feb 1903.

38. Ibid.

**68,** 2. Agnes Fry, *A memoir of the Rt hon. Sir Edward Fry* (1929) 137.

12. Order in Council, 16 Feb 1903.

20. Diary, 18 Feb 1903; *Memoirs*.

27. 'The civic university' in *The conduct of life and other addresses* (1914) 63-95 [Address delivered in Oct 1912].

39. Fitzroy to the duke of Devonshire, 14 Jan 1903; Harold Cohen Library, Univ. of Liverpool, MS. 2.96(13).

**69,** 11. Haldane to Fitzroy, 3 Apr 1903; ibid., MS. 2.96 (28).

19. *Memoirs*.

27. Enclosure to memo on Liverpool and Manchester draft charters, of 7 May 1903; PC 8/605/90602.

**70,** 19. PC 8/605/94286.

26. Fitzroy, diary, 29 May 1905; *Memoirs*.

33. *Maurice*, I, 144.

39. P. 90.

**71,** 8. Alfred Hopkinson, *Penultima* (1930) 122.

13. J. R. B. Muir, *Ramsay Muir: an autobiography and some essays*, ed. S. Hodgson (1943) 48.

19. *Our partnership*, p. 247.

**72,** 5. P. 146.

11. 11 Aug 1902; H.Pp., 5905.

32. Haldane to Joseph Chamberlain, 18 Sep 1902; Joseph Chamberlain Pp., JC 11/15/3.

37. 18 Sep 1902; H.Pp., 5905.

**73,** 2. J. L. Garvin and J. Amery, *The life of Joseph Chamberlain*, VI, (1969) 516.

8. Cf. Haldane in his address to the 'Eighty' Club at Cambridge in May 1904; *Constructive liberalism* (1904).

29. 'The making of a university', *Cornhill*, XIV (Jan – Jun 1903) 530–40.

37. *Autobiography*, p. 146.

**74,** 7. 'National education' in *After-war problems*, ed. W. H. Dawson (1917) 81.

16. *H. C. Debs*, 14 Jun 1898, col.233f.

34. Ref. **67,** 8.

**75,** 8. Introduction to Norman Lockyer, *Education and national progress: essays and addresses, 1870–1905* (1906).

22. 3 Feb 1901; T 1/9653B/3328/1901.

**76,** 4. 14 Aug 1902; Joseph Chamberlain Pp., JC 11/15/2.

8. 12 Mar 1905; ibid., JC 11/15/4.

31. Transcript of notes of reply by the chancellor, 17 Feb 1904; T 1/10215B/3211/1904.

**77,** 38. T 1/10370/22413/1905.

**78,** 18. Ibid.

31. *U.Cs Grants, Try cttee, 3rd rept;* 1905 [Cd 2422] LX.

**79,** 33. Confidential print, 17 Mar 1905; CAB 37/75.

**80,** 4. 'Observations by Mr Higgs', 31 May 1905; analysis of replies from university colleges by R. G. Hawtrey, 27 May 1905; T 1/10370/22413/1905.

7. Memo by Murray, 27 Jun 1905, ibid.; Try minute, 1905 [Cd 2621] LX.

33. *H. L. Debs*, 6 July 1915, col. 275.

36. Ibid., 31 Jul 1918, col. 218.

**81,** 30. Fitzroy, diary, 28 May 1902; *Memoirs*.

**82,** 8. *H. C. Debs*, 24 Mar 1902, col. 900; 5 May 1902, col. 703.

28. Ibid., 8 May 1908.

31. 'The education bill: a symposium', *Nineteenth Century*, LII (Jul – Dec 1902) 602–24.

35. *H. C. Debs*, 6 May 1902.

**83,** 4. *The Times*, 9 May 1902.

8. B. Webb, diary, 21 Jul 1902; *Our partnership*, p. 245; cf. ref. **82,** 31.

25. Ibid., 25 Apr 1902; p. 233.

31. Ibid., pp. 244–5.

36. P.Pp., IV.

**84,** 17. Enclosure in Haldane to B. Webb, 2 Oct 1902; P.Pp., II, 4b, 44.

20. Haldane to B. Webb, 2 Nov 1902; ibid., II, 4b, 47.

23. *Our partnership*, pp. 248–9.
28. Dated '30 Jan 1903' but seemingly in error for 3 Jan; P.Pp., II, 4b, 63.
31. 7 Jan 1903; ibid., II, 4b, 56.
32. *Our partnership*, p. 257.
34. Ibid., pp. 257–8.
38. P.Pp., II, 4b, 72.

**85,**  2. Ibid., II, 4b, 74.
6. Ibid., II, 4b, 76.
8. *Our partnership*, p. 263.
17. 18 Apr 1903; P.Pp., II, 4b, 93.
28. H. C. *Debs*, 28 Apr 1903, col. 703.
35. Yoxall, ibid.
39. *Our partnership*, p. 265.


Chapter 5: At the cabinet table
**86,**  6. *The Student*, no. 378 (2 Nov 1905) 26.
7. Ibid., NS, XI (1913–14) 84.
11. Ibid., NS, IV (1906–7) 371.
22. Ibid., NS, IV special Union no. (2 Nov 1906) 41.
29. 15 Sep 1901; P.Pp., II, 4b.
**87,** 12. *Autobiography*, p. 170.
14. *Our partnership*, pp. 325–6.
27. L. S. Amery, *My political life* (1953) 227.
30. Osbert Sitwell, *Laughter in the next room* (1949) 98.
**88,**  3. *Autobiography*, p. 262.
32. Alex Hill to Selby-Bigge, private, 6 May 1913; ED 24/1941.
**89,**  2. Haldane to Selby-Bigge, 9 May 1913; ibid.
5. 13 Jun 1914; ibid.
27. See above p. 63.
29. 5 Feb 1902; *University for the West of England* (Bristol, 1902).
**90,** 17. Morris W. Travers, *Autobiography* (unpubd typescript): Bristol Univ. Library, DM 389.
**91,** 10. PC 8/618/95729. The memorandum was minuted by Crewe: 'I agree'; and copies were transmitted to Birrell, at the board of education, and to Haldane. Cf. ED 24/511; ED 24/514.
28. Fitzroy to the lord president, 13 Nov 1908; PC 8/672/101390.
30. Appended note, ibid.
35. Runciman to Fitzroy, 15 Dec 1908; PC 8/172/101635.
**92,**  4. Minute by Fitzroy, 16 Dec 1908, and by Haldane, 21 Dec 1908; ibid.
21. Ibid.
25. 22 Mar 1909; ibid.
**93,**  2. 'The civic university' in *The conduct of life and other addresses* (1914) 63–95.
20. *Civil Service, R. com.*, appx to first rept, q.1761; 1912–13 [Cd 6210] xv.
**94,** 25. Asquith Pp., 10.
**95,**  7. *U.Cs Grants, Try cttee, rept*, p. 7; 1909 [182] LXIX.
14. Secretary, board of education, to treasury, 17 Dec 1908; T 1/10942A/22002/1908.

17. Morant to Murray, 17 Dec 1908; ibid.

33. T. L. Heath to Murray, 14 Jan 1909; ibid.

**96,** 4. Cf. H. F. Heath, 'Outline of the history of the transfer of the Treasury Grants to the Board of Education', 24 Jan 1912; ED 24/1938.

11. ED 24/567.

16. V. Nash to Runciman, 30 Jul 1910; ED 24/519.

38. Ibid.

**97,** 16. 9 Jan 1912; ED 24/519.

22. Ref. **96,** 4.

27. Murray to Runciman, 21 Apr 1911; ED 24/568.

35. Runciman to Murray, 23 May 1911; T 1/11525/4849/1913.

**98,** 1. ED 24/519.

27. Ibid.

33. Ibid.

**99,** 3. Ibid.

17. Minute by Pease; 11 Jan 1912; ED 24/1938.

24. Selby-Bigge to Pease, 25 Jan 1912; ibid.

36. 1 Feb 1912; ibid.

40. 2 Feb 1912; ibid.

**100,** 10. T. L. Heath to the secretary, board of education, 21 Feb 1912; T 1/11525/4849/1913.

32. Diary, 27 Feb 1912; Austen Chamberlain, *Politics from inside* (1936) 429.

**101,** 39. F. G. Ogilvie to Morant, 1 Sep 1906; ED 24/532.

**102,** 9. Morant to Sir William White, 1 Nov 1906; ED 24/531.

11. J. Sykes to Morant, strictly confidential, 13 Feb 1907; ibid.

23. Private, 15 May 1906; ibid.

29. Ref. **102,** 11.

35. 13 Feb 1907; ED 24/531.

40. McKenna to Sir Francis Mowatt, 19 Feb 1907; ibid.

**103,** 2. 21 Feb 1907; ibid.

10. B. Webb, diary, 19 May 1908; *Our partnership*, p. 411.

14. Morant to G. E. Buckle, 16 Feb 1909; ED 24/174.

25. Webb to Haldane, 3 Feb 1909; ibid.

32. Webb to Morant, 5 Feb 1909; ibid.

**104,** 1. Morant to Haldane, 4 Feb 1909; ibid.

3. Ibid.

5. Morant to Webb, 5 Feb 1909; ibid.

14. Abraham Flexner, *I remember* (New York, 1940) 140ff.

18. Ref. **103,** 14.

25. *Univ. educ. in London, R. com., final rept*, p. 26; 1913 [Cd 6717] XL.

36. Cf. *H. L. Debs*, 29 Jun 1926; col. 637.

**105,** 9. *Univ. educ. in London, R. com., final rept*, q.15809; 1913 [Cd 6718] XL.

14. *Univ. educ. in Wales, R. com., appx to 2nd rept*, q.8898; 1917–18 [Cd 8699] XII.

17. Ibid., *appx to final rept*, q.13973; 1918 [Cd 8993] XIV.

21. *Univ. educ. in London, R. com., appx to 3rd rept*, q.10130; 1911 [Cd 5911] XX.

25. Ibid., q.7807.

**107,**   9. Ref. **105,** 9; paras 64, 65, 69.

**109,**   4. Ibid., para. 85.

24. Ibid., para. 395.

28. Ibid., para. 291.

**110,**   3. Ibid., para. 403.

17. Ibid., para. 410.

25. Cf. letters to his mother, e.g. 20 Nov 1912; H.Pp., 5988; also *Maurice,* I, 325.

29. H. H. Bellot, *The University of London: a history* (1969) 21.

39. Q.4639; 1911 [Cd 5528] xx.

**111,**   4. Q.4291; ibid.

13. 17 Apr 1913; H. Pp., 5989.

15. *T.E.S.,* 6 May 1913.

28. *The Times,* 21 Apr 1913.

35. *H. C. Debs,* 17 Jul 1913, col. 1420.

40. Minute by J. A. Pease, president of the board of education, 14 Aug 1913; ED 24/1171.

**112,**   5. First report, 20 Apr 1914; ibid.

13. Webb to Haldane, 19 May 1914; ED 24/2019.

15. Ibid.

**113,**   4. 'Universities and schools in Scotland' in *Education and empire* (1902) 39–87.

9. *University for the West of England* (1920).

10. *The Times,* 12 Sep 1903.

13. Ibid., 12 Nov 1904.

26. Confidential print, 'Education Bill: Cabinet Committee', 12 Jan 1906; CAB 37/82.

32. *Autobiography,* p. 219; cf. Fitzroy, diary, 25 Apr 1906; *Memoirs.*

**114,**   5. *National education: speeches . . . delivered at the 'Eighty' Club Dinner, April 4 1913* (1913).

9. *Lord Haldane's education proposals: from Lord Haldane's speech before the Manchester Reform Club . . . 10th January 1913* (1913).

14. Cf. Pease to Selby-Bigge, confidential, 5 Dec 1912; ED 24/628. The first meeting was held in Haldane's room at the house of lords on 19 December; ibid. The appointment of the committee was disclosed in *The Times* on 24 January 1913, and attracted further comment in the 'Political Notes' of that paper on 25 April.

23. Selby-Bigge to Pease, confidential, 6 Dec 1912; ED 24/628.

**115,**   1. Ibid.

6. 9 [sic for 10] Jan 1913; H.Pp., 5989.

22. Ref. **114,** 9.

39. C. P. Scott, diary, 16 Jan 1913; *Political diaries* (1970) 68–9.

**116,**   6. 10 Mar 1913; H.Pp., 5989

9. *H. C. Debs,* 17 Mar 1913.

28. *The Times,* 31 Mar 1913; *T. E. S.,* 1 Apr 1913; ref. **114,** 5.

34. Draft bill, 26 Apr 1913; ED 24/638.

36. 1 May 1913; ED 24/628.

**117,**   4. 4 May 1913; ibid.

7. Haldane to Selby-Bigge, 9 May 1913; ibid.
14. *H. C. Debs*, 22 Jul 1913, col. 1907.
16. Sir James Yoxall; ibid., col. 1944.
19. ED 24/638.
32. ED 24/628.
36. Ibid.

**118,** 5. Haldane to Lloyd George, 26 Apr 1914; Lloyd George Pp., C 4/17/6.
22. *The inwardness of the budget; speeches delivered by the Rt Hon. Viscount Haldane . . . and the Rt Hon. D. Lloyd George at the National Liberal Club on June 26, 1914* (1914).
33. C. Addison, *Four and a half years* (1934).

**119,** 3. Ibid.
5. Diary, 11 Dec 1914; ibid.
18. C. Addison, *Politics from within* (1924) 48.
19. Addison to Pease, 20 Mar 1915; ED 24/1581.
24. Diary, 30 Mar 1915; ref. **118,** 33.
28. Cf. J. A. Pease 'Proposals for a national scheme of instruction and research in science, technology and commerce', 6 Apr 1915; confidential print, ED 24/1581 (also pubd, with minor changes, refs **118,** 33; **119,** 18.)
33. Cf. Selby-Bigge to Addison, 18 Jun 1915; ED 24/1576.

**120,** 8. *The Times*, 11 Jun 1912.
17. Quoted Koss, *Lord Haldane*, p. 90.


Chapter 6: On the periphery of power
**121,** 13. Fitzroy, *Memoirs*.
19. Haldane to Webb, 27 Jul 1891; P.Pp., II, 2, 33.
23. C. P. Scott, *Political diaries*.

**122,** 5. M. Belloc Lowndes, *A passing world* (1948) 130.
10. H.Pp., 5912; copy, P.Pp., II, 5.
17. Quoted Heuston, 'Lord Haldane' in *Lives of the lord chancellors*, pp. 183–240.
21. P.Pp., II, 4g, 14.
30. Selby-Bigge to Fitzroy, 16 Jul 1915; PC 8/1129.
34. Haldane to Lloyd George, 4 Apr 1916; Lloyd George Pp., B 17/1/1.

**123,** 14. A. J. P. Taylor, *English history 1914–1945* (Oxford, 1965) 73.
18. *Maurice*, II, 45.
21. H.Pp., 5997.
25. 15/16 Mar 1917; *Political diaries*.
32. ED 119/82.

**125,** 2. *Univ. educ. in Wales, R. com., final rept*, p. 24; 1918 [Cd 8991] XIV.
9. *H. C. Debs*, 16 Jun 1899, col. 1388.
13. 'The soul of a people' in *Universities and national life* (1911) 1–32.
22. *T.E.S.*, 6 Jun 1916.
34. Haldane to Gosse, 2 Jul 1916; Gosse Pp.
39. *H. L. Debs*, 24 Jul 1918, col 1136.

**126,** 3. 28 Jun 1916; Lloyd George Pp., I 2/2/46.

19. Qs 6817, 6818: *Univ. educ. in Wales, R. com., appx to 2nd rept;* 1917–18 [Cd 8699] XII.

25. Q.5191; ibid.

**127,** 18. *The ideal of the university* (1920).

32. Ref. **125,** 2; para. 176.

**128,** 2. Ref. **127,** 18.

24. Ref. **125,** 2; para. 105.

38. Qs 14003ff., *appx to final rept;* 1918 [Cd 8993] XIV.

**129,** 13. Ref. **125,** 2; para. 190.

18. Ref. **127,** 18.

33. Q.12222; *appx to final rept.*

**130,** 7. *The University and the Welsh democracy* (1922) [Address delivered at the Central Hall, Swansea on 25 Nov 1921].

23. *T.E.S.,* 22 Aug 1918.

17. C. Addison, diary, 19 Mar 1915; *Four and a half years* (1934) I, 70.

**131,** 3. *T.E.S.,* 22 Aug 1918.

9. H. J. W. Hetherington, *The life and letters of Sir Henry Jones* (1924).

13. ED 24/2026.

15. PC 8/890.

21. *T.E.S.,* 24 Oct 1918.

27. D. Emrys Evans, *The University of Wales: a historical sketch* (Cardiff, 1953) 84.

37. Gosse Pp.

**132,** 15. *H. L. Debs,* 12 Jul 1916, col. 668.

26. MS diary, 7 Apr 1916; P.Pp., I, I, vol. 33.

**133,** 23 *The student and the nation* (1916).

38. Ref. **135,** 27; col. 679.

**134,** 17. *H. C. Debs,* 9 Aug 1917, cols 561–2.

25. 5 Apr 1916; H.Pp., 6012.

29. 4 Apr 1916; Lloyd George Pp., D 17/1/1.

40. Ibid., D 17/1/2.

**135,** 5. Memo by V. Nash, 8 May 1916; RECO 1/14/27.

8. 'Notes on the proposal for a Royal Commission on Education', 29 May 1916; enclosed in Selby-Bigge to V. Nash, 31 May 1916: ED 24/1173; RECO 1/14/56.

12. Extract from conclusions of meeting of 23 Jun, transmitted to the board of education on 11 Jul; RECO 1/14/73.

24. 22 May 1916; quoted Koss, *Lord Haldane,* p. 229.

27. *H. L. Debs,* 12 Jul 1916, cols 655–705.

**136,** 13. Adjourned debate; ibid., 26 Jul 1916.

25. 13 Jul 1916; *The Times,* 14 Jul 1916.

35. 15 Jul 1916; Michael Sadleir, *Michael Ernest Sadler* (1949) 273.

40. RECO 1/14/168.

**139,** 9. Arthur Henderson; *H. C. Debs,* 18 Jul 1916, col. 975.

11. Ref. **136,** 40.

19. Gosse Pp.

20. Cf. Haldane to Gosse, 5 Sep 1916; ibid.

27. Ref. **136,** 40.

35. Undated memo by V. Nash, ibid.

**140,** 1. Haldane to Gosse, 11 Aug 1916; Gosse Pp.

7. 'Confidential. The reform of our system of education', 17 Aug 1916; ED 24/1461. Cf. Haldane to Gosse, 18 Aug 1916; Gosse Pp.

29. Gosse Pp.

33. Ibid.

37. *H. C. Debs*, 10 Oct 1916, col. 15.

**141,** 3. Ref. **136**, 40.

14. *Diaries, 1912–1924* (1952) 98.

16. Cf. minutes of meetings; ED 24/1461, ED 24/1473.

19. RECO 1/14/534; second draft [6 Dec 1916] ED 24/1473.

**142,** 6. ED 24/1473. Cf. RP No. 6, Confidential, Board of Education, 'Development of the National System of Education', initialled L.A.S.B., Dec 1916; ED 24/1461.

9. 'Comments on Memorandum of 6 Dec', initialled L.A.S.B., 7 Dec 1916; ED 24/1473.

22. H. W. Orange. 'Remarks on a Memo. unsigned and undated, recd on Dec 12 1916'; ibid.

30. Extract from minutes of meeting of war cabinet, 15 Feb 1917; RECO 1/40.

36. *T.E.S.*, 1 Feb 1917.

**143,** 3. Cf. Haldane's acknowledgement, 28 May 1915; Fisher Pp.

8. *Maurice*, II, 45–6.

11. H. A. L. Fisher, *An unfinished autobiography* (1940) 95.

32. Lloyd George Pp., F 22/5/1.

**144,** 1. *T.E.S.*, 11 Jan 1917.

4. Ibid., 18 Jan 1917.

11. *H. C. Debs*, 19 Apr 1917, col. 1910.

15. Address to representative managers of LCC schools on 23 Apr 1917; *T.E.S.*, 26 Apr 1917.

17. *H. L. Debs*, 9 May 1917, col. 2.

**145,** 6. *H. C. Debs*, 10 Aug 1917, col. 795.

10. 13 Aug 1917; Fisher Pp.

16. 23 Aug 1917; Gosse Pp.

20. *T.E.S.*, 4, 18, 25 Oct 1917.

26. Ibid., 15 Nov 1917.

n. Ref. 145, 10; ref. 144, 17.

**146,** 8. *H. C. Debs*, 14 Jan 1918, col. 55.

13. 4 Jul 1918, Fisher Pp.

22. *H. L. Debs*, 24 Jul 1918, col. 1131.

28. Ibid., col. 1140.

**147,** 15. Selby-Bigge to Haldane, personal, 21 Aug 1917: enclosure in Haldane to Gosse, 23 Aug 1917; Gosse Pp.

Chapter 7: Ebb-tide

**148,** 9. 15 Nov 1925; P.Pp., I, 2, vol. 39.

11. 6 Jan 1927; ibid., I, 2, vol. 41.

12. 30 Mar 1926; *Diaries, 1924–32* (1956) 87.

30. 12 Aug 1926; P.Pp., 1, 2, vol. 40.

**149,** 5. 'The portrait of a lady', *Observer*, 28 Mar 1926.
   9. 30 Mar 1926, *Diaries, 1924–1932*, p. 86; and further reflections, ref. **148,** 30.
   21. Ref. **148,** 12.

**150,** 1. *Maurice*, II, 77.
   3. Ibid., p. 114.
   16. 30 Sep 1918; W. R. Inge, *Diary of a dean* (1949) 47.
   18. 9 Jul 1918; ibid.
   29. 13 May 1919, enclosed in T. Jones to M. Hankey, 14 May 1919; Lloyd George Pp., F 23/4/62.

**151,** 24. Fisher to Bonar Law, 19 Dec 1918; T 1/12324/20290/1919.
   30. Ibid.
   36. Ibid.

**152,** 8. See above, p. 100; cf. R. O. Berdahl, *British universities and the state* (1959) 57–8.
   10. ED 24/1968.
   19. H. A. L. Fisher, *An unfinished autobiography* (1940) 116.
   27. *H. L. Debs*, 21 Jul 1920, col. 399.
   34. Draft to Snowden, undated and marked 'Not sent'; ED 24/1977.
   40. Roy Jenkins, *Asquith* (1964) 483.

**153,** 5. Quoted Koss, *Lord Haldane*, p. 237.
   9. *H. L. Debs*, 19 Apr 1923, cols 741–8.
   25. PC 8/1001.
   32. Memo by A. H. Kidd, 26 Jul 1918, on the request from the 'Committee for the furtherance of University Education in the South-West' to send a deputation to the president of the board of education; ED 24/1946.
   33. Minutes of proceedings of the deputation, 12 Nov 1918; ibid.
   40. Fitzroy to McCormick, 10 Jan, 11 Apr 1921; PC 8/1075.

**154,** 10. 14 May 1923, *Memoirs*.
   23. *H. L. Debs*, 8 Feb 1922, cols 66–77.

**156,** 1. *Maurice*, II, 77.
   5. Ibid., pp. 114–15; *The Times*, 15 Jun 1922.
   13. 26 Nov 1921; *The University and the Welsh democracy* (1922).
   28. 16 Jan 1922, Asquith Pp.; quoted *Maurice*, II, 108–9.
   38. Haldane to B. Webb, 23 Jan 1925; P.Pp., II, 4h, 26.

**157,** 35. 'Educational reform: general proposals'; Lloyd George Pp., F. 77.
   37. Enclosure to confidential print on 'London University' drawn up by Fisher and circulated to the cabinet on 1 Aug 1918; ED 24/2007.

**158,** 10. Ibid.
   12. Ibid.
   16. 'London University: memorandum by Mr H. A. L. Fisher' 1 Nov 1918; ibid.
   18. E. C. Perry, vice-chancellor, University of London, to Kidd, board of education, 18 Jan 1919; ED 24/2019.
   19. ED 24/1196.
   n. ED 24/2007.

**159,** 11. Ref. **158,** 19.

13. Ibid.

15. Eustace Percy to Hilton Young, 6 Feb 1925; minute of appointment, 16 Feb 1925; ED 24/1196.

39. *H. C. Debs*, 19 Nov 1926, col. 2113ff.

**160,** 15. F. J. C. Hearnshaw, *The centenary history of King's College* (1929) 453.

25. H. H. Bellot, *The University of London: a history* (1969) 33.

28. Douglas Logan, *Haldane and the University of London* (1960).

**161,** 22. *The nationalisation of universities* (1921).

27. Ref. **160,** 28.

31. Ibid.

35. *H. L. Debs*, 29 Jun 1926, col. 635ff.

**162,** 33. 'Universities and the schools in Scotland' in *Education and empire* (1902) 39.

**163,** 4. *H. L. Debs*, 8 Feb 1922, col. 66ff.

19. Albert Mansbridge, *The dedication of life* (Haldane Memorial Lecture, 1930).

21. E. C. F. Collier, ed., *A Victorian diarist: later extracts from the journals of Mary, Lady Monkswell, 1895–1909* (1946) 208.

**164,** 16. *Univ. educ. in Wales, R. com., appx to final rept*, q.12016ff.; 1918 [Cd 8993] xiv.

23. Violet Bonham Carter, 'Haldane of Cloan: Scottish lawyer who shaped the British army', *The Times*, 30 Jul 1956.

27. Cf. ref. **161,** 22.

**165,** 11. *H. L. Debs*, 21 Jul 1920, col. 229ff.

29. *Autobiography*, p. 296.

**166,** 5. Presidential address to British Institute of Adult Education, 20 Sep 1924; *The Times*, 22 Sep 1924.

13. *Autobiography*, p. 330.

18. Ibid., p. 300.

22. *H. L. Debs*, 18 Mar 1925, col. 589ff.

28. *The Times*, 27 Jun 1925.

29. Haldane to B. Webb, 18 Oct 1925; P.Pp., II, 4h, 40.

30. B. Webb, diary, 8 Nov 1926; P.Pp., I, 2, vol. 41.

36. Ibid., 19 Nov 1925; I, 2, vol. 39.

**167,** 9. *H. L. Debs*, 9 Mar 1927, col. 419ff.

18. P.Pp., II, 4h, 41a.

33. 'A vision of the future' in *The way out*, ed. Oliver Stanley (1923).

**168,** 2. 'The higher education of the people', *Journal of Adult Education*, I, i (Sep 1926) 10.

10. *Hibbert Journal*, XXVI (1928) 193–207.

Chapter 8: Epilogue

**170,** 15. 'The dedicated life' in *Universities and national life* (1911) 65–110 [Rectorial address, 10 Jan 1907].

**171,** 27. 'The soul of a people', ibid., pp. 1–32 [University College of Wales, Aberystwyth, 14 Oct 1910].

**172,** 1. Cf. Webb to Haldane, 13 Jun 1921; H.Pp., 5915; copy, P.Pp., II, 5.

5. Ref. **171,** 27.

13. Cf. his speech at the annual dinner of the court of the University of Leeds on 17 Feb 1912; *The Times*, 19 Feb 1912.

16. Ref. **170**, 15.

**173,** 13. Agnes Fry, *A memoir of the Rt hon. Sir Edward Fry, G.C.B.* (1921) 238.

**174,** 12. 8 Dec 1905; R. S. Churchill, *Winston S. Churchill*, II companion vol. (1969) 720.

13. A. G. Gardiner, *Prophets, priests and kings* (1908) 205.

16. *The Student*, XI, no. 5 (19 Nov 1913) 83.

17. Haldane to Gosse, 23 Aug 1917; Gosse Pp.

18. *Maurice*, II, 71.

22. B. Webb, *Diaries, 1924–1932*, p. 88.

**175,** 37. *D.N.B.*

**176,** 11. 9 Sep 1928; P.Pp., II, 4i, 31.

23. B. Webb to Haldane, 14 Aug 1928, H.Pp., 5917; copy, P.Pp., II, 5.

26. P.Pp., II, 4i, 30a.

# Index